Digital Architecture Beyond Computers

Digital Architecture Beyond Computers

Fragments of a Cultural History of Computational Design

Roberto Bottazzi

BLOOMSBURY VISUAL ARTS
LONDON • NEW YORK • OXFORD • NEW DELHI • SYDNEY

BLOOMSBURY VISUAL ARTS
Bloomsbury Publishing Plc
50 Bedford Square, London, WC1B 3DP, UK

BLOOMSBURY, BLOOMSBURY VISUAL ARTS and the Diana logo are trademarks of Bloomsbury Publishing Plc

First published in Great Britain 2018
Paperback edition first published 2020

Cover design by Daniel Benneworth-Gray

A catalogue record for this book is available from the British Library.

Library of Congress Cataloging-in-Publication Data
Names: Bottazzi, Roberto, author.
Title: Digital architecture beyond computers: fragments of a cultural history of computational design / Roberto Bottazzi.
Description: New York: Bloomsbury Visual Arts, An imprint of Bloomsbury Publishing Plc, 2018. | Includes bibliographical references and index.
Identifiers: LCCN 2017049026 (print) | LCCN 2017049495 (ebook) | ISBN 9781474258166 (ePub) | ISBN 9781474258142 (ePDF) | ISBN 9781474258135 (hardback: alk. paper) | ISBN 9781474258128 (pbk.: alk. paper)
Subjects: LCSH: Architectural design–Data processing. | Architecture–Computer-aided design. | Architectural design–History.
Classification: LCC NA2728 (ebook) | LCC NA2728 .B68 2018 (print) | DDC 720.285–dc23
LC record available at https://lccn.loc.gov/2017049026

ISBN: HB: 978-1-4742-5813-5
PB: 978-1-4742-5812-8
ePDF: 978-1-4742-5814-2
eBook: 978-1-4742-5816-6

Typeset by Deanta Global Publishing Services, Chennai, India

Contents

Preface

Despite digital architecture having carved out an important position within the contemporary discourse, it is perhaps paradoxical that there is still little awareness of the history, fundamental concepts, and techniques behind the use of computers in architectural design. Too often publications concentrate on technical aspects or on future technologies failing to provide a critical account of how computers and architecture developed to converge in the field of digital design. Even more overlooked is the actual medium designers utilize daily to generate their projects. Software is too often considered as just a series of tools; this superficial interpretation misses out on the deeper concepts and ideas nested in it. What aesthetic, spatial, and philosophical concepts have been converging into the tools that digital architects employ daily? What's their history? What kinds of techniques and designs have they given rise to?

The answer to these questions will not be found in technical manuals but in the history of architecture and sometime adjacent disciplines, such as art, science, and philosophy. Digital tools conflate complex ideas and trajectories which can span across several domains and have evolved over many centuries. *Digital Architecture Beyond Computers* sets out to unpack them and trace their origin and permeation into architecture. In introducing the possibilities afforded by the emergent CAD software, W. J. Mitchell (1944–2010) noticed that "the application of computer-aided design in architecture lagged considerably behind applications in engineering. Hostility to the idea amongst architects and ignorance of the potentials of computer technology, perhaps contributed to this (1977, p. 40)." Some twenty years later, it was Greg Lynn's (1999, p. 19) turn to highlight that "because of the stigma and fear of releasing control of design process to software, few architects have attempted to use computers as a schematic, organizing, and generative medium for design." The present situation seems to both contradict and confirm these remarks. If, on the one hand, CAD software has become the media of choice for spatial designers, therefore removing any stigma; on the other, most architects have simply replaced traditional media with new ones, without any substantial effect on their design process or outputs. The conceptual and practical experimentation with computational tools remains a marginal activity in regard to the building industry as a whole. One reason is the still polarized nature of the debate on digital technologies between detractors and devotees. Both being equally ineffective, albeit in different ways, these factions suffer from the common tendency of approaching the role of digital tools in design too narrowly and, consequently, conjure up "premature metaphysics" of computation (Varenne 2013, p. 97). The former group stubbornly resists acknowledging that digital tools can be used generatively and therefore struggle to grasp the wider, often not even spatial, issues at stake when designing with computers. The latter group, on the other hand, attributes to computers such degree of novelty and internal coherence to self-validate any outcome.

Transformations in the medium of expression of any creative discipline has always had rippling effects on its discourse be it theoretical or practical. For instance, the slow introduction of perspective in the fifteenth and sixteenth centuries elicited the formation of new schools, professions, and reorganization of the building site. Strictly starting from the analysis of the actual design process, the discussion of the case studies eventually branches out to include—whenever relevant—its cascading impact on related fields, such as division of labor, the emergence and propagation of new forms of knowledge or learning, the need for new or different figures, and their impact on public knowledge at large. In fact, the relation between tools for representation and design has always been a fluid one in which the means of expression available at any given time determine the bounds of architectural imagination. As for language, we cannot articulate feelings or ideas for which we have no words; so architects have not been able to build or even imagine forms beyond what is allowed by the tools they employed. The introduction of CAD in the design process has deeply altered the confines of what is possible, but has not altered this basic principle. In Alexandro Zaera-Polo's words "nothing gets built that isn't transposed onto *AutoDesk AutoCAD*." The ambition of this study is to move beyond this sterile position to critically survey the relation between digital means of representation and architectural and urban ideas and forms—whether built or not. The central focus of this research is therefore software, not only understood as an active component of the design, an unavoidable media managing the interaction between designers and designs, but also impacting on the very cognitive structure of design. As such software is always imbued of cultural values—as Lev Manovich (2013) noted—demanding a materialistic, which critically examines its very structure, impact. Whereas critical theory privileges the cultural and social impact of software overlooking its intrinsic qualities and the ideas that actually shaped it, technical manuals offer little scrutiny of the very tools they introduce. This does not necessarily mean that the cultural and social dimensions of digital design will be categorically omitted in the study; rather they will not act as primary engines for innovation and development in this field. Despite the results achieved by the application of critical theory to many fields, including architecture, when it comes to digital architecture this approach seems structurally unable to grasp the intrinsic qualities, constraints, and issues related to generating spatial ideas with digital devices.

Structure and organization of the book

In introducing his thoughts, Blaise Pascal warned the reader that they should not have accused him of not having said anything original: what was new in his work was the disposition of the material. Likewise, here the reader will recognize names that have been largely discussed in many scholarly works, occasionally they will encounter genuinely new discussions or topics. Regardless, it is the very frame within which these conversations take place to constitute the ultimate novelty of this work: the range of precedents discussed here is brought together for the first time under the agenda of computational and digital design. The formula digital architecture conflates two fields—architecture and computation—whose origins, scopes, and developments are very different from each other and have only recently merged. Modern computers—which only appeared in their modern incarnation during the Second World War—are significantly younger than architecture and built without a precise aim to fulfill—Alan Turing often talked of them as universal machines. By accepting this basic principle, the book expands the history of "digital" architecture beyond the history of computers to highlight how the current generation of digital architects is experimenting with or evolving ideas and techniques that can be traced as far back as the baroque or the Renaissance. The characterization of these episodes is independent of the physical existence of computers at the time, thus implicitly constructing a more cultural history of digital architecture rather than a purely technical one.

Eight chapters, each dissects specific techniques or concepts currently in use in digital architecture and design. As the encounter between architects and computers is opportunistic rather than predetermined, linear and chronological accounts are utilized as little as possible. Instead, the book proposes a sort of archaeology of digital-design processes and methods in which multiple narratives articulated through eight fragments—each corroborated by numerous case studies—through which the discontinuous and fluid trajectory of techniques and ideas can be more carefully articulated. The discussion of each theme contextualizes the use of tools in design: whether it has a generative, representational, operations, or methodological impact. Some tools have limited range of use (e.g., contour), whereas others have impacted several aspects of design. The discussion of these latter types of tools, such as databases, voxel, and randomness, will be limited to their impact on spatial design and organization.

The eight categories identified, one in each chapter are found in the most popular CAD applications designers employ (morphing, pixel, parametrics, etc.), yet they are not specific to any proprietary piece of software. They form an original and accurate vantage point from which to examine what is at stake when designing with computers. The perimeter of the investigation is software; that is, the interface between the digital—be it computers or other digital devices, such as scanners—and design—its culture, techniques, and communication methods. This is understood in its present configuration, acknowledging that ideas forging them have changed from period to period. The book contains inevitable gaps. This is not only because such "vertical" history privileges the evolution of concepts over an even chronological distribution, but also we abandoned the idea of an encompassing history of the relation between design and computation and only discussed those examples that had a paradigmatic effect on design procedures.

The chapters are arrayed in alphabetical order and it will be left to the reader to conflate, hybridize, evolve, and critically dissect the notions, concepts, episodes, and practice listed in the various chapters. This method will not only mirror the very trajectory through which the practices analyzed came into being in the first place; but will also be a more earnest structure to capture the discontinuous relation between design and computation. As for inventions in other fields, advancements in digital and pre-digital tools often resulted from the more or less smooth fusion of previously separate notions or devices. Out of this process of conflation new affordances emerged; a process which also explains why same episodes, names, or contraptions are recalled in more than one chapter, albeit within a different context.

The book opens with a short overview of the concepts forming the architecture of the modern computer. Besides the key chronological developments, the discussion will also focus on the flexibility and "plasticity" of computation. Computation in fact finds its root in formal logic, a field straddling between sciences and humanities. Its basic architecture underpinning all software architects and designers daily use stems out of a very concise and defined series of the shared procedures. Although for users *Photoshop* and *Grasshopper* may look like very different, if not antithetical, pieces of software, their procedures are not. The chapter on databases—a central component of any piece of software—focuses on the long history of techniques utilized to spatialize data and their, at times, direct impact on architecture. The chapter on networks can be seen as the extension of the previous one. Whereas databases look at the spatialization of data at the architectural scale, networks are here understood as territorial mechanisms coupling space and information. The growth in scale and complexity of networks is one of the implicit outcomes of this chapter; whereas the long narrative woven by these first two chapters clearly reveals how much the success of embedding information depends on the theoretical framework steering its implementation. Throughout the various cases discussed what emerges is not only an outstanding series of techniques to spatialize data; but also, contrary to common perceptions, how data has always needed a material support to exist, which has often been provided by architecture. "Morphing" discusses a series of techniques to control curves and surfaces which have had a direct impact on the formal repertoire of architects. Part of this conversation overflows into the fourth chapter on the timely theme of parametrics. This is certainly the most popular theme discussed in the book but, possibly for the same reason, the one riddled with all sorts of complexities and misunderstandings. Starting from the great examples of the Roman baroque, the chapter will sketch out a more material, design-driven understanding of parametric modeling. Some of the chapters are not dedicated strictly to computational tools but embrace the composition of the modern computer, which includes digital devices that have little or no computational power. The chapters on pixels and scanners both fit this description, as they chart how technologies of representation ended up impacting design and providing generative concepts. Randomness—the sixth chapter—is unavoidably the most abstract and complex of the whole book. Besides the technical complexity in generating genuine random numbers with computers, it is the computational and philosophical issues which are foregrounded here. Finally, the last chapter discusses notion of voxel tracing both its development and impact on contemporary digital design. The chapter on scanning returns to examine how representational technologies have evolved from mathematical perspective to the laser scanner. Despite being central to many digital procedures, this concept has only recently been explicitly exploited by designers, whereas its historical and theoretical implications have been so far completely overlooked.

Acknowledgments

This book brings together several strands of research that have been carried out over the past fifteen years or so. Many institutions, colleagues, professionals, and students have influenced my views for which I am very thankful. I am particularly thankful to Frédéric Migayrou not only for providing the afterword to the book, but also for giving me the opportunity to develop my research and for sharing his time and immense knowledge with me. At The Bartlett, UCL—where I currently teach—I would also like to thank Marjan Colletti, Marcos Cruz, Mario Carpo, Andrew Porter, Mark Smouth, Bob Sheil, Dr. Tony Freeth, and Camilla Wright. At the University of Westminster—where I also work—I am particularly grateful to Lindsay Bremner for broadening the theoretical territory within which to discuss the role of computation in design, Harry Charrington, Richard Difford, Pete Silver, and Will McLean. During the ten years spent at the Royal College of Art, Nigel Coates was not only first to believe in my research, but also communicated me a great passion for writing and publications in general. I am also grateful to Susannah Hagan—whose *Digitalia* injected a design-driven angle to the work—Clive Sall. Amongst the many outstanding projects I followed there, Christopher Green's had an impact on my conception of digital design. Parallel strands of research were developed whilst at the Politecnico of Milan where I would like to thank Antonella Contin, Raffaele Pe, Pierfranco Galliani, and Alessandro Rocca. The section on experimental work developed in Italy in the 1960's and 1970's is largely based on the generosity of Leornardo Mosso and Laura Castagno who gave me the opportunity to analyse their work, Guido Incerti, and Concetta Collura. The research on the use of digital scanners on architecture was also developed through conversations with ScanLab and Andrew Saunders. Over the years some key encounters have changed my views of architecture which have eventually opened up new avenues for research which have converged in this book. These are: Oliver Lang, and Raoul Bunschoten.

A special thank you to my teaching partner, Kostas Grigoriadis for his insights, commitment, and help. I am also grateful to Bloomsbury Academic for the opportunity they provided me with; particularly, James Thompson—my editor—who supported this project and nurtured it with is comments, Frances Arnold, Claire Constable, Monica Sukumar, and Sophie Tann.

Finally, I would like to thank my parents for their continuous support. My deepest gratitude goes to my wife Stefania and my children Aldo, and Emilia who have not only endured the hectic lifestyle which accompanied the preparation of the book, but have also supported and encouraged me in every which way possible. Stefania followed the entire process of this book providing invaluable knowledge and critical insights at all levels: from the intellectual rationale framing the work to the detailed feedback on the actual manuscript. Without their unconditioned love and help all this book would not have existed. It is to them that this book is dedicated to.

Illustrations

Introduction: Designing with computers

A machine is not a neutral element, it has got its history, logic, an organising view of phenomena

Giuseppe Longo (2009)

Before venturing into the more detailed conversations on the role of digital tools in the design of architecture and urban plans, it is worth laying out a series of the key definitions and historical steps which have marked the evolution and culture of computation. Whereas each chapter will discuss specific elements of computer-aided design (CAD) software, here the focus is on the more general elements of computation as more abstract and philosophical notions. Built on formal logic, computers are unavoidably abstracting and encoding their inputs; whatever media or operation is eventually transformed into strings of discrete 0s and 1s. What is covered in this short chapter is in no way exhaustive (the essential bibliography at the end of the chapter provides a starting point for more specific studies) but clarifies some of the fundamental issues of computation which shall accompany the reader throughout all chapters.

First, computers are logical machines. We do not refer to a supposed artificial intelligence computers might have, but rather, literally, to the special branch of mathematics that some attribute to Plato's *Sofist* (approx. 360 BC), which concerns itself with the applications of principles of formal logic to mathematical problems. Whereas formal logic studies the "structure" of thinking, its coupling to mathematics allows to broadly express statements pertaining to natural languages through algebraic notations, therefore coupling two apparently distant disciplines: that of algebra and—what we now call—semiotics. It is this century-long endeavor to create an "algebra of ideas" that has eventually conflated into the modern computer, compressing a wealth of philosophical and practical ideas spanning over many centuries. The common formal logic from which digital computation stems also accounts for the "plasticity" of software: beyond the various interfaces users interact with, the fundamental operations performed by any software eventually involve manipulation of binary code consisting of two digits: 0 and 1. This also explains why an increasing number of software can perform similar tasks: *Photoshop* and visual scripting language *Grasshopper*, for instance, allow to manipulate similar media objects, such as geometries and movies.

What's a computer, anyway? It is easier to see how the etymology of the word derived from the act of computing, of crunching calculations; however, whenever we buy a computer we actually purchase a series of devices only some of which actually compute. Computers in fact also include input devices—keyboard, mouse, etc.—and output ones—monitor, printer, etc.—allowing us to interact with the actual computing unit. Computation is therefore an action which is not exclusive to computers; likewise, the word "digital" does not solely pertain to the domains of computer, as it derives from digits, discreet numerical quantities (such as those of the fingers of our hands).

Perhaps unsurprisingly given these initial definitions, modern computation is a rather old project whose foundation can be identified with the groundbreaking work of Gottfried Leibniz in the seventeenth century. In Herman Goldstine's words (1980, p. 9), Leibniz's contribution can be summarized in four points whose power still resonate with the work of digital designers today: "His initiation of the field of formal logic; his construction of a digital machine; his understanding of the inhuman quality of calculation and the desirability as well as the capability of automating this task; and, lastly, his very pregnant idea that the machine could be used for testing hypothesis." It is this very last point to both reveal the importance of Leibniz's thinking and set a richer context for digital design: this field is still somehow stigmatized for its "impersonal," rigid rules stifling the design process, whereas anybody fairly fluent in digital design would know that the opposite is also true. Computers' ability to take care of the "inhuman quality of calculations" frees up conceptual space for the elaboration of alternative scenarios. As for testing hypotheses, it implies an experimental, open, iterative relation between designer and computer aiming at fostering innovation.

Before surveying some of the steps toward the construction of modern computers, it is important to clarify some of the key concepts we will repeatedly utilize throughout the book.

Analogical and digital computing

Prior to the invention of modern computers in the first part of the twentieth century, the most advance calculating machines utilized analogous or continuous computation. Analogue forms of computation were based on continuous phenomena. All empirical phenomena are analogical; they always occur within a continuum. For instance, time flows uninterrupted regardless of the type of mechanism we are using to measure it. Analogue computers execute calculations adopting continuous physical elements whose physical properties are measured—for example, the length of rods is recorded or different current voltage. As Goldstine (1980, p. 40) reminds us, analogue computing goes hand in hand with nineteenth-century mathematics: the developments in the field of mathematics required new types of machines—precisely, analogue machines—in order to compute the set of equations describing a certain physical phenomenon. "The designer of an analogue device decides what operations he wishes to perform and then seeks a physical apparatus whose laws of operation are analogous to those he wishes to carry out." The slide ruler is an example of analogue computing in which logarithms are calculated by sliding two markers along a graded piece of wood, effectively measuring their position along a graded edge. The two markers physically represent established mathematical properties of logarithms stating that the logarithm of a product of two numbers is the sum of the logarithms of the two numbers. Through these examples it is possible to discern how computational machines are always an embodiment of theory, and they are not natural but designed artifacts, informed by theoretical preoccupations as well as physical limitations.

Modern computers, on the other hand, are digital machines; they operate with digits combined according to algebraic and logical rules. They do not operate with continuous quantities—like their analogue counterparts—but rather discrete ones which capture through numbers what would otherwise be a continuous experience. The invention of the Western alphabet could very well mark the introduction of the first discrete system: whereas when we speak the modulation of sounds is continuous, the alphabet dissects it into a number of defined symbols—letters. The abacus, Leibniz's calculating machine, and Charles Babbage's (1791–1871) *Analytical Engine* (proposed in 1837) are examples of discrete computing machines in which basic calculations such as additions and subtraction are executed and the results carried over to complete other operations. In the case of Leibniz's wheel numerical quantities are engrained on metal cogs which click to position to return the final desired results. Quantities are finite and discreet, no longer continuous. Modern computers always discretize; they reduce continuity to the binary logic of 0s and 1s creating a problematic conceptual and, at times, practical gap between the natural and the artificial. These problems are at the center of studies on how computers operate as ontological and representational machines; though these conversations affect all areas of computations, this book will particularly concentrate on its impact on design, especially in the use of computer simulations and parametric modelers to design architecture.

The elegance of binary code

As we mentioned, all data input in or output by computers are formatted in binary code. The elegance of this system brings together several disciplines and knowledge which have matured over many centuries. We know that the invention of binary code greatly precedes its introduction in Leibniz's work. The German philosopher's was, however, motivated by a different desire; that of conceiving the shortest, in a way the most economic numerical system able to describe and return the largest number of combinations. Leibniz in fact saw binary numbers as the starting point of a much bigger endeavor: that of expressing philosophical thoughts and even natural language statements through algebraic expressions. Leibniz did make several attempts to both define such a system and test its applications—for instance, to resolve legal disputes—without much success: this would fundamentally remain a dream—to borrow Martin Davis' expression—that would be quickly forgotten after his death.

Uninterested in Leibniz's philosophical ambitions, French textile worker Basile Bouchon developed a system of perforated cards in 1725 to control the weaving patterns of mechanical looms, which was shortly after improved by Jean-Baptiste Falcon. Once the cards were fed through the machine, the loom would automatically alternate the combination of threads to obtain a desired pattern. Binary logic would find an ideal partner in the material logic of perforated cards as the unambiguous logic of either holed or plain cells mirrored that of 0s and 1s. Despite the invention and rapid diffusion of microprocessors, mainframe computers still used punch cards as material support for software instructions.

Whether aware of Leibniz's work or not, binary numbers were also the decisive ingredient in British mathematician George Boole's (1815–64) work whose logic basically marked the modern foundation of this discipline and indelibly shaped how computers work. Boole's (1852, p. 11) own words well capture the importance of his work: "The design of the following treatise is to investigate the fundamental laws of those operations of the mind by which reasoning is performed: to give expression to them in the symbolical language of Calculus, and upon this foundation to establish the science of Logic and instruct its method; . . . and finally to collect from the various elements of truth brought to view in the course of the inquiries some probable intimations concerning the nature and constitution of the human mind." Boole's invention consisted of employing algebraic notation to express logical statements; such connection was just a brilliant example of scientific thinking but also provided a clear and coherent bridge between algebra and natural languages. Using the four arithmetical operations, Boole could translate statements in natural language. For instance, the * symbol describe a "both" condition: the group of all red cars could be expressed as, for instance, $x = y * z$ or $x = yz$; in which y describes the group of "red objects," whereas z denotes that of "cars." The + symbol described and/or conditions, from which it was possible to quickly infer how the symbol could also be utilized. The famous exception to the algebraic notation—which had already been anticipated by Leibniz—was the expression $x^2 = xx = x$, as adding a group to itself would not produce anything different or new. Boole (1852, pp. 47–48) introduced binary numeration as "the symbol 0 represents Nothing," whereas the symbol 1 represents "'the Universe' since this is the only class in which are found *all* the individuals that exist in *any* class. Hence the respective interpretations of the symbol 0 and 1 in the system of Logic and *Nothing* and *Universe*" (italics in the original).

From the point of view of computation, Boole's logic basically allowed to program a computing machine: it supplied a syntax to correctly turn instructions—linguistics—into machine commands—numbers. It is therefore not a coincidence that further work in this area—particularly by Gottlob Frege (1848–1925)—also marked the beginning of modern studies on semiotics. However, the full realization of this potential would only occur in 1910–13 when Bertrand Russell (1872–1970) and Alfred North Whitehead (1861–1947) would publish their *Principia Mathematica* taking up Boole's logic (another failed dream, in some respect).

The nineteenth century was also characterized by progresses made in the development of electricity. Electric circuits would eventually be employed to control machines and become the "engine" of the modern computer. Switches in electrical circuits also only have two positions: they are either open or close. Peirce first intuited that binary code could have been the ideal language to control the position of the switches. Its application to computation would, however, only occur in the 1930s when Claude Shannon's essential work on information—also discussed in the chapter on randomness—would relate formal logic (by now, programming), electrical circuitry, and information transmission under the unifying language of binary numbers. After Shannon's work it was possible to compute with a modern computer: that is, to determine a set of logical steps, translate them into a programming language engendered with both semantic and syntactic characteristics, which could instruct the electric apparatus of the computer.

This short foray into the evolution of basic programming language for computers shows how computers came to exploit disparate notions which eventually converged; since the Jacquard's loom, computation has been consisting of a hardware (computing mechanism) and a software (set of instructions), which will be briefly discussed here.

Data and information

Information is one of the key words of the twentieth century. Its relevance has increased exponentially not only through the proliferation of new media, but also through the parallel interest expressed by more established disciplines, such as philosophy and ethics. The invention of the modern computer surely played a significant part in growing its popularity: in fact, the computer essentially performs nothing but manipulations of stored information. The wealth of knowledge on the subject has not always been beneficial, as several definitions of the same words emerged responding to the very contexts in which they were analyzed. Information and data have been defined in semantic, statistical terms often presenting contrasting definitions.

Rather than attempting to reconcile these differences, we concentrate on the very material nature of the modern computer and on its intrinsic qualities and limitations. Computational information is purely a quantitative phenomenon, unrelated to qualitative, sematic concerns: it can claim no meaning, and even less truthfulness. To understand the nature and properties of digital data and information, we have to cast a larger net of categories over the subject. Contrary to the superficial notion that data is abstract, immaterial entity, computers first and foremost are material constructs: data stored in computers exist as the combinations of physical properties. Most often these are alternate voltages switching between two currents corresponding to binary numeration. Binary digits—better known as bits—are the building blocks of digital data. There are sequences of 0s and 1s, without any precise meaning: they could be characters in a text, songs, 3d models, etc. Groups of bits form patterns used as codes. Structured and coded strings of bits are finally defined as data, whereas information is generally defined as data in context. In this "epistemological chain" of digital data, information marks the threshold in which the material properties are stored in the hardware can designed. This specific act is performed through algorithms which allow information to be "interpreted, manipulated, and filled with meaning" (Ross 1968, p. 11; quoted in Cardodo Llach 2012, p. 42). Strictly speaking, digital media only deal with information as this is the deepest editable layer of content in the computer; for this reason we have a specific field of studies dedicated to information—i.e., informatics—but not to data.

Brief history of computers

The modern computers emerged out of the millennia-long development of artificial apparatuses to assist human calculation. Its origin is found in the development of calculating machines first manually operated and then based on activating mechanical parts. Among the most ancient computing devices we can count the Antikythera mechanism—perhaps the first ever—an analogue computing orrery discovered on the homonymous shipwreck in Greece. Made of about thirty interconnected bronze cogs, this device could have been made between 150 and 100 BC and used for astronomical calculations. The abacus, a calculating machine based on discrete quantities, emerged much later, around 1200 in China. The emergence of mechanical calculating machines is generally understood to coincide with Blaise Pascal's (1623–62) device built in 1642—at the age of twenty—for his father. The machine, based on a series of rotating wheels, could solve additions and subtractions. Not long after, in 1673 Leibniz completed his version of a similar type of machine—often referred to as "Leibniz wheel" because of its operating principle—which extended its functions to all four basic mathematical operations.

Falcon's perforated cards were further developed by Joseph Marie Jacquard (1752–1834), who connected them to a weaving loom neatly separating the set of instructions to compute—marking the birth of the notion of software—the

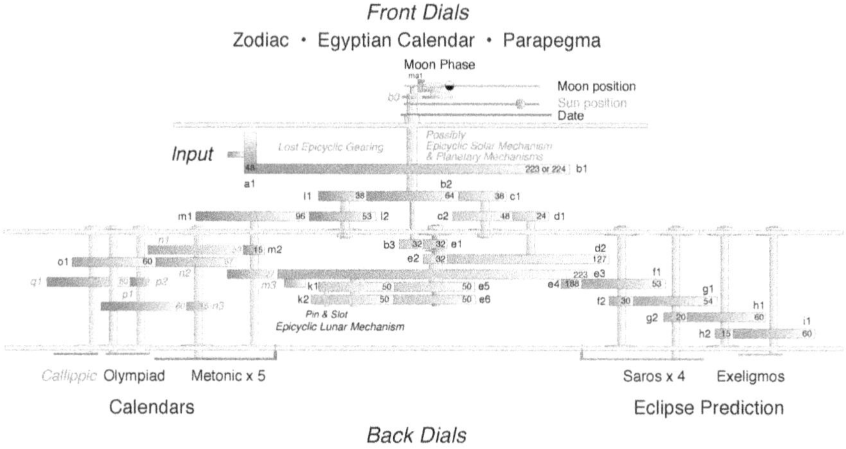

Figure 0.1 Antikythera Mechanism. Diagram by Dr. Tony Freet, UCL. Courtesy of the author.

device physically computing it—from hardware. This division still in use was central not only to the application of computing technologies to everyday tasks but also to the emergence of information as a separate field in computational studies. It is interesting to point out the impressive penetration that this machine had, once again demonstrating that computation is not a recent phenomenon: in 1812 there were 11,000 Jacquard looms in use in France.[1]

The principles of the Jacquard loom were also at the basis of Charles Babbage's *Difference Engine* (1843). Operated by punch cards, Babbage's machine could store results of temporary calculations in the machine's memory and compute polynomials up to the sixth degree. However, the *Difference Engine* soon evolved into the *Analytical Engine* which Babbage worked on for the rest of his life without ever terminating the construction of what can be considered the first computer. Its architecture was in principle like that of the Harvard Mark I built by IBM at the end of the Second World War. The working logic of this machine consisted of coupling two distinct parts, both fed by perforated cards: the store, which computed the logical steps to be operated upon the variables, whereas the mill stored all the quantities on which to perform the operations contained in the store. This not only meant that the same operations could be applied to different variables, but also marked the first clear distinction between computer programs—in the form of algebraic scripts—and information. This section would not be complete without mentioning Augusta Ada Byron (1815–52)—later the Countess of Lovelace—whose extensive descriptions of the *Analytical Engine* not only made up for the absence of a finished product, but also, and more importantly, fully grasped the implication of computation: its abstract qualities which implied the exploitation of combinatorial logic and its application to different type of problems.

The year 1890 was also an important year in the development of computation, as calculating machines were utilized for the U.S census. This not only marked the first "out-of-the-lab" use of computers but also the central position of the National Bureau of Standards, an institution which would play a pivotal part in the development of computers throughout the twentieth century: as we will see later, the Bureau will also be responsible for the invention of the first digital scanners and pattern recognition software. The technology utilized was still that of perforated cards, which neatly suited the need to profile every American citizen: the organization in rows and columns matched the various characteristics the census aimed to map. The year 1890 marks not only an important step in our short history, but also the powerful alignment of computers and bureaucracies through quantitative analysis.

Whereas the computing machines developed between 1850 and the end of the Second World War were all analogue devices, the ENIAC (Electronic Numerical Integrator and Calculator), completed on February 15, 1946, emerged as the first electronic, general-purpose computer. Contrary to Vannevar Bush's machines developed from the 1920s until 1942, the ENIAC was digital and already built on the architecture of modern computers that we still use. This iconic machine was very different from the image of digital devices we are accustomed to: it weighed 27 tons covering a surface of nearly 170 square meters. It consisted of 17,468 vacuum tubes—among other parts—and was assembled through about 5,000,000 hand-soldered joints needing an astonishing 175 kilowatts to function. It nevertheless brought together the various, overlapping strands of development that had been slowly converging since the seventeenth century, and, at the same time, paved the way for the rapid diffusion of computation in all aspects of society.

The final general configuration of modern computers was eventually designed by John von Neumann (1903–57) whose homonymous architecture would devise the fundamental structure of the modern computer as an arithmetic/logic unit—processing information; a memory unit—later referred to as random-access memory (RAM); and input and output units (von Neumann 1945). The idea of dedicating separate computational units to the set of instructions contained in the software from the data upon which they were operated allowed the machine to operate much more smoothly and rapidly, a feature we still take advantage of.

The 1970s finally saw the last—for now—turn in the history of computers with the emergence of the personal computer and the microprocessor. Computers were no longer solely identified with colossal machines that required dedicated spaces, but rather could be used at home and tinkered with in your own garage. This transformation eventually made processing power no longer "static" but rather portable: today roughly 75 percent of the microprocessors manufactured are installed not on desktop computer but on portable machines like laptop, embedding computation into the very fabric of cities and our daily life.

Brief history of CAD

It was the development of specialized pieces of software that marked the advent of CAD tools. The invention of CAD should be seen as one of the products of the conversion of the military technologies developed during the Second World War to commercial uses as needed by the US government in order to capitalize on the massive investments made. This decision had a profound effect on postwar academic research. Tasked with transferring technologies conceived for very specific purposes (e.g., ballistic calculations), software designers stripped these tools down to their more general features in order to make them applicable to as many problems as possible, including unforeseen ones. This would be a common habit in software development which has only grown in time with more accurate and faster client feedback and through "error reports" or forums.

CAD was also a necessity as computer-controlled machines—broadly grouped as computer-aided manufacturing (CAM)—were also being developed. These machines were operating on a numerical rather than manual basis; no need for dials and levers to control them but rather an interface which also operated on a numerical basis: the computer. It is within this context that the DAC-1 by IBM and *Sketchpad* were designed. *Sketchpad* (1962)—the result of Ivan Sutherland's (1938–) research at MIT—not only marked a historic benchmark for digital design but also exemplified how digital tools migrated from military to civilian uses. The software was deliberately conceived as a generic interface for design in order not to foreclose any potential area of application. However, since his first presentation, Sutherland (2003) realized the design potential of CAD; designing objects with a computer was "essentially different" from hand drafting, he stated. The step-by-step formal logic of emerging software could not have been fully exploited without also changing the way in which objects were conceived. The ambition was for both design process and representation to radically merge traditional practices with the advantages afforded by computation. Just as the following two decades would be characterized by many experiments developed within academia—which will occupy large parts of the discussion in the book—CAD has also slowly been developed in the corporate world. Here the emphasis was not so much on innovative design methods or theories, but on efficiency, on streamlining the transmission of information between design offices and building sites to make projects possible and/or cheaper. Architecture practices rarely involved computers though, and, as a result, CAD only began to penetrate the world of architecture in the 1980s when software packages such as AutoDesk *AutoCAD* were first released.[2] A rare exception was American corporate practice Skidmore, Owings & Merrill (SOM), which not only acquired mainframe computers since the 1960s, but also developed their own pieces of software to assist both design and construction. During this period, however, other disciplines such as automobile, aeronautical, and naval design were leading the way in the implementation of CAD. It is not a coincidence that the term "computer graphics" was invented at Boeing by William F. Fetter (1928–2002), for instance. Computer graphics would eventually branch out to form the field of image visualization and animation, which found fertile

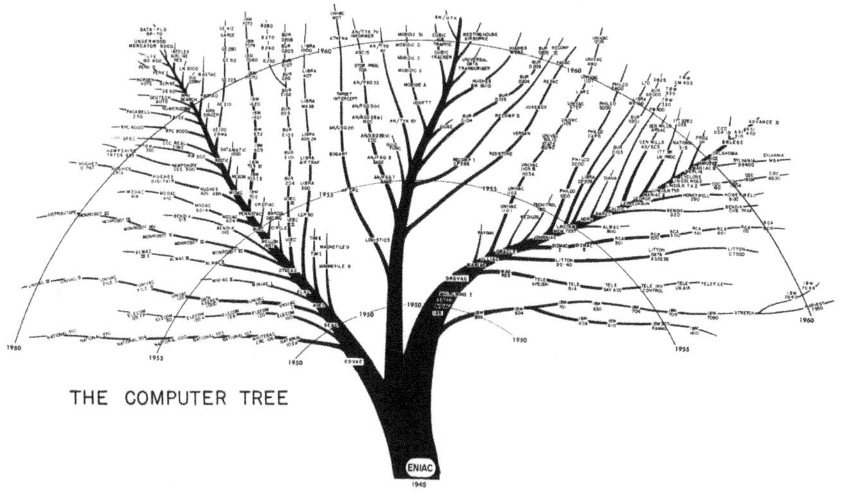

Figure 0.2 The Computer Tree, 'US Army Diagram', (image in the public domain, copyright expired).

ground in the movie industry.[3] This is not an anecdotal matter as the very context within which software packages developed would deeply impact its palette of tools and general architecture. When later on architects started appropriating some of these software packages they had to adapt them to fit the conventions of architectural design. Cardoso Llach (2015, p. 143) usefully broadly divided software for design into two categories: CAD solely relying on geometry and its Euclidean origins; and simulation software based on forces and behaviors inspired by Newtonian physics. Every *Rhinoceros* or *Autodesk Maya* user knows all too well the frustration caused by respectively having to model architecture in environments conceived for different disciplines: the default unit of engineering design is millimeters, whereas in the animation industry scale does not have physical implications. Likewise, it is not surprising that computer programs conceived to design airplanes' wings or animated movie characters did have such advanced tools to construct and edit complex curves and surfaces. In all the design fields mentioned, aerodynamics is not a matter of aesthetic caprice but rather a necessity! However, much of both the criticism and fascination for these tools have argued their position by using the most disparate fields such as philosophy, aesthetic, or even psychology but very rarely computation itself, with its intrinsic qualities. As the market demand grew so did the range of bespoke digital tools to design architecture, with some architects such as Frank Gehry, Peter Eisenman, or Bernard Cache going the extra mile and were directly involved with software manufacturers to customize CAD tools.

Understanding both the evolution of computing and its application to design is not only a key step to appreciate its cultural richness, but also crucial to deepen architects' understanding of what is at stake when designing with computers.

Notes

1. *Encyclopaedia Britannica* (1948), s.v. "Jacquard, Joseph Marie" (Quoted in Goldstine 1972, p. 20).
2. Developed since the late 1970s, the first release of *AutoCAD* was demonstrated at the COMDEX trade show in Las Vegas in November 1982. *AutoCAD 1.0 December 1982*. Available at: http://autodesk.blogs.com/between_the_lines/ACAD_R1.html (Accessed August 15, 2016).
3. This connection will be explored in the chapter on pixels.

Chapter 1

Database

Introduction

The use of databases is a central, essential element of any digital design. Any CAD package designers routinely use, manage, and deploy data in order to perform operations. This chapter not only deconstructs some of the processes informing the architecture of databases; but, more importantly, also maps out their cultural lineage and impact on the organization of design processes and physical space. The task is undoubtedly vast and for this reason the chapter extends onto the study of networks discussed in a different chapter: the former traces the impact of data organization on form (physical structures), whereas the latter analyzes the later applications of data to organize large territories, such as cities and entire countries. Since the initial attempts to define and contextualize the role of digital information as a cultural artifact, theoretical preoccupations have been as important as technical progress; for instance, when introducing these issues to a general audience, Ben-Ami Lipetz did not hesitate to state that "the problem [of data retrieval] is largely an intellectual one, not simply one of developing faster and less expensive machinery" (Lipetz 1966, p. 176).

A database is "a large collection of data items and links between them, structured in a way that allows it to be accessed by a number of different applications programs" (BCS Academy Glossary Working Party 2013, p. 90). In general parlance, databases differ from archives, collections, lists, and the like, as the term precisely identifies structured collection of data stored digitally. Semantically, they also diverge from historical precedents, as they are simpler data collections than, for instance, dictionaries or encyclopedias. Much of the semiotic analysis of historical artifacts concerned with collecting data has been focusing on the difficulties arising to unambiguously define both the individual elements—primitives—of a list and the rules for their aggregation or combination—formulae. This issue is not as crucial in the construction of a database as both primitives and formulae are established *a priori* by the author. This will be true even a database is connected to other ones or its primitives are actually variables. This should not be seen as a negative characteristic; rather it circumscribes the range of action of databases to a partial, more restricted, domain in contrast to the global ambitions of validity of, for instance, the dictionary. Databases construct their own "world" within which most of the problems highlighted can be resolved: a feature often referred to as semantic ontology (Smith 2003).

Given the wide time span we will be covering in this chapter we will unavoidably refer to both archives and collections as databases, or better proto-databases. Key characteristics of databases are hierarchy (data structure) and retrieval system (algorithm), which determine how we access them and how they will be visualized. It is the latter that indicates that similar, if not altogether identical, databases may appear to be radically different if their retrieval and visualization protocols change. This is a particularly important point constituting one of the key criteria to analyze the relation between databases and space. By excluding that databases are just sheer accumulation of structured data—a necessary but insufficient condition; we will concentrate on the curatorial role that retrieval systems have to "spatialize" a collection of data on the flat confines of a computer screen or in physical space. In the age of Google searches in which very large datasets can be quickly aggregated and mined, data curation becomes an evermore essential element to navigate the deluge of data. However, rather than limiting it to the bi-dimensionality of screens, we also will concentrate on its three-dimensional spatialization; that is, on how changes in the definition of databases impacted architecture and the tools to design it. In fact we could go as far as to say that design could be described as the art of organizing and distributing matter and information in space. To design a building is a complex and orchestrated act in which thousands of individual elements have to come together in a coherent fashion. Vitruvius had already suggested that this ability to coordinate and anticipate the result of such an operation was the essential skill that differentiated architects from other design professions. This point is even more poignant if we consider that most of these elements making a building are not designed by architects themselves and their assembly is performed by other professionals. This analogy could also hold true for designing with CAD, as this process can be accomplished by combining architectural elements existing both as textual and as graphic information, as it happens in Building Information Modeling (BIM).[1] Here too hierarchy of information plays a crucial role to produce coherent designs accessible to the various professions participating in the construction process.

Hierarchy and retrieval eventually provide the *form* for the database. Form here should be understood to have both organizational and aesthetic qualities, whether the database contains abstract or visual information. These databases—referred to as practical or "pragmatic" by Umberto Eco (1932–2016)—possess three characteristics (2009, p. 45). First, they are referential, as they stand for objects which are external to the database itself. Their type of external links set can vary: items on databases are indexical, they stand for real objects or values (e.g., the specific weight of steel in a software for structural analysis), while at other times they are purely virtual (as in the case of mathematical operations routinely carried out to perform specific tasks). Secondly, they are finite: their limit is always known and fixed. This does not mean that databases cannot have dynamic qualities—a key feature of digital databases which we will explore in the chapter on parametrics—rather this means that at any given moment their form is finite. Consequently, their final property establishes that they cannot be altered without also changing any of the conditions forming them. There is nothing incongruous in a database; its closed world does not tolerate blurry boundaries. The combination of these three factors represents their form which defines the aesthetics of the database. We should note in passing that the "introverted" definition of database will contrast with the open, infrastructural definition of networks which will be used later on. The relation between the content and the form of a database is an active element which can be legitimately defined as an act of design; all the examples dissected in the chapter will focus on how these databases were designed and how they gave rise to abstract or concrete spatial configurations. Finally, the retrieval logic of the database—the element differentiating databases from other historical modes of structuring information—gives rise to five types of spatial configurations according to their degree of flexibility: hierarchical (arranging data in tree structure and parent/child relations), network (close to the previous model but use "sets" to allow children to have more than one parent as well as many-to-many relationships), relational (based on a graph model of nodes and relationships), client/user (in which multiple users can remotely and simultaneously access and retrieve information), and object oriented (in which the objects in the database appear as programming language) (Paul 2007, p. 96). Rather than emphasizing technical differences, we should understand this categorization as an example of combinatorial logic which greatly precedes the invention of databases and constitutes their philosophical and aesthetic foundation.

Finally, to design a database always also involves issues of data compression. As we will see, since the early experiments with memory theaters, organizing information invariably also meant reducing it. Two elements here are relevant to the discussion of the role of databases vis-à-vis digital design. First is the notion of metadata—that is, data on data—forming a much reduced dataset used by software to perform searches on the database itself. The second technique—appearing as early as the sixteenth century—is cryptography, which allows replacing symbols with other symbols to both reduce the database size and protect data.

As mentioned, databases are at the core of computer software regardless of whether the end user can interact with them. Some applications, however, make list management an explicit feature. Parametric modelers such as *Grasshopper* do provide a series of tools to manage lists of numbers which can be associated to geometrical properties of objects. It is however with scripting software (e.g., *Processing*) or languages that such tools acquire a more prominent role, as users do not interact with a graphic interface but directly manipulate the data structure. Out of the many scripting languages allowing direct operations on databases, AUTOLISP deserves greater attention, as it provided basic software architecture for *AutoCAD*. LISP was invented by John McCarthy (1927–2011) in 1958 and is one of the oldest high-level programming languages still in use. Its evolution into AUTOLISP was designed around the organization and connection between numerical lists. *AutoCAD* employed it between 1986 and 1995, as it gave the possibility to directly manipulate lists, still an essential feature for modeling complex structures. These features are also at the core of BIM, which makes the most direct use of databases; pieces of software such as *Revit* adopt an object-oriented modeling allowing to associate text-based information to building components such as doors and windows. BIM models building parts as much as databases formatted in a non-visual, text-based media: these lists can not only be interacted with by various parties, but also be outputted separately from the actual drawings.

Such techniques should not be regarded as strictly technical procedures bereft of aesthetic potential. Some examples of this are Marcel Duchamp's (1887–1968) decision to abandon painting to become a librarian at the Sainte Genevieve Library in Paris conceiving art as the manipulation of data toward an aesthetic objective, Le Corbusier's (1887–1965) enthusiastic appreciation for the Roneo filing system (Le Corbusier, 1987), or Buckminster Fuller's (1895–1983) *Dymaxion Chronofiles*, which all speak of architects' interest in data organization both as a cultural manifestation and as a design method.

When mapped onto architecture, the closest point of comparison is the library. Libraries are an established building type to store and retrieve books; and more recently, other types of media. The primary concern in the design of a traditional library is the organization of books, an issue restaging the same conversations on information hierarchy and access we just saw. Contrary to the museum—also a type concerned with the organization of cultural artifacts—the objects contained in a library are extremely consistent in form and physical properties, making organizational issues even more relevant. There are multiple computing mechanisms at work in a library. The cataloging system operates on the abstract level but it nevertheless has both cultural and physical connotations. The way in which books are ordered reflects larger cosmologies: from the spiraling, infinite Tower of Babel to more recent cataloging structures such as the Dewey system[2] according to which each item has a three-digit code ranging from 000—philosophy—to 900—history and geography—reflecting an imaginary journey from the heavens down to earth. In the library we can observe how architecture can also present direct computational properties: the very spatial layout adopted allows users to retrieve information, facilitate ad hoc connections between disparate objects, and, more generally, produce an image of culture as expressed through the medium of books. The recent addition of electronic media has revamped discussions on both access to information and their public image in the city. Among the many examples of libraries the recently completed Utrecht University Library (2004) by Wiel Arets (1955–) and the Seattle Public Library (2004) by the Office for Metropolitan Architecture (OMA) are exemplary outcomes restaging this discussion. Wiel Arets distributed 4.2 million books in suspended concrete volumes, each thematically organized, creating a very suggestive series of in-between spaces and constructing a theatrical set of circulation spaces for the user's gaze to meander through. Koolhaas' office conceived the library as an extension of the public space of the city, which flows from the street directly into the foyer and along the vertical ramp connecting the various levels of the library. Along the same line we should also include the impressive data visualizations generated by mining large datasets: the works of Lev Manovich, Brendan Dawes, Senseable City Lab at MIT represent some of the most successful works in this area.

Ramon Llull's wheels

Though first emerged in the work of the Greek Simonides and Aristotle, the first systematic account of techniques to gather and retrieve data appeared in three books: the *Ad Herennium* written by anonymous, Cicero's *De Oratore* (55 BC), and Quintilian's *Institutio Oratoria* (AD 95). *Ars memorativa*—the sum of techniques to artificially remember notions—was at the center of all three examples. Memory was constructed by transforming notions into icons, which then were "placed" in the rooms of imaginary buildings. By recalling how the rooms were furnished, one could unfold the small units of information "stored" in each object to eventually aggregate them all into a comprehensive narrative. Since these early examples, it is possible to see how architecture—though only in its virtual form—played a central role in the history of databases: it was an organizational as much as a generative device to store and retrieve information. Architecture would provide the formal structure to store notions regardless of their topic or meaning. Architecture would provide the formal structure to store notions regardless of their topic or meaning. In this sense we could say that architecture *computed*; icons ornated the walls of the palaces whose structure allowed information to be "played back" to reconstruct more articulate notions. Room layouts, luminosity, typological organization, etc. all facilitated storing information in virtual building, reducing the amount of notions to retain to memorize a complex event or concept. The use of architecture as retrieval and computational system is clearly stated in the *Ad Herennium* (c.80 BC) when the author states that "the places are very much like wax tablets or papyrus, the images like the letters, the arrangement and the disposition of the images like the script, the delivery is like the reading" (Yates 1966, p. 179).[3] Similarities have been drawn between the memory palaces and formal logic: the separation between the layout of the architecture chosen (algorithm) and images populating it (data), the semi-automatic properties of the device conceived, and the need to develop techniques to compress the information stored.

An important precursor of the innovations that the Renaissance would diffuse was Ramon Llull (Majorca 1232–c.1315). Born in Majorca on the border between Christianity and Islam, Catalan Ramon Llull occupies an important place both in the history of the organization of knowledge and that of proto-computational thinking, as he introduced abstract and combinatorial logics which still play a central role in the design of databases. His work is situated at the end of the Middle Ages—between the end of the thirteenth and the beginning of the fourteenth centuries—and in many respects anticipates themes and issues that will gain popularity from the fifteenth up to the seventeenth century. His vast production was a result of lifelong studies ranging from astronomy to medicine, to some very early developments on electoral systems. Often met with either adulation or complete rejection, Llull's *Ars Magna* was a system to organize knowledge—referred to as memory—to demonstrate to other religions the superiority of Christianity, an aspect to keep in mind as we venture into more detailed descriptions of the *Ars*.

Llull invented a system based on a series of basic lists that could be aggregated or combined by using a series of concentric wheels with letters marked along the perimeter. (Probably inherited from the very Muslim culture he was seeking to convert.) The random combinations of letters returned by each spin of the wheel were encoded to give rise to philosophical statements answering the fundamental metaphysical questions. At the basis of this construction were the basic primitives: nine attributes of God called *dignities*: *Bonitas*, *Magnitudo*, *Eternitas*, *Potestas*, *Sapientia*, *Voluntas*, *Virtus*, *Veritas*, and *Gloria*.[4] Letters from B to K were given to each attribute and eventually organized along the first wheel. The *Tabula Generalis* established six groups of nine elements each and provided the general structure of the *Ars*: *Principia assoluta* (dignities), *Principia relativa*, *Quaestiones*, *Subjecta*, *Virtutes*, and *Vita*. They combined through a small machine in which three concentric circles literally computed combinations in exceptionally large numbers (despite the outer wheel was static). The groups were each associated to the nine-letter system, a fixed characteristic of Llull's *Ars*. By spinning the wheels, new configurations and possible new ideas were generated: for instance, the letters representing *dignities* in the outer ring were connected through *figures* to generate seventy-two combinations allowing repetitions of a letter to occur. The *Tabula Generalis* allowed decoding the random letters generated by the wheels: for instance, BC would translate as "*Bonitas est magna*," whereas CB would be "*Magnitudo est bona*." At this level of the *Ars Magna* both combinations were accepted: this apparently secondary detail would have profound implications, as it allowed each primitive to be either a subject or a predicate. Geometry also played a central part in formalizing this logic and was clearly noticeable in the illustrations accompanying the description of the first wheel: the perfect circle of the wheel, the square denoting the four elements, and the triangle linking the *dignities* according to the *ars relata* which described the types of relations between primitives and arched back to Aristotle's *De memoria et reminiscentia* (c.350 BC). Triangular geometry allowed Llull to devise, perhaps for the first time, both binary and ternary relations between the nine letters by applying his *Principia relativa* and three-letter combinations—named *chambers*—were listed in the *Tabula Generalis*. Llull added a series of rules—a sort of axiomatics formed by ten questions on religion and philosophy and their respective answers—to discriminate between acceptable and unacceptable statements generated through the wheels. Llull introduced here a tenth character, the letter T as a purely syntactic element in each chamber. The position of T altered how the ternary combination read: its role has been compared to that of brackets in modern mathematical language, as it separated the combinations into smaller entities to be "computed" independently to be then aggregated (Crossley 2005). The letter T also changed the interpretation of the letter in the group: each letter to the left of T must be interpreted from the list of *dignities*, while the reader should have used the *Principia relativa* for letters to the right of T. The letter T in Llull's *Ars* represented one of the first examples of symbolic logic with purely syntactical function. The table eventually listed 1680 four-letter combinations divided in columns of twenty elements each.

As we have seen, the overall structure of the *Ars* was fixed, with constant relations and recursive "loops" that allowed to move across the different scales of being (*Subjecta*). *Deus, Angelus, Coelum, Homo, Imaginativa, Sensitiva, Vegetativa, Elementativa, and Instrumentativa* were finally the nine primitives (scales) of the universe; to each of them Llull applied his godly attributes.[5] The recursive logic of this system was also guaranteed by the very nature of the geometrical figures chosen to measure it: a geometrical structure defined each step or iteration and related to one another. This allowed the user to move up and down the chain of being: from the sensible to the intelligible, from material reality to the heavens, in what Llull himself called "*Ascensu et Descensu Intellectus*" (ascending and descending intellect) and represented as a ladder.[6] It is this aspect that prompted Frances Yates to affirm that Llullian memory was first to inject movement into memory, an absolute novelty compared to the previous medieval and classical methods (Yates 1966, p. 178). Llullian recursion was mostly a rhetorical device rather than a logical one, as its main aim was to disseminate its author's doctrine and religious beliefs: any random spin of the wheel would confirm the validity and ultimate truth of Llull's system and metaphysics. This system was therefore only partially generative, as some of the options were excluded in order not to compromise the coherence of any final answer delivered by the wheels. The more one played with the wheels, the more its logic became truer.

Besides the introduction of complex binary and ternary relations, Llull's *Ars* was also the first known example of use of parameters. Whereas in Aristotle primitives had a fixed meaning, in Llull these slightly varied according to syntactical rules: statements such as "*Bonitas est magna*" and "*Magnitudo est bona*" were only possible if subjects and predicates could morph into each other. This was in turn only possible if the meaning of letters from B to K *varied* changing the overall reading of the letters in different combinations. The importance of variables and parametrics in mathematics and digital design cannot possibly be overstated and will find a proper formal definition only with François Viète (1540–1603) in the mid-sixteenth century.[7]

The combination of letters obtained by spinning the wheels was fundamentally independent of their application to the *Tabula*: it was in this sense that Llull spoke of "artificial memory," a definition that was close to that of formal language. As Yates noticed, the self-referential system conceived by Llull no longer needed to heavily rely on spatial or visual metaphors—as classical and medieval memory edifices had done up to that point—but rather on abstract symbols (letters) and geometry (circles, squares, and triangles)(Yates 1966, pp. 176–77). This point was also corroborated by the lack of visuals accompanying Llull's rhetoric (his treatise on astronomy made no use of visual material). Even when drawings were employed, they lacked the figurative qualities so abundant in the classical and medieval tradition; in fact, it may be more appropriate to refer to them as diagrams, indicating geometrical relations between various categories through careful annotations. The relevance of this point is twofold and far exceeds that of a mere philosophical dispute as, first, it marks a sharp departure from any other medieval tradition—and will have a lasting influence on Renaissance and baroque thinkers shaping the emergence of formal logic, which will play an important role in defining the ideas and methods of computation.[8]

The efficacy of logical thinking to model either empirical phenomena or theoretical ideas is an essential part of computational thinking and its ability to legitimately represent them. This book touches upon this theme in several chapters (parametrics, randomness, and networks), as it affects both how real objects are translated into the logic of computational language and whether logical steps can represent them. Llullian machines were purely computational devices strictly calculating combinations regardless of inputs and outputs; they literally were computers without peripherals (mouse, keyboard, or monitor).

However, the *Ars* was not an actual generative system, as not all statements produced by the wheels were semantically acceptable: consequently it could not yield "new" realities, rather only answer a limited number of fundamental questions in many different ways. Its purpose was to convert whoever interacted with it to Christianity and the very idea of "generating" new combinations also presented a completely different and potentially undermining problem: that of having conceived of a machine that could create new knowledge and be consequently accused of heresy. Llull's methods differed from classical ones as they were not so much addressed to remembering notions, but rather to remember "speculative matters which are far remote not only from the senses but even from the imagination" (Yates 1966, p. 194). In other words, Llull's method concerned "how to remember, how to remember"—that is, recursive logic. The power of logical abstract thinking resonates with that of modern computers, which also have developed to abstract their operational logic to become applicable to as many problems as possible. By abstracting its methods and making them independent of individual applications, Llullism widened its domain of applications to become an actual metaphysics. To witness an actual "open" exploration of the unforeseen possibilities yielded by combinatorial logic, we will have to wait until the fifteenth century when Pico della Mirandola (1463–94) will venture into much more audacious exercises in "materialist permutations" (Eco 2014, p. 414), freeing Llull's work from its strictly theological and rhetorical ambitions and paving the way for the logical work of Kircher and Leibniz.

Llull's machine also reinforced the use of wheels as mechanical devices for analogue computation; already present in the Antikythera orrery, wheels freely spun in a continuous fashion. A whole plethora of machines would make use of this device: from the first mechanical calculating machines by Pascal and Leibniz, to *Analytical Engine* by Charles Babbage respectively completed in the seventeenth and nineteenth centuries. Leibniz's admiration for Llull persuaded him to directly work on the *Ars*: Leibniz in fact calculated all the possible combinations that Llull's wheel actually allowed if no semantic rule was applied to curtail them: the number he came up with was 17,804,320,388,674,561 (Eco 2014, p. 424). Finally, Llull indirectly influenced architects too: in 2003 architect Daniel Libeskind (1946–) was inspired by the rotating devices in his design for an artist studio in Palma—Llull's birthplace—which he used as a metaphor for connecting cosmology and architecture.

The cosmos in 49 squares[9]

L'Idea del Theatro written, apparently, in only seven days is Giulio Camillo Delminio's (1480–1544) main work which was only published posthumously passing away in 1544 in Milan. The book constitutes one of the most intriguing, enigmatic, and relevant precedents shaping the relation between information and design. In this book Camillo described a project that had occupied his entire life: the construction of a theater containing all the best exemplars of the knowledge known at the time. Despite such a grand project, Camillo would have found this description still rather underwhelming, as he also referred to it as a library, a translating machine, and, most importantly, a creative device. By the time he started dictating his memories he had already spent several years in Venice—in which he became a close friend of Titian (1488/90–1576), Lorenzo Lotto (c.1480–1556/7), and Sebastiano Serlio (1475–c.1554) (Olivato 1971)—and France where François I—a great admirer of the Italian Renaissance—invited him with the idea of finally constructing the theater.[10] In many ways, Camillo built on several of the precedents we have already discussed—particularly Ramon Llull' *Ars*—but this would not do justice to his work and to the new elements he brought to the relation between knowledge, memory, and creativity. The first of these elements was the range of media through which Camillo's system materialized: Camillo directly utilized architecture—in the form of a classical theater—to organize and "compute" the information stored. Contrary to previous examples, *L'Idea* is a complete work of art including painting—201 drawings by Titian accompanied one edition of the book[11]—and machines. Camillo's ideas had great traction—thanks to the charismatic, almost mystical tone with which he illustrated his project—which extended to architects too as Serlio was deeply influenced by it. The theater was a physical place as much as a mental map, an externalization of the cognitive and associative processes constantly at work in the brain; a notion that still resonates with how we experience the World Wide Web.

The basic organization adopted by Camillo was a grid divided into seven columns and rows. Seven were the known planets of the universe occupying each column; whereas each row—which Camillo refers to as "degrees or gates, or distinctions"—described the mythical figures organizing knowledge from the Heavens down to Earth. More precisely the 7 degrees are:

1 The seven *Planets*—sun excluded;
2 The *Banquet*—in which the oceans transport the "water of knowledge" in which ideas and prime elements float;
3 The *Niche*—in which the Nymphs weave their fabrics and bees "combine" the prime elements bringing them down into the natural world;
4 The *Gorgons*—the three mythical figures with only one eye representing the three souls of men and, consequently, their internal dimension;
5 *Pasifae*—symbolizing the soul descending into the body;
6 *Talaria*—Mercury's winged shoes—representing human actions on earth;
7 *Prometheus*—representing all the products of arts and sciences (Bolzoni 2015, p. 22).

Variedly combined these categories provided all the "places" to store the knowledge of the theater, each marked by the insertion of a painting. The combination of places and images added another layer of interpretation to the theater, as the same image could have different meanings according to its position. Providing the theater of a structure was not only a practical expedient to give access to its inner workings, but it was also necessary to make all knowledge easier to remember. Camillo was not just interested in cataloging past and present ideas; the arrangement in columns and rows was also instrumental to allow the "audience" of his theater to generate new works by combing existing elements, also providing them with some guidance to place potentially new images and words in the theater. The architecture of the theater with rows and seats maintained a tension between both individual parts and the whole—that is, how the celestial scales of the cosmos and earthly ones are related, and between singular notions and multiple—that is, combinatorial and complex—knowledge. Camillo was always adamant to point out the wealth of materials contained in the theater. Numbers detailing the quantities of items regularly punctuated his description: for instance, in his letter to Marc'Antonio Flaminio, he boasted that his theater had "one hundred more images" than Metrodoro di Scepsi's (140–170 BC), whose system for ordering memory was still based on the 360 degrees of the zodiac.[12] As we progress through the *Idea* more space is given to ever-longer lists enumerating every item that ought to be included in the theater. The *Theatro* was a perfect device not only because of the sheer quantity of knowledge it contained, but also because this knowledge was indeed "perfect"; that is, directly derived from classical texts representing the highest point in a specific area of inquiry.

The grid was then re-mapped onto the architecture of the classical theater as already described by Vitruvius. However, there was a radical departure from the model inherited: the spectators did not occupy the seats, but they were meant to be on stage watching the spectacle of memory unfolding before their eyes. Camillo was certainly interested in utilizing a converging geometry to enhance the mesmerizing effect of images on memory and knowledge to impact on the users of his theater, but the reason for this inversion seems to run deeper. Camillo looked for a spatial type able to order his "database" while being able to induce in the viewer the impression that what was displayed was the very spectacle of the images stored in their brain. The powerful image which the theater was meant to evoke was that of a "*Magnam mentem extra nos*" (Camillo 1587, p. 38)[13] demanded a spatial structure able to give both a totalizing impression and persuasiveness that allowed users to grasp its organization in a single glance. Camillo referred to Socrates' metaphor of an imaginary window opening onto the human brain to illustrate how he understands his creation: the possible confusion of all the images stored in the brain ideally seen all together was counterbalanced by its structure organization, which brought legibility to an otherwise cacophonic space. Camillo's theater multiplied Socrates' image presenting itself as a theater with many windows: both an image and a place where it would have been possible to both touch all the knowledge but see the flickering spectacle of the brain unfolding (Bolzoni 2015, p. 38).

Replacing the seats of a traditional theater were small cabinets with three tiers of drawers—organizing texts by subject ranging from heavens to earth—covered by drawings announcing their content. The books in each drawer were specially designed to enhance their visual qualities: images decorated the covers, diagrams were inserted to show their content and structure, and finally tabs were introduced to indicate the topics discussed. The works contained in the theater directly came from the classical Greek and Latin tradition.

Camillo often described the *Theatro* not only as a repository of knowledge, an externalized memory, he insisted that the *Theatro* was also a creative machine that would educate its users to produce novel forms of artistic expression. On the one hand, this could be achieved by only storing the great classics of Latin literature which Camillo regarded as models to aspire to; on the other, the classical world of Cicero was distant enough to that of Mannerist culture to avoid direct comparisons which would have not been beneficial for either those who used the theater or to the longevity of the knowledge stored in it. Camillo actually described how the *Theatro* would have worked as an engine for creative writing. Besides the books and paintings composing its space, Camillo also mentioned the introduction of machines to facilitate creativity, especially when the model to draw inspiration from proved particularly challenging. Though never precisely described, these machines could be imagined to have been dotted around the theater, sitting next to the cabinets with drawers. In the *Discorso in materia del suo theatro* (1552) Camillo talked of an "artificial wheel" which users would spin in order to randomly shuffle chosen texts. The mechanism of these automata—apparently depicted in drawings and models—could deconstruct a given text into its constituent parts, revealing its rhetorical mechanisms; an artificial aid supporting the creative process. This description closely echoed that of Llull's wheels, which had already gained popularity in the fifteenth century, through the use of combinatory logic: new knowledge and creativity resided in the ability, whether exercised by a human or not, to recompose existing elements. What Camillo's theater added to these long-standing conversations was not so much a different logic, but rather an aesthetic dimension; the circle—the geometry chosen to play with randomness—but also metaphor of a "whirlpool," a source—as Lina Bolzoni suggests (2015, pp. 70–71)—from which novel forms emerge. This conception of creativity never really ceased to attract interest as the works of Giordano Bruno in the sixteenth century and Leibniz a century later will eventually become fundamental figures of the formal logic of computation.

The ambition to make the theater far more than a "simple" container for knowledge opens up an important, and in many ways still contemporary, issue on the relation between information and creativity. As mentioned, the theater

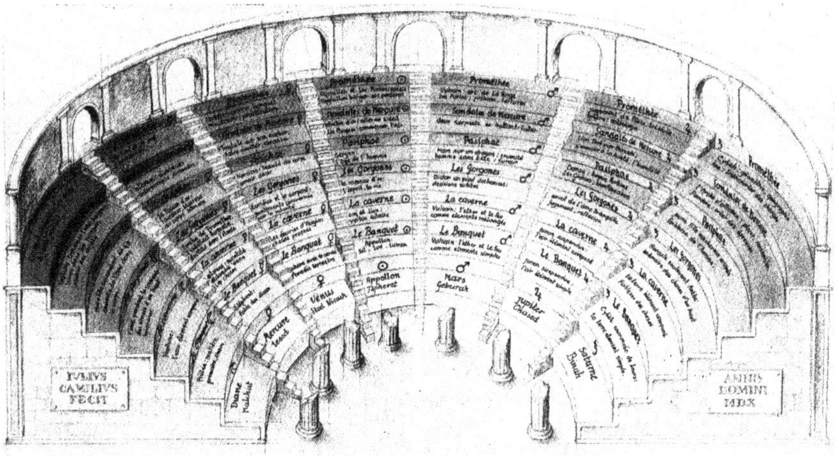

Figure 1.1 Reconstruction of Camillo's Theatre by Frances Yates. In F. Yates, The Art of Memory (1966). © The Warburg Institute.

only contained classical works—Petrarca and Virgilio from the vulgar tradition and Aristotle and Plinio from the classical one—considered by Camillo the highest point in their respective languages and, therefore, a reliable model for inspiration. Several contemporaries—particularly Erasmus—dismissed his positions as anachronistic, unable to reflect the very contemporary reality of the time the theater was meant to be used. However, Camillo's intentions were different; as for the experiment in logical thinking we have already seen or are about to, Camillo too was looking for a language of "primitives" that could return the greatest variety and therefore value; that is, the most reliable and succinct source of elements able to yield the greatest and most novel results (in logical terms, the range of symbols yielding the highest number of combinations). This operation first involved highlighting the deeper, invariant elements of knowledge and rhetoric onto which the combinatorial game could have been performed. In his *Trattato dell'Imitazione* (1544), Camillo noticed that all concepts existent were more than 10,000 that can be hierarchically organized in "343 governors, of which 49 are captains, and only 7 are princes" (1544, p. 173, quoted in Bolzoni 2012, p. 258). Having passed the test of time, these literary sources paradoxically guaranteed users to be freer while performing their literary creations. The very structure of the theater—as a combination of architecture and paintings—provided the mechanisms to deconstruct the content of texts studied and give rise to the very associative logic through which to mutate the lessons learned. Once the elemental rhetorical figures had been revealed, the theater revealed to the user a chain of associations to move from text to text causing the initial ideas to morph and gain in originality. Camillo called it *topica*; a method which we could broadly define as the syntax binding the vast material stored in the theater, a logic causing the metamorphosis of ideas. The theater revealed itself in all its grandiose richness, its detailed and rigorous structure allowing the user to first dissect—almost anatomically in Camillo's language—a specific author, theme, etc., and then, through the *topica,* to revert the trajectory to link unique observations back to universal themes, to timeless truths. Different from Llull or Leibniz, Camillo did not fund his logic on purely numerical or algebraic terms, rather on a more humanistic approach as the arts were used to dissect, structure, and guide the user. The role of automata must be read in conjunction with the logic of the *topica*: the role of machines here was not simply that of computing a symbolic language.

The theater did produce almost "automatic" results through its accurate—perfect, Camillo would have argued—map of knowledge and methods to dissect and reorganize it. The definition of the theater as a closed system of classical texts in which creativity emerged out recombining existing elements echoes with the "introverted" notion of databases in which novel constructs result from aggregating, combining existing items. The model for creativity presented through the *Theatro* also applies to digital databases: this is the one in which the "new" is already present within the given set of elements, somehow "hidden" within the endless combinations available, a virtual form to actualize.

Its organization and iconography suggested vertiginous correlations between images, moving from natural to mythical subjects, relating minute objects or observations to vast themes so as to prompt the user to possibly create their own images grounded on the classical tradition. Here the database was seen as an aesthetic device: the implementation of logical protocols gave rise to aesthetic effects. This is the most relevant part of Camillo's work, one we are also daily confronted with when we design through digital tools as we can clearly notice the presence of a data structure and a retrieval mechanism. The ideas posed here go beyond issues relate to the sheer ability to store large quantities of data or devising efficient retrieval mechanisms; the focus is rather on what images—we could say, metadata, in today's digital parlance—are appropriate to experience such collection of information and which elements can elicit creativity. In this sense, Camillo is an important precedent to also understand Aby Warburg's (1866–1929) *Mnemosyne Atlas* started in the 1920s in which visual material would come to completely replace the role that text had had in organizing large collections of material.

Camillo had a profound effect on the artistic scene. Gian Paolo Lomazzo (1538–92) constructed his *Idea del Tempio della Pittura* (1590) around seven columns. But it was architecture to be even more profoundly affected because of the close friendship between Camillo and Sebastiano Serlio. Camillo thought that his theater would be applicable to not only literary works but also other types of artistic production, such as paintings and architecture. The method of the topics would have been as effective to dissect text as other types of media, such as drawings and paintings; these too had deep rhetorical mechanisms to unveil and appropriate. Serlio's *Seven Books of Architecture*—whose first tome was published in 1537—echoed Camillo's theater in more than one way: first, the use of the number seven to structure the work; it also proceeded from particular to universal by deriving the primitives of his language from Vitruvius—custodian of the classical tradition—to then recompose them according to the principles of the aggregational logic (Carpo 2001, pp. 58–63). Although similar ideas were also to be found in the *Idea dell'eloquenza* (1544), Serlio's book was the first architecture book to consciously couple the conceptual tenets put forward by Camillo with the technological advancement of modern printing to inaugurate the modern tradition of the architectural treatise accessible to a wider audience (Carpo 2001). Finally Serlio's treatise also supported a design method based on *ars combinatoria* based on the idea that the architect must have been able to correctly bring together and articulate elemental pieces whose legitimacy had already been sanctioned by history.

The fascination with the theater was not only confined to Mannerist artists, but also found renewed interest at the arrival of the internet, which also posed similar questions regarding access to information and its relation to creativity. Several recent installations celebrated the pre-digital character of Camillo's databases. For instance, Robert Edgar's *Memory Theatre One* (1986)—programmed in *GraForth* on *Apple II*—updated the model of the memory theater according to 1980s' computer technology. Agnes Hegedüs (with Jeffrey Shaw) added virtual reality to her *Memory Theatre VR* (1997) consisting of a virtual museum in the shape of an eight-meter-diameter cylindrical space (Robert 1985). Despite several centuries having gone by since Camillo's work, these examples still confirm how deep the relation between architecture and information is and how they have influenced one another.

Leibniz and the *Ars Combinatoria*

German polymath Gottfried Wilhelm Leibniz (1646–1716) occupies a special place in the history of computers having largely contributed to both the birth of infinitesimal calculus and set the basis of formal logic through binary numeration. We have already seen how Llull's work influenced not only Leibniz's thinking on logic but also the design of his calculating machine. However, Leibniz's work had far greater implications for computation, as it moved the development of formal logic further and virtually lay the foundation to coding as the "algebra of ideas". Since *Dissertatio de art combinatoria* (1666), Leibniz demonstrated his interest in devising a universal language based on the simplest—i.e., the shortest—lexicon to express the largest, perhaps even infinite, number of statements; an idea that carried through his oeuvre and formed the basis of his most famous and enigmatic work *The Monadology* (1714). Different from what we have examined so far, Leibniz ventured outside the strict confines of science and sought to apply his language to philosophy: symbolic logic—based on algebraic operations—was developed and applied to thoughts rather than just numbers (at some point in his life, Leibniz even tried to apply it to juridical cases) (Leibniz 1667). He conceived it as the "alphabet for human thought" to which he eventually referred to as *characteristica universalis*: a discipline separate from the actual act of calculating (*calculus ratiocinator*), which he imagined to become more and more a mechanized activity. This separation was essential for both the development of more sophisticated logical thinking and for the actual development of the architecture of the modern computer. The basis of the *characteristica* should have been rooted in real phenomena, but the power of this type of thinking made immediately evident that "new realities" could have also been calculated and logically inferred through mathematical operations. This brilliant observation not only laid the foundations for computation but also opened up the possibility to generate new numerical combinations. This intuition promised to invest machines (proto-computers, in fact) with the potential to augment our cognitive capabilities and imagine different cultural and even social realities; a promise that still seems partially fulfilled today.

In defining his combinatorial logic, Leibniz developed his own symbols, out of which the ⊕ deserves closer attention. This symbol signifies the aggregation of two separate sets of statements, which can be combined according to a series of predetermined rules. The second axiom of the *Ars* enigmatically states that $A \oplus A = A$. Contrary to algebraic mathematics in which $1 + 1 = 2$, here we are adding concepts rather than numbers and therefore adding a concept to itself does not yield anything new. We have already seen how influential these considerations have been in the history of computer and, in particular, in George Boole's work.

The task of expressing thoughts through algebraic notation proved more complicated than expected as Leibniz realized that the problem was twofold: on the one hand, to map out all the domains to be simulated by defining their characteristics; on the other, to detect with univocal precision the primitives of such language. The task of naming such primitives was replaced by the idea of postulating them instead to concentrate all the efforts on the syntax of the logic to compute them. The result was used by Leibniz to describe with mathematical—algebraic, quantitative—precision qualitative phenomena: the *characteristica* allowed "running calculations, obtaining exact results, based on symbols whose meaning cannot be clearly and distinctively identified" (Eco 2014, p. 56). The clear separation between describing a problem through logic and calculating it is still an essential characteristic of how computers operate, but also—from the point of view of the history of databases—provided a way forward to manage the increasing number of notions and the unavoidable difficulties in defining them. As we will discuss in greater depth in the chapter on randomness, symbolic logic implicitly contains a wider range of application which is not strictly bound by reality; it can also be used to test propositions, almost as a speculative language for discoveries that, with the help of a calculating machine, take care of its "inhumane quality" (Goldstine 1972, p. 9).

Aby Warburg's *Mnemosyne Atlas*

The next historical fragment in this journey through the evolution of databases takes us to the beginning of the twentieth century to investigate a particular classificatory system whose methods to link and retrieve information have been often seen as precursors of the modern hyperlink.[14] To discuss this important element of digital design we have to venture into the idiosyncratic world of Aby Warburg. Abraham Moritz Warburg was part of one of the wealthiest German families in the late nineteenth century; being private bankers, the Warburgs' interests and fortunes extended far beyond Germany's borders, as they also had offices in London and New York. The story goes that Aby—the first descendant—renounced his rights to take over the family business and passed them on to his brother in exchange for financial backing to pursue his artistic interests. Unencumbered by financial pressures, Warburg could devote himself to studying antiquity—particularly Italian Renaissance—travelling the world, and, most importantly for us, supporting his research by methodically collecting books, objects, and images. In his native Hamburg, in 1933, Warburg managed to open the *Kulturwissenschaftliche Bibliothek Warburg*, a library and research institute whose layout reflected Warburg's own cataloging system. The very architecture of the institute was an embodiment of Warburg's archival practice as its four-story structure purposefully matched the division by media predicated by Warburg: Image (on the ground level), Word, Orientation, and Practice (on the top floor). The very classification system was also an ontological one that moved from religious themes to applied ones as one walked up the building. None of this original scheme survived in Hamburg: the rise of Nazism forced the institute to quickly relocate in London, where it still operates.

Despite having produced a very limited number of papers and publications, Warburg's research was restless and unique, warranting its own classification system in order to store and retrieve documents. It is still possible to explore the vast card collection kept by Warburg; contrary to traditional systems, cards were not annotated by bibliographical references but by theme, privileging their content—and potential associations—over the individual piece of information. The library too operated according to a complex and unique classification system in which books were organized by theme, forming small clusters around specific subjects. The very meaning of each book in this complex web directly depended on its position within the library; again, architecture and, in this case, pieces of furniture such as shelves *computed* the very information they contained. To make matters more difficult, Warburg understood this relation to be dynamic and constantly relocated books to reflect his latest ideas, or, in a more "generative" fashion, to test hypotheses. Whoever visits the Warburg Institute at University College London can either enjoy—as I did—or despair in trying to navigate such a unique system.

While working with his close assistant Fritz Saxl on a lecture on Schifanoia, Warburg started brainstorming ideas by pinning different materials on large black canvases. Besides the practical advantages of this way of working, the two saw the potential to foreground a different methodology to carry out art history studies. The project was given the name of *Mnemosyne Atlas* directly linking it to classical culture—"Mnemosyne" is the Greek goddess of memory the memory theaters of the Renaissance, and the format of the *Atlas*, a media whose popularity had been growing in Germany since the second half of the eighteenth century. Their ambition was to write a history of art without text; that is, to utilize iconology, the study of images, their migration and metamorphosis to trace cultural motifs through history. These mutating figures were termed "dynamograms" and the methodology tracing their reappearances and movement took the captivating name of "pathos formulas" to foreground the importance of symbolism. It is in this very quality of the project that many have seen the first incarnation of the digital hyperlink. By the time Warburg passed away there were seventy-nine panels, each dedicated to a particular symbolism traced in its mutations. As for the task of recording the content of each composition, these panels were constantly changing; a feature encouraged by the very media utilized. This journey involved collecting visual material of radically different sources: Plate 79, for instance, was dedicated to the theme of the Eucharist covering it both in time—with materials spanning from the ninth century to 1929—and space—with iconography from Germany, Japan, and Italy (Fig. 1.2). The panel featured—among other items—an image of Rafael's *The Mass at Bolsena* (1512) (part of the rooms he painted in the Vatican), the *Last Communion of St. Jerome* (1494–95) by Sandro Botticelli, two clippings from the *Hamburger Fremdenblatt* of 1929, and several photographs of Saint Peter's Square (probably taken from other publications). There was no hierarchy between copies and originals as well as between high and low cultural references or disciplines: Warburg combined Rafael and newspapers clippings; some panels also featured sketches, genealogical trees, and maps. The project took full advantage of the new media of the time—photography—to rethink the idea of memory, and mnemonics, in the light of increasingly more accessible images. As mentioned, the construction of the *Atlas* required not only a cross-disciplinary approach, but also an ability to evaluate different types of media which had not been available and that had to be invested with rigorous examination. Likewise, chronological ordering was abandoned not only because

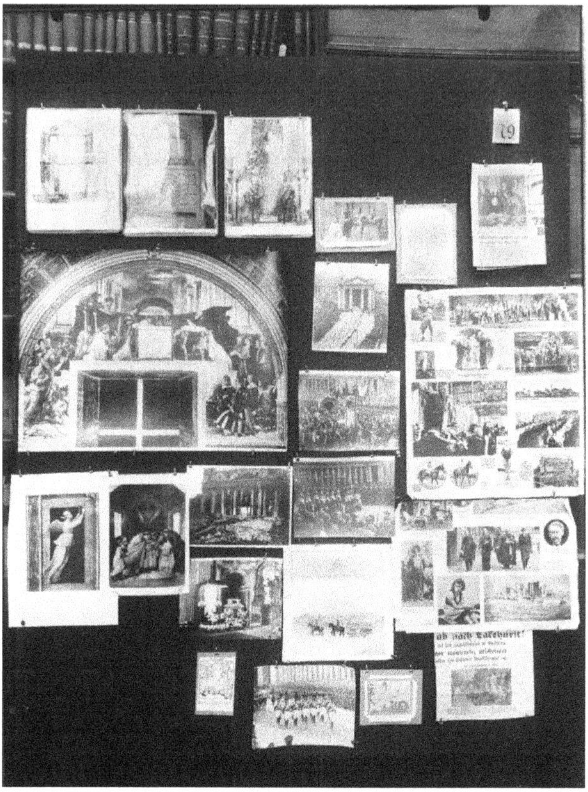

Figure 1.2 Image of Plate 79 from the Mnemosyne series. © The Warburg Institute.

of the heterogeneous sources employed—fragments collected followed both a diachronic and synchronic system—but also because the spatial arrangement adopted was that of an open network: there was no starting or vantage point through which to grasp an overall narrative. The meaning of each panel was neither to be found in the individual fragments collated—as archetypes—nor in the overall image the whole of the artifacts gave rise to; rather, what mattered was not the origin of the material but the relations established by each element (Agamben 2009, pp. 28–30). Contrary to other studies on iconology, Warburg ventured beyond mere visual affinity between disparate fragments to foreground the importance of their relationships. There was no *a priori* meaning which the plates were to reinforce; fragments were proposed for their "found" qualities, in the most objective fashion. The act of interpretation through writing was seen as an additional layer superimposed to open up a conversation to attribute more specific meanings to the material gathered. The *Atlas* was an example of information management elevated to the level of philosophy, as it was tasked to deliver both content and form; both of which were in a state of flux, as relations between all the elements could be explored in different ways. The overlay of text onto the images was at time employed to frame a field of interpretation; this too could have been intended as temporary or permanent part of the plates.

Warburg's "retrieval system" went far beyond the examples we have seen so far. The plates delivered an "open" set of materials revolving around a theme, which was then arbitrarily "fixed" by Warburg when the accompanying text was produced. The rigid logic of the memory theater had found a coherent new paradigm to replace it: the *Atlas* was a pliable method, more uncertain and complex. The arrangements of the plates were susceptible to alterations over time (new objects could be added or removed) and necessitated an interpreter to overlay a textual depth to the otherwise purely visual nature of each plate. The image describing this type of database was no longer that of the tree or circle; the relations between objects could no longer be imagined to be sitting on a flat surface, but rather moving in a topological space regulated by the strength of the connections linking the individual fragments, an ever-expanding landscape dynamically changing according to the multiple relations established by the objects in the database. This space did not have predetermined limits; it could constantly grow or shrink without changing its nature. In principle, any object could be connected to any other and changed at any time; in experiencing each plate, one would have learned about connections as much as content. Warburg's plates mapped a network of relations as much as a number of artifacts; any form of knowledge extracted would only have a "local" value depending on the shape of the network at the time the interpretation was produced, making any more general claim impossible. Pierre Rosenstiehl (1933–) saw in this condition similarities to the world of computation when he likened the navigation through a network to that of a "myopic algorithm" in which any local description could only be valid as a hypothesis of its general configuration; in other words, in a network we can only avail of speculative thinking. The similarities of this way of thinking information and the organization of the World Wide Web are striking: not only because of the dynamic nature of internet surfing, but also because of the convergent nature of the web in which disparate media such as sound, images, videos, and texts can be linked to one another (Rosenstiehl 1979, cited in Eco 2014, pp. 64–65). The conceptual armature to map and operate in such conditions found a mature formulation when Gilles Deleuze and Felix Guattari compared such space to a rhizome (1976). The impact of the internet on the arts goes well beyond the scope of this work; however, it is compelling to recall how David Lynch used the complex logic of the hyperlink as a narrative structure for his *Inland Empire* (2006). These are important examples of technological convergence, one of the key qualities brought about by digital media as it deviates from modern and premodern media in its ability to blend different formats giving rise to hybridized forms of communication (Jenkins 2006). Essential to this way of working is what we could define as "software plasticity"; that is, the possibility to convert different types of media into each other as well as transfer tools from software to software. These possibilities exist because of the fundamental underlying binary numeration at the core of digital computation, a sort of digital Esperanto that allows powerful crossovers between previously separate domains. The effects of this paradigm shift are noticeable in the most popular pieces of software designers daily use: the difference between, for instance, *Photoshop*, *Rhinoceros/Grasshopper*, or *Adobe After Effects* are thinning, as the three software packages—respectively designed to handle images, digital models, and videos—have gradually been absorbing each other's tools to allow end users to collapse three previously separate media into new types of hybrids.

To conclude, all left today of this ambitious projects are a series of photographs still part of the Warburg Institute's collection, as Warburg was among the few that at the end of the nineteenth century could afford a personal photographer to keep accurate records of his work, including the *Atlas*. For a long period Warburg's original approach received little attention; but the emergence of the World Wide Web in the 1990s reignited interest in the *Mnemosyne Atlas* given its strong resonance with the notion of the hyperlink. In 1997, the "Warburg Electronic Library" was launched to effectively materialize and explore what was always latent in the original work of Warburg and Saxl. The fluidity Warburg had explored within the physical boundaries of his institute could relive—albeit on an exponential scale—on the web where all the material could be rearranged according to personal interests by the algorithms guiding the retrieval of information. Similar to Camillo's, Warburg too saw his construction as a "laboratory of the mind" an externalizing mechanism through which to think and speculate, a quality that the internet has only enhanced.

Contemporary landscape

The ever-larger amounts of data we can now store and process at incredibly high speeds have only accreted the importance of databases. Lev Manovich (1960–), whose work in this area is of particular relevance, was first to put forward the idea that databases were the media format of our age (Manovich 2007). A whole science for analyzing astronomically large datasets has also emerged under the broad notion of Big Data to replace the scientific model based on hypothesizing/testing with correlational thinking. The implications of such transformations have not been fully grasped yet; however, it seems to us that a radical reversal of the historical relation between databases and design is taking place. Some compelling and elegant data visualizations are, for instance, being produced by the likes of Lev Manovich and Brendan Dawes to couple data mining techniques and aesthetic preoccupations.

In all the historical examples we observed how the structure of databases was derived from some "external" inspiration or metaphor: these had mostly come from nature, from the branching structure of trees, to anatomical parallels, etc.; but also from geometrical shapes charged of computational models are rather "exported" to and implemented as physical spaces. Nowhere is this more evident than in the organization of Amazon Fulfillment Centers in which items are stored in massive generic spaces according to a random logic which finds no link to historical models for arranging information be it that of libraries or museums. The precedent for this mode of organization—which Amazon tellingly refers to as "the cloud" (Lee 2013)—is rather to be found in the architecture of the magnetic core memory as it first emerged at the beginning of the 1950s (Fig. 1.3). A core memory unit arranged a series of fine wires in three-dimensions by threading them both vertically and horizontally. Among the many advantages this small piece of technology introduced there also that "access to any bit of a core plane . . . [was] as rapid as the any other"; hence the name random (Ceruzzi 1998, pp. 50–53). This technology was the first to imagine a highly abstract space no geometrical figure could represent. Similarly, files stored in the computer memory started being fragmented in order to be stored wherever there was sufficient space on the

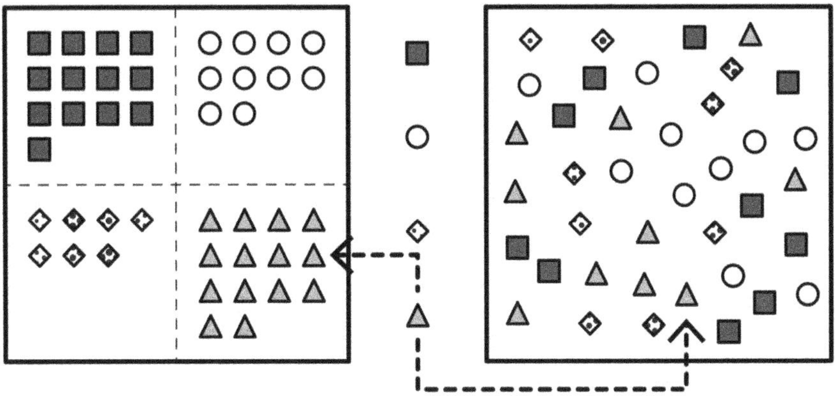

Figure 1.3 Diagram comparing the cloud system developed by Amazon with traditional storing methods. Illustration by the author.

computer hard drive, an operation end users are never really aware as they interact with the file as if this was a single element. Not only were files stored randomly but even individual files could be broken down into smaller parts and scattered whenever there was enough space to store it. The success of this brilliant idea was immediate and to this very day hard drives still operate according to the same principle. The Amazon Warehouse can be understood as nothing but the physical translation of this principle, a new kind of space whose principles are no longer mutated from nature but are rather taken from the very artificial logic of computers.

In our narrative this marks a profound shift. First, it completely puts an end to mnemonic methods to locate and retrieve information. Despite steadily losing their centrality in the history of information since the Renaissance, mnemonics still plays a part in our everyday experience of cities and buildings: the legibility of a city—through street patterns, landmarks, etc.—relies on its persistence in time. If, on the contrary, objects are constantly moving and finding their position according to no consistent logic, this very quality of space is lost. Secondly, *ars oblivionalis*—the need to forget in order to only remember what is deemed important—stops casting its menacing shadow which, incidentally, had brought Camillo to the verge of madness. Everything can be remembered as limitations in storing capacity, and mining techniques keep increasing at an exponential pace. Consequently, traditional media to navigate space such as maps see their usefulness has been eroded. It is not possible to draw a conventional map of a space which has no order whatsoever and is in constant flux. Maps' role is taken up by algorithms, what was communicated visually is now turned into computer code, in other words, into the abstract syntax of logics, the structure of databases. In the Amazon Warehouse, this is implemented by tagging all items with Radio Frequency Identification (RFID) labels which both contain data describing the product and send signals picked up with scanners. In this specific scenarios robots move through the warehouse filling shelves or loading items attached to an order. Maps have been replaced by search engines; that is, by models for querying databases. The logic of databases finds here its reified implementation as it coincides with architecture itself. The spatiality of this literally inhuman piece of architecture bears relations to no architectural precedent but it is rather the last iteration in the long history of organizing information. Out of the two fundamental elements of databases—hierarchy and retrieval—only the latter survives to absorb all the cultural and aesthetic qualities of databases.

The aesthetic of the database seems then to have taken yet another turn in which the computer can be naturalized and exploited in all its creative potential. Once again, as Ben-Ami Lipetz promptly noticed at a time in which the potential of modern computation could only be speculated, its success will depend more on the intellectual agenda accompanying its progresses rather than technical developments alone.

Notes

1. "Building Information Modeling (BIM) is a process involving the generation and management of digital representations of physical and functional characteristics of places. Building information models (BIMs) are files (often but not always in proprietary formats and containing proprietary data) which can be extracted, exchanged or networked to support decision-making regarding a building or other built asset." *Building Information Modeling. Wikipedia* entry. Available at: https://en.wikipedia.org/wiki/Building_information_modeling (Accessed May 16, 2016).
2. This cataloging method was conceived by Melvil Dewey (1851–1931) in 1876. His decimal classification system introduced the notion of relative index which cataloged book by content rather than acquisition as well as allowed new books to be added to the system.
3. Anonymous, *Ad Herennium,* c. 80 BC, quoted in Yates (1966, p. 179).
4. Goodness, Greatness, Eternity, Power, Wisdom, Will, Virtue, Truth, and Glory (Yates 1966, p. 179).
5. Gods, Angels, the Zodiac and the seven known planets, Man, Imagination, the Animal Kingdom, the Vegetable Creation, the Four Elements, and the Arts and Sciences (Yates 1966, pp. 180–81).
6. *The Ladder of Ascent and Descent* (Llull 1512).
7. Crossley was first to indicate Llull as the first to use variables, a statement that has not always been met with unanimous consensus. However, the transformation of subjects into predicate is a unique feature of Llull's system which, in our opinion, also indicates the presence of a logic of variation (See Crossley 2005).
8. Key figures to understand such mutation are: Pico della Mirandola, Giulio Delminio Camillo's *Theatro*, Giordano Bruno's *Medicina lulliana* (1590), Gottfried Leibniz's *Ars Combinatoria* (1666) as well as Athanasius Kirchner.
9. Paraphrased from Cingolani (2004). Most of factual and critical account of Camillo's work is based on the outstanding work that Lina Bolzoni has been developing on the Mannerist thinker. (See Bolzoni 2015).
10. Here we also know that a wooden model of the theater was built, though almost immediately after Camillo's return to Italy all traces of this artifact were lost.
11. None of the paintings was ever made. However, we know that one copy of the *L'Idea del Theatro* contained 201 drawings executed by Titian; the book, possibly destroyed, was part of the library of the Spanish ambassador in Venice—Diego Hurtado de Mendoza (Bolzoni 2015, p. 30).
12. Quintilian, *Institutiones oratoriae*, XII, 2, 22 (Quoted in Bolzoni 2015, p. 23).

13. A great brain outside ourselves. Translation by the author.
14. A hyperlink is defined as a link between different media formats on the internet. The hyperlink can connect to another location or another part of the same hypertext. Hyperlinks do not have to only link texts, but other media such as images can act as triggers.

Chapter 2

Morphing

Introduction

A discussion on morphing and contouring techniques will bring us to the very core of CAD tools. Not only because most software packages have such or similar commands, but also because contouring and morphing tools have at some point been used by any digital designer to either generate or describe a particular geometry. Contouring and morphing, out are in fact both generative and representational tools. Regardless of which one we intend to use, these techniques are apt to describe particularly complex forms, whose intricacy cannot be accounted for by Euclidian solids. Contouring suspends geometrical categorization, to replace it with a rigorous instrument to explore, almost search, or even define, the actual shape of the object designers wish to represent or create. It is therefore not a coincidence that the most popular use of contouring lines is mostly employed to describe the surface of the earth: physical maps feature contour curves, which are extracted from the imaginary intersection between topography of the earth and a series of horizontal planes. The earth—as all natural forms—has an irregular, hardly ever repeating form requiring a more complex set of surveying tools to greatly expand the reductive geometries of primitive forms to take into consideration their unique formal complexity. The efficacy of this method has since been extended to many other domains particularly to meteorological and climatological studies, as the environment too gives rise to hardly simplifiable shapes.

By shining light on the origins of these tools we also begin to clarify their relevance for design disciplines. From nautical design, to animated characters in movies, to architecture, there is a whole plethora of fields that have in fact made use of these techniques. On a superficial level, we could claim that CAD tools have simply appropriated methods to contour objects which vastly predated the invention of computers. However, a closer examination will reveal how in the process of absorbing them, CAD software also opened up a new or more sophisticated series of operations. For instance, the possibility to recursively contour an object—almost at *inifinito*—or to endow this operation with dynamic qualities has altered how contouring tools can be used and made into generative tools.[1] We can therefore speak of quantitative innovation, as it is possible to handle more information (e.g., more control points describing contour paths) that has eventually given rise to a qualitative difference: in fact, more complex techniques such as layering, caging, fields, and morphing have since emerged based on this new affordance. The ease with which digital tools have allowed to control large sets of curves has also been instrumental in facilitating the reversal of this process; if contour lines have commonly been used to describe three-dimensional forms, the opposite process has also been streamlined.

We will move from the static use of these techniques of contour lines, to two and a half-dimensional ones of layering, and finally to morphing, understood as both a dynamic and three-dimensional generative technique. As defined earlier, contour lines are generated by intersecting a three-dimensional object with planes: this operation simplifies the original shape without reducing it to any primitive form. Layering is a more complex technique which has sometime been referred to as two and a half dimensional: that is, three-dimensional depth can be alluded to by manipulating bi-dimensional elements (Colletti 2013, pp. 169–80). Layered elements begin to register the traces of a potential or latent transformation within a shape, and blur the precise boundaries of discrete forms creating undefined, ambiguous spaces or shapes which can be exploited by designers. Morphing allows such an allusion to movement to be manipulated directly: it in fact describes the seamless transformation of a form or object into another one. This can be communicated through drawings or more directly through videos. As we shall see, morphing techniques emerged alongside modern computers, but have become part of the cultural and architectural imaginary only in the 1990s when the movie *Terminator 2* (1991) demonstrated their full visual and generative potential. The journey that will take us to contemporary examples of digital morphing and layering will be a long and articulated one that will cross as varied disciplines as naval design, art, cinema, and sciences.

Layering: Seeing irregularities

The idea of superimposing semitransparent sheets upon each other in order to modify and evolve a piece of design is a very old one. The architecture of CAD software, however, only offers the visual effect of overlaying different objects. What software actually does is to tag the objects composing the scene so that they can be separated and interacted with only in subsets.

The overall composition is therefore broken down into parts, "disembodied." This operation, undoubtedly, has practical advantages, however we will rather dwell in its deployment to generate novel formal configurations. Toward the end of the nineteenth century a series of scientific discoveries and hypotheses impacted on the cultural imaginary of artists and designers, who would begin to radically question the received notion of aesthetics and creativity. It will only be with the emergence of historical avant-garde movement that such agitation will manifest. It is worth noticing in passing that these very same concerns will also determine the initial definition of a proto-voxel spatiality, which will be discussed in the last chapter of the book.

The first example emerging in the nineteenth century coincided with the advent of photography which opened up new representational domains. Though artists greatly contributed to the idea of capturing a subject in all its formal complexity, the first examples of layering photographs were not completed by an artist. Francis Galton (1822–1911)—Charles Darwin's cousin—was a well-established British polymath, who, among other activities, in 1877 concentrated on physiognomy studies by taking photographs of British criminals and overlaying them onto each other. He called them "Composite Portraits" and worked on them until the beginning of the twentieth century to uncover recurrent features in facial traits. Galton's work could be one of the first uses of layering in the same fashion in which such command features in contemporary pieces of software such as *Adobe Photoshop* or *Autodesk AutoCAD*. Besides technical affinities, Galton's use of layering was not really exploring the unique and distinctive characters of human facial traits; rather he sought to "normalize" their irregularities, to think of them "statistically" to extract an ideal, average, and yet abstract type resulting from the process of sheer quantitative accumulation. Rather than an exploratory process, Galton interpreted it as a rigorous principle to reduce complexity and tease out persistence within different forms. Galton's exercise had larger social implications, as it sought to justify and promote the emergent field of eugenics (the idea of social betterment through breeding manipulation), which eventually would produce catastrophic results in the twentieth century. Jeffrey Kipnis (1951–) spoke of "phenomenological reduction" in Galton's work as "all of the variations between the particular noses were cancelled, only the form of the ideal nose would remain. The ideal proportions of the nose would never exist in any single nose, yet they would become the transcendent order hidden in all noses in general."[2]

Photography was not solely used for the purpose of social engineering as around the same time Étienne-Jules Marey (1830–1904) developed a series of long exposure photographs of moving subjects, such as flying birds or human subjects performing some physical activity. These images too made use of layering techniques: the individual positions of the subjects recorded at regular intervals were overlaid by making each still semitransparent and therefore legible both as an autonomous image and as a part of the continuous trajectory of movement. Though similar technically, Marey's images no longer pursued an ideal geometry through reduction, but rather allowed the viewer to experience and explore the complexity of movement and trajectories in their formal complexity. Contrary to Galton's, Marey's images did not average out differences between successive stills but rather foregrounded the intricate qualities of movement and transformation. As we will also discuss in the chapter on voxels, other technologies emerged toward the end of the eighteenth century to cast a new eye on matter and material processes. Layered or composite photographs—but also X-ray scans—not only recorded the irregular geometries of the internal parts of the body but they also flattened them by showing different organs as if placed on a single plane. These processes provided artists with a scientific medium to investigate transparency and play with depth. The idea of transparency also prompted artists to question the status of objects whose boundaries looked increasingly uncertain, a condition well captured by Kazimir Malevich's (1878–1935) observation that objects had "vanished in smoke" (cited in Bowlt 1987, p. 18).

Modern architecture was also influenced by these developments; particularly, the theme of transparency well suited the technological advancements in the use of glass in buildings. As pointed out by Colin Rowe (1920–99), the work of Lázló Moholy-Nagy (1895–1946) provided an extended definition of transparency no longer bound with its physical dimension only. György Kepes (1906–2001) defined it as: "If one sees two or more figures overlapping one another, and each of them claims for itself the common overlap part, then one is confronted with a contradiction of spatial dimensions. To resolve this contradiction one must assume the presence of a new optical quality. The figures are endowed with transparency: that is, they are able to interpenetrate without an optical destruction of each other. Transparency however implies more than an optical characteristic, it implies a broad spatial order. Transparency means a simultaneous perception of different spatial locations. Space not only recedes but fluctuates in a continuous activity. The position of the transparent figures has equivocal meaning as one sees each figure now as the closer, now as the further one" (1944, p. 77. Cited in Rowe and Slutzy 1963). This kind of spatiality utilized layering techniques in order to suggest a less hierarchical, more dynamic spatial organization as well as three-dimensional depth through strictly bi-dimensional manipulations. Rowe would detect the more interesting architectural results of this new spatial sensibility in the work of Le Corbusier both in his *Villa Stein* (1927) in Garches and in the proposal for the palace of the League of Nations in Geneva (1927) (Rowe and Slutzy 1963).

Layering techniques also enhanced more traditional techniques such as tracing, which could now be charged with greater conceptual depth. The work of Bernard Tschumi (1944–) and Peter Eisenman (1932–) used tracing techniques to respectively add a cinematic and an archaeological dimension to design. Tschumi initially developed such an approach through more speculative studies captured in his *Manhattan Transcripts* (1981), whereas Peter Eisenman consistently made use of tracing techniques: first in the series of houses marking the beginnings of his practicing career, and then in the *Aronoff Center* at the University of Cincinnati (1988–96) in which the addition of digital tools greatly expanded the possibilities to study figural overlays and geometrical transformations. The overall plan of the building was obtained through successive superimpositions of different alignments, grids, and distortions which were amalgamated in the final architecture by performing Boolean operations of addition and subtraction. Carefully placed openings, shifted volumes, and distribution of colors were employed to indexically record the transformations performed during the design process. The complexity and control over the use of such techniques would find an ideal ally in *Form·Z*, the software package developed by Chris Yessos with the direct input of Eisenman himself. The more mature and in a way flamboyant integration of layering techniques and digital tools is perhaps best exemplified in *Guardiola House* (1988), in which the game of tracing the superimpositions of the rotating volumes was explored in all its full three-dimensional qualities.

Finally, a particular combination of layering and wireframe modes of visualization has sometime appeared in the work of Rem Koolhaas' OMA. The first use of this technique appeared in the drawings prepared for the competition entry for *Parc La Villette* in 1983 and then 1989 for another competition for the *Très Grande Bibliothèque*, both in Paris. The plan for the Parisian park is particularly effective not only because the layering techniques well served the design concepts which is based on the direct accumulation of a series of elements, but also because the office did not hesitate to publish the plan as it appears on the computer screen of the computer program utilized. This is one of the first times in which the electronic, digital aesthetic of CAD software is deliberately used as an aesthetic device (Fig. 2.1). Since then the office has often published their proposal by using the wireframe visualization mode—often the default visualization option in 3D-modelers. These images simultaneously depict all the elements irrespective

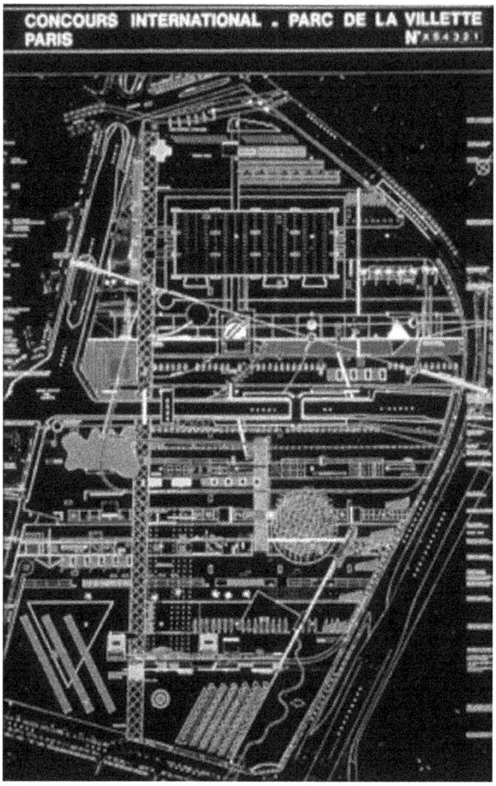

Figure 2.1 OMA. Plan of the competition entry for Parc La Villette (1982). All the elements of the project are shown simultaneously taking advantage of layering tools in CAD. © OMA.

of whether they are interior or exterior ones; this effect particularly suited the overall concept of OMA's entry for the library in Paris, as it showed a series of interior spaces as organs floating within the overall cubical form of the building. This type of representation had a lasting effect on the aesthetic of the Dutch office since the 2011 show; *OMA/Progress* at the Barbican Art Gallery in London still showed some drawings developed with this technique.

Contouring: Exploring the irregular

Though the emergence of scientific perspective will be discussed in depth in the chapter on scanning, it is worth noticing here how the methods developed by Filippo Brunelleschi (1377–1446) first and then theorized by Leon Battista Alberti (1404–1472) suited well the representation of rectilinear objects such as buildings but presented significant shortcomings when applied to irregular figures. Vaults, columns were likely to be the more complex parts of buildings, but also objects such as the mazzocchio—similar to a chaperon—all proved much more difficult to draw according to the new method. The most complex of these was certainly the human body which, after all, was also the most prominent element in paintings. Alberti himself had indicated that the body could have been treated as a series of triangular facets that the artist could have smoothen out by controlling the distribution of light on them. The application of perspectival rules to the depiction of the human body found a much more precise resolution in Piero della Francesca (1416–92) whose "Other Method," also discussed in the chapter on scanning, was tested to portray—among several examples—the human head. In this chapter we will not concentrate on the "proto-computational" qualities of the method, as it allowed to recalculate the coordinates of the points surveyed, but rather on the steps proposed by Piero to plot points and extract contour curves describing the head. In order to survey its irregularities without reducing it to primitive shapes such as the triangles as proposed by Alberti, Piero measured the position of sixteen points along eight horizontal virtual planes intersecting the head. Constructed in this way, the geometry of the head was not reduced to an ideal set of primitives, which would have implied the existence of a series of *a priori* forms to which irregular shapes had to conform. By using contour lines, Piero conceptually inverted the process operating from the "inside out"; he proceeded from the detail (point) to move to more complex geometrical entities that allowed him to eventually survey the whole head: points were strung together by curves and eventually lofted to give rise to surfaces. The process was rigorous but could not anticipate what the next step would produce. It was an exploratory method in which the artist "learned" about the shape of the human while producing a representation of it. If Alberti started from the ideal geometries of triangular facets to eventually "deforming" them to approximate the actual silhouette of the body, Piero inverted the process by injecting more geometrical control at every step. He implicitly accepted the exceptional nature of the object surveyed and devised a method able to explore its shape rather than constraining it. The rigorousness of this process eventually produced a set of information that could be both drawn and transmitted. This was technically obtained by lowering the degree of complexity of the geometrical entities utilized: if Euclidian solids would have been too overdetermined and inflexible, points provided the necessary agility to survey the head without immediately having to discard a whole series of information. From there, he could work incrementally, first by adding more points along each plane to approximate the head's outline with greater precision and then by increasing the dimensions of each new geometry introduced by moving from lines (contours), surfaces (skin), and volume (head). In contemporary digital parlance, we could say that the process allowed Piero to produce a high-resolution survey. First of all because using points allowed him to retain a whole series of information that Alberti's method would have had to immediately discard. Moreover, the whole process was more flexible, allowing Piero to add as many intersecting planes as necessary, therefore controlling the "resolution" of the drawing obtained: the more points and planes dissecting the figure, the higher is the fidelity of the final representation.

It is therefore not a surprise if the other major application of contouring techniques was in topographical survey, as the earth like the human body is an irreducibly irregular object. The development of contour maps of sea beds emerged in 1738 when cartographer Philippe Buache (1700–73) dedicated himself to apply a similar method to marine maps. If the datum in Piero's experiment was represented by the eight intersecting planes, Buache utilized the water surface from which soundings were emitted. Once again by incrementally increasing the number of soundings a more detailed relief of the seabed could be constructed. Besides running lines between the points, Buache began to calculate the actual position of contour lines which eventually constituted the main piece of information included in the final marine charts (Booker 1963, p. 71). These techniques have been consistently employed since. For instance, on April 24, 1890, Joseph E. Blather patented a new technique to contour topographical landscapes, which is still largely employed to make physical models as the works of artist Charles Csuri (1922–) and architect Frank Gehry (1929–)—to name a few—demonstrate. The method proceeded from bi-dimensional topographical maps of a certain area that were cut out along their contour lines out of wax plates. Eventually the plates were stacked on top of each other forming a three-dimensional relief. The same procedure could be inverted to generate the negative landscape to utilize as a mold. Finally a piece of paper was to be pressed between the two molds to obtain a three-dimensional relief of the area. A variation of this principle was developed in Japan by Morioka who projected a regular pattern—parallel lines or grid—on the subject to portray. The deformations caused by the uneven topography of the face—effectively utilized here as a projection screen—would be contour lines to be traced over and reproduced, stacked, and carved to form a complete three-dimensional relief (Beaman 1997, pp. 10–11).

Again, these examples show how contouring was consistently employed whenever Euclidian solids did not suffice to describe forms. Complex pieces of architecture did not constitute an exception to this rule as Hans Scharoun's (1893–1972) Philarmonie built in Berlin between 1956 and 1963 also confirms. The initial design presented nearly insurmountable difficulties arising from the complexity and irregularity of its geometries. The gap between the information contained in the drawings and that required to actually build the concert hall became all too evident when the architect realized that the set of points for the nearly completed foundations were so off that the whole process had to be restarted as it could not be fixed anymore (in Evans 1995, pp. 119–21). Scharoun had to invent a working process to survey his own design, one that could avoid reducing both the amount of information recorded and complexity of the shapes proposed. Instead of cutting the building at conventional points, the three-dimensional model was sliced at very close and regular intervals to produce sort of depth-less sections more akin to profiles than traditional sections. It is not a coincidence that the car industry also utilized the same method to prepare shop drawings: the car's chassis—also a complex and irregular shape—was sliced at approximately 100 millimeter intervals. However, Scharoun's method also shared similarities with that of Blanther or Morioka as the contour lines were applied after the object had been modeled and, therefore, did not have any structural or regulating qualities but were purely utilized for representational reasons. It is interesting to notice that some CAD packages—for example, *Rhinoceros*—offer a contouring tool able to slice both two- and three-dimensional objects. This command can be utilized according to either of the two paradigms just illustrated: that is, as a surveying tool as developed by Scharoun, or as a guiding principle to apply a structural system as in the case of the design of a hull.

A more recent, perhaps curious example of exploratory contouring was the unusual brief set by Enric Miralles (1955–2000) instructing his student on "how to lay out a croissant" (Miralles and Prats 1991, pp. 191–92). Despite the blunt, straightforward nature of the task, the brief was also a beautiful example of contemporary practitioners still exploiting the spatial qualities of morphing techniques. In introducing the exercise, Miralles was adamant to emphasize its exploratory nature; the croissant is an object conceived with no regard for geometrical purity or composition, whose visual appeal combines with its olfactory qualities resulting from the natural ingredients and artificial processes: after all, Miralles noted, "a croissant, or half moon [*sic*] in Argentina, is meant to be eaten" (Miralles and Prats 1991, p. 192). Similar to the experiments carried out since the fifteenth century, geometrical constraints were gradually inserted only when necessary in the process: after an initial phase in which the surveyor should "emphasise the tangents, . . . let the constellations of centrepoints [*sic*] appear without any relation between them," Miralles begin to lay out a series of more controlled steps that will allow to draw up sections, axes, etc. The experiment is a distilled example of Miralles' poetics and formal repertoire as similar techniques can be detected in some of his most successful buildings, such as the *Barcelona Olympic Archery Range* completed with Carme Pinos (1955–) in 1991.

Today, not only are contouring commands included in many software packages, but some even provide specific tools to automatically extract cross sections from a set of guiding profiles.[3] As for the historical examples already mentioned, the immediate advantage of these tools endowed the user to proceed both in a descriptive fashion—from object to representation—and in a projective mode to design. In these instances described, contouring proved a powerful technique to both reduce the complexity of an otherwise complicated form and control its formal and material qualities in greater detail.

Lofting: Building the irregular

The first design discipline to make use of contouring techniques was naval design. As early as the sixth and seventh centuries, we find documentations confirming the use of this technique. This is not entirely surprising though as the shape of a boat's hull is also an irregular surface impossible to represent through primitive geometries. Moreover, the overall shape did not result from abstracted geometries or aesthetic proportions, but rather it was the result of the very interaction between material affordance and dynamic forces the hull had to withstand once in use. As we will see, contouring techniques were used to form a surface out of a series of wooden elements representing the cross sections through the hull. However the great improvement in drawing techniques that took place between the fifteenth and sixteenth centuries allowed ship builders to invert this process therefore working from either cross sections or the overall surface of the hull. Peter Jeffrey Booker (1924–) illustrated this development through the work of Matthew Baker (1530–1613) who, in 1586, published a sort of textbook on ship draught which summarizes state of the art ship-building techniques in the sixteenth century (Booker 1963, pp. 68–78). The method transmitted in the book had already been in use for several centuries and consisted in drawing up the cross-section profiles of the hull—ribbed sections—place them at regular intervals, and finally lofting them by applying the outer surface of the hull. The shape of each cross section was composed of arcs and lines, and the template drawings showed the various centers and respective radii to use to reproduce and, most importantly, scale up the sections. In fact, these had to be redrawn at 1:1 scale on the floor of large column-less spaces—that is, lofts—before joining them together.[4] What resonates with contemporary digital tools is not so much the possibility of repeatedly sectioning a shape, but rather the techniques to transform profiles into the ruling surfaces of the hull. In the sixteenth century contouring started being used to generate rather than describe irregular forms. This was mainly due to the improvement of drawing techniques—mostly those of combined orthographic projections—which could have been used as analogue computing devices to extract information from a basic set of sections. Over the basic cross sections was overlaid a virtual plane (datum) representing the water line. Through orthographic projections from one set of sections it was possible to extract the complementary ones—that is, the plan and the elevation views. In order to understand the conceptual implications of this process, Booker asks us to imagine the volume contained by the hull as a solid through which a series of evenly spaced orthogonal planes were sliced to obtain the basic two-dimensional profiles that would then be carved out of wood. As Michael Young (2013, p. 126) pointed out in describing the role of contouring lines in this process: "The curve becomes the primary representational element not as boundary edge, but as a notation of the edgeless condition interior to a surface of freeform curvature, a contour." This technique was extremely advanced, comparable to the Monge's Descriptive Geometry; however, secrecy was an essential ingredient of the trade and only the publication of manuals allowed it to circulate. The combination of contouring and projections well survived the introduction of many representational and technological evolutions and can still be seen in drawings of hulls produced around 1900.

As we will see in much greater detail in the chapter on parametrics, *S. Carlino alle Quattro Fontane* by Francesco Borromini (1599–1667) represented an important example of continuity and differentiation in the baroque. *S. Carlino*'s internal elevation was neatly separated into three segments whose middle one presented the most complex and irregular geometrical features. Whereas the use of complex geometries to connect different parts of building had been used for centuries, *S. Carlino* presented these problems at the scale of the whole building, not simply to resolve particular details. Besides alluding to a four-crossed layout, this section mainly acted as a transition between the other two segments, morphing from the distorted octagonal outline of the lower third to the oval profile of the intrados of the dome. In this section we find an early example of digital lofting: given a start and an end outline, most 3D-modelers can generate the interpolating surface connecting them. In Borromini's cases, it is however more appropriate to speak of swiping, a modeling function also available in many 3D-modelers, which also found its origins in construction techniques utilized to compute surfaces generated out of nonplanar edges. Such surfaces could be obtained by making an open rectangular box with two different profiles as long sides and then filled with sand. A separate piece was cut out and used as a cross-sectional profile—called "rail"—and then run along the top of the box in order to skim off the excess sand. If repeated, a continuous surface and yet locally varying surface could have been plotted.[5] Swiping is therefore a more accurate description of *S. Carlino*'s middle third, as it provides a greater geometrical control over the curve followed to connect the top and bottom profiles. Again, swiping provided a robust technique to break down complex, irregular forms, reducing them to a series of simpler geometries that could be more easily controlled. Digital swiping still offers such advantages, but it also allows to invert the process; in fact, rather than deconstructing irregular surfaces into its basic components, such tools can also proceed in the opposite direction to explore the effects of varying basic parameters onto the final geometry.

Caging objects

A more advanced type of three-dimensional distortion—more than lofting and railing—is often referred to as caging. Such a tool offered, for instance, by CAD programs such as *Rhinoceros* and *Autodesk 3DSMax* allows to wrap a single or a group of objects in a bounding box with editable control points. Rather than deforming the individual objects, this tool transfers the transformations applied to its control points to whatever is included in it. Again, such tools can be very effective in the design process, as they allow the user to only perform elementary operations on control points, leaving to the algorithmic processes to transfer them to the final object(s). Besides the practical advantages of this way of working, we should also consider the conceptual ones as the designer can concentrate on the "strategic" formal moves leaving to the software the complex task of applying them the final objects. An early example of this way of conceptualizing form and its evolution was provided by the famous diagrams prepared by Sir D'Arcy Thompson (1860–1948) showing the morphological relations between different types of fish (Thompson 2014).

Fields theory and spatiology

The use of contouring, layering, and morphing tools in design found an interesting and unusual precedent in the work of Paolo Portoghesi (1931–). Portoghesi's international fame is mainly associated with postmodernism which he championed in the 1980 Venice Architecture Biennale he curated. Far less known, but by no means any less original or relevant, is his work on the history of technology and baroque architecture. It is at the intersection of the these two apparently disjoined fields that Portoghesi placed his "field theory" (Teoria dei Campi) in which we find an innovative use of contouring and layering techniques applied to architecture (Portoghesi 1974, pp. 80–94). The method—developed in the first half of the 1960s—conceived of space as a volumetric phenomenon.

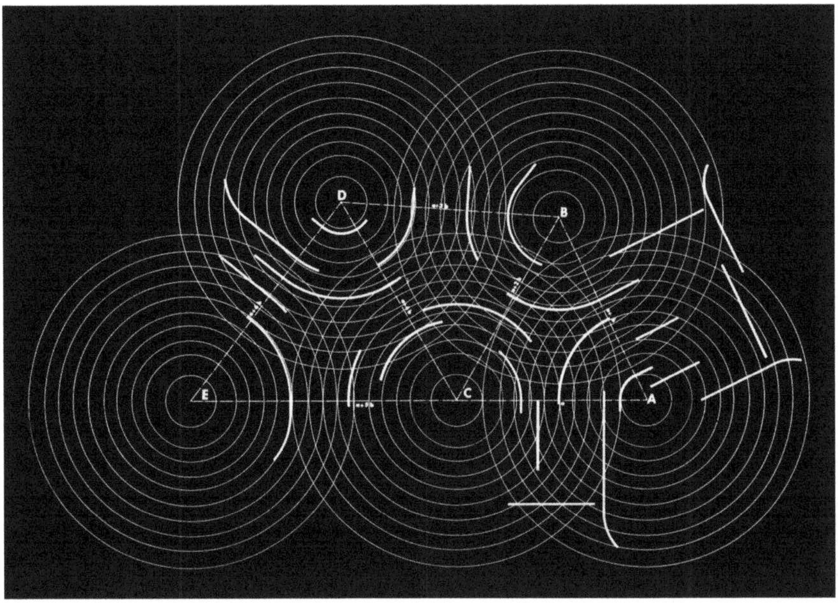

Figure 2.2 P. Portoghesi (with V. Giorgini), Andreis House. Scandriglia, Italy (1963-66). Diagram of the arrangement of walls of the house in relations to the five fields. © P. Portoghesi.

It however departed from other similar ideas, as it did not consider space to be a homogeneous substance, but rather differentiated one, affected by the presence of, light, air, sound as well as architectural elements, people, and activities. While studying the role of hyper-ornated altars—the *retablos*—in the organization of baroque churches in Mexico, Portoghesi intuited that these architectural elements could have been imagined as "emanating" some sort of weaves through the space of the otherwise sober interiors of these churches. Traditional orthographic drawings of the physical parts of the buildings would not have captured this ephemeral spatial quality and a more abstracted, diagrammatic language was necessary. The series of studies that followed imagined space as traversed by rippling weaves concentrically departing from specific points—similar to the surface of a pond rippling when stones are thrown in. Expanding outward in form of circles, these diagrams could have also been interpreted as regulatory templates to determine the presence of walls, openings, orientation of roofs, etc. but also choreographing the more immaterial qualities of space such as light and sound. Most importantly, Portoghesi—at the time working closely with Vittorio Giorgini (1926–2010)—began to realize that the field method could have been used to generate architecture. The method was not only suggesting a more open, porous spatiality, but also turned the initial part of the design process into an exploration of spatial qualities in search of a formal expression.

The *Church of the Sacred Family* in Salerno (1974) is perhaps one his best projects in which the results of the method are clearly legible. However, it was in the *Andreis House* (1963–6) in Scandriglia that the method was first applied (Portoghesi 1974, pp. 149–59). The organization of the house loosely followed the template constructed through the circles; however, the final layout achieved a much greater spatial richness, as the internal circulation unfolded freely between the various volumes of the house. By working in this way, Portoghesi could rethink the rigid division between architecture and the space it contains: not only solid and void could be played against each other, but also interior and exterior could be conceived in a more continuous, organic fashion. This resulted in a different approach to context: the circles propagated outwardly to eventually "settle" along the topographical features of the site. This method certainly drew inspiration from the organic plans of F. L. Wright and the experiments De Stijl was carrying out in the Netherlands both of which had taken place in the first part of the twentieth century; however a mere historiographic analysis would not do justice to Portoghesi's results. To better appreciate his work, we could set up a quick digital experiment in which contemporary digital software is used to re-enact Portoghesi's theory. We could in fact imagine to literally simulate the dispersion of some sort of fluid from a series of specific points carefully placed within a topographical model of a site. The software settings would allow us to control the liquid's speed, viscosity, its distribution, etc.; whereas the topographical undulations of the terrain would affect its dispersion. The architecture would emerge from freezing this time-based experiment at an arbitrary moment, presumably when other concerns, much harder to simulate—programmatic organization, client's desires, personal preferences—were also satisfied. As for other experiments involving contouring and morphing, this process too would presuppose an exploratory attitude toward architecture, as the overall configuration would not be possible to anticipate without running the simulations. Besides understanding design as an exploratory process, the field method also implied space as subjected to continuous deformation, almost a metamorphic transformation borne out of the radiating circles. Portoghesi himself pointed out how all the geometrical elements of the diagrams could have been understood as evolving manifolds containing a variety of curves occasionally coinciding with "simple" lines. In other cases, the nature of curves would provide the architect with indications regarding the directionality of spaces, their connections with both other interior or exterior spaces.

Vittorio Giorgini's role in this collaboration was greater than simply assisting Portoghesi and the full implication of these ideas conjured for *Andreis House* would only reveal themselves in full later on in his academic activity at Pratt,

New York, between 1971 and 1979. This research would culminate with the invention of *Spaziologia* (spatiology): a design discipline informed by the study of natural forms, by their topological understanding, and by a personal interest in both architecture and engineering. More precisely, long before moving to the United States, Giorgini had already completed and designed several projects in which these ideas prominently featured. *Saldarini House* (1962) was a daring biomorphic structure borne out of Giorgini's interest in topological transformations, which could be compared to Kiesler's *Endless House*.

In fact if a criticism were to be directed at Portoghesi's work, it would point at the relatively traditional family of forms utilized to interpret his field diagrams; these experiments were calling for a new, fluid, perhaps even amorphous spatiality. This missing element was actually at the center of Giorgini's work—even prior to his collaboration with Portoghesi—and would also continue afterwards finding both greater theoretical grounding and formal expression. Giorgini worked on the topological premises of form to devise a new formal repertoire that could reinvent architecture anew. The bi-dimensional diagrams of *Field Theory* turned into three-dimensional topological spaces subjected to forces and transformations. The formal and mathematical basis of such geometries first appeared in the work of Felix Klein (1849–1925) in 1872 and then with Henri Poincaré (1854–1912) and found a direct, global expression in the work of Giorgini. These very themes reemerged in the 1990s when architects such as Greg Lynn sensed that the introduction of animation software was giving a renewed impetus to these conversations. This is an important point, as it marks the limit of layering, caging techniques to account for formal irregularities: as we have seen these had been powerful tools as long as form was conceived in its static configuration. Topologies, on the other hand, were dynamic and evolving constructs subjected to forces which could be conceptualized by a new generation of software: layer and fields gave way to morphing techniques.

Morphing: The dynamics of form

Of all the techniques considered in this chapter, morphing constitutes the most seamless one to explore formal irregularities, as it allows to transform an image or a form into a different one. The emergence of actual, generative morphing techniques for design is linked to that of computers. Though its foundations go as far back as the middle of the eighteenth century, the speed and volume of calculations that computers could execute allowed morphing to be included in the digital tools available to designers, and therefore popularize it.

As mentioned, morphing techniques emerge out of studies on topology, which is concerned with the preservation of spatial properties of objects undergoing continuous deformation. The first example of this way of conceptualizing space was sketched out by Swiss scientist Leonhard Euler (1707–83) in 1735 while trying to resolve how to walk around the city of Königsberger in Prussia crossing all its seven bridges only once. To resolve the problem Euler removed all geography and abstracted information into a list of nodes and connections. Without entering a detailed discussion of the problem, it suffices to notice that Euler moved away from the geometrical description of form to replace it with a description of its inherent capacity to vary. Toward the end of the nineteenth century this work would find greater rigor and expansion in the work of Felix Klein and, most importantly, Henri Poincaré.

Rather than concentrating on the pure mathematical roots of the problem, it is interesting to trace how morphing penetrated design disciplines to affect both their processes and outcomes. As we have seen, historical avant-gardes were deeply influenced by these new scientific insights on space, which would only come to fruition with the introduction of computers after the Second World War. The advent of digital art provided the milieu for these experiments. The cross-disciplinary Computer Technique Group—founded in Tokyo in 1966—completed one of the first examples of proto-morphing with their *Running Cola is Africa* (1967/68) in which the profile of a running man transformed into that of a Coca-Cola bottle to eventually turn into the outline of the African continent. In this work—which the group compellingly termed "metamorphosis"

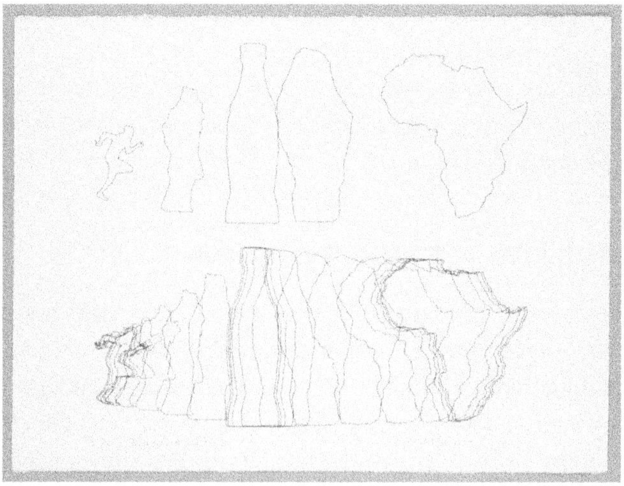

Figure 2.3 Computer Technique Group. Running Cola is Africa (1967). Museum no. E.92-2008. © Victoria Albert Museum.

(Tsuchiya et al. 1968, p. 75)—we can begin to appreciate how digital morphing opened up new semantic territories for forms and images; any intermediate state between its initial and final configuration provided outlines which escaped fixed meaning and opened themselves up to new interpretations and speculations: neither a person nor a continent, yet it contained partial elements of both. It is along these lines that we can trace a continuity between layering, contouring, and morphing as they all—with different levels of sophistication—deal with complex forms, and their exploration for both generative and representational purposes. In the light of these examples, it is interesting to revisit another early example whose elusive forms have often escaped traditional classifications. We refer to one of Gian Lorenzo Bernini's (1598–1680) earliest works: the *Fontana della Barcaccia* by the Spanish Steps in Rome.[6] Given that this small project greatly precedes both Euler's experiment and the invention of digital morphing, rather than a literal comparison we are interested in investigating the formal and semantic ambiguities of this project. Barcaccia is Italian for "little boat"; however, a close examination of this object reveals that very little elements are borrowed from naval architecture. There is neither bow nor stern and all the elements determining the edges of the boat have strong biomorphic connotations: once again, we would not be able to link them to the anatomy of any particular animal though. Paraphrasing Pane's (1953, pp. 16–17) description, we could call them "fleshy architectural elements," as they inflect, or rather, morph as if they were muscles in tension. The overall shape of the boat seems to be breathing, capturing movement in the static constraints of marble. All these elements seem to have morphed and frozen halfway in their transformation. This project obviously anticipated some of the central themes of the baroque, which we will also see explored by Borromini—albeit in a more controlled and less metaphorical fashion. The geometrical and semantic dynamic, irregular qualities of this project have often puzzled art critics who could not definitely resolve as to whether the Barcaccia was a piece of sculpture or architecture. The famous Viennese art historian Alois Riegl (1858–1905) in fact opted for an intermediate category when he spoke of "a naturalistic interpretation of a nonliving subject, a boat and therefore an inanimate thing" (1912, 34–36). The metamorphic quality of its forms clearly escaped disciplinary divisions, anticipating one of the most interesting potentials of morphing techniques in design. Finally, it was not perhaps a coincidence that such an exuberant design was proposed for a fountain. Water was considered as the most mutating of substances: its form and appearance would have never repeated itself, always escaping geometrical reduction and constantly adding a further element of dynamism to the composition of the fountain.

Digital morphing techniques found their ultimate field of experimentation in the invention of digital animations. Computers have been utilized to assist in several steps of animations: coloring, editing, motion dynamics, etc. However, the step that interests us here is the very first one: the translation into digital tools of manual animation techniques. Prior to the advent of animation software, animations were invariably carried out by dividing the workload between the head designer who would sketch out the "key frames" of a scene, and the assistants that would fill the gaps de facto interpolating between the key sketches. Digital key-frame animations worked in the exact same way except that algorithms rather than interns generated all the frames to join key frames. Such type of software was first developed at the legendary Xerox PARC in Palo Alto, California, as well as by Tom de Fanti (1948–) at the Computer Graphics Research Group at Ohio State University since the early 1970s. Peter Foldes (1924–77) was also an important figure in the development of digital morphing techniques: in 1971 he completed *Metadata*, an animated short movie in which the sequence of scenes morphed into one another. It would only be with *Hunger* (1974) that Foldes would achieve the technical sophistication he was after: the eleven-minute movie featured the endless transformations of a character and its surrounding. The movie—awarded at the Cannes Film Festival—completely relied on software to interpolate the key-shots, which were often manipulated drawings obtained from tracing footings of real actors. Foldes described his relation with digital software suggesting that: "in my films, I made metamorphosis . . . . With a computer, I can still make metamorphoses, but with control over each line of the drawing, which I can move as I please. And I work faster, because the machine frees the artist from the fatigue of labour" (in Bendazzi 1994, p. 66).

Contemporary landscape

The realization of a proper three-dimensional digital morphing would once again come from the movie industry. A proto-version of three-dimensional, transparent objects was anticipated by the so-called "water snake" or "pseudopod" in the movies *The Abyss* (1989) by James Cameron (1954–). However, it will be with *Terminator 2* that digital morphing techniques would reach a new level, not only in terms of realism, but also in the degree of manipulation and the dynamics of form. The character T-1000 gained the reputation of one of the most insidious villains in movies because of its ability to morph into everyday objects or humans in order to acquire their capacities or knowledge. Advancements in fluid simulation software were coupled with animation tools to make T-1000 take different shapes. The exquisite quality of the renderings—the character was rendered as mercury—had a tremendous impact on both the industry of special effects and culture at large. This was also a time in which software and hardware capable of morphing objects were within reach of architects who started speculating on their use to design architecture. As mentioned, Peter Eisenman was perhaps first in exploring such possibilities, but also François Roche (1961–) who developed a series of schemes in the early 1990s in which morphing techniques were utilized to generate a more profound relation between site conditions and architecture. Since the competition entry for the Bundestag in Berlin in 1992, Roche had been working with either natural or artificial grounds, mobilizing them through digital morphing to create actual interventions. Greg Lynn also made extensive and very original use of key-frame animation techniques to explore issues of motion and continuity in architecture. In projects such as that for the *Artist Space Installation Design* (1995) not only was he among the first architects to use digital morphing, but he also coupled it with the use of contour lines (Lynn 1999, pp. 63–81). It is worth noticing in passing how the analysis of both intentions and instruments of these projects once again confirms how contouring and morphing tools allowed the exploration of irregular, "post-geometrical" configurations. The final form of the spaces of the gallery emerged from the interaction between volumes and forces: the composition resulted in a series of geometries irreducible to Euclidian forms that were therefore contoured in order to be manufactured.

It is in the conflation of morphing techniques and simulation tools to perhaps provide the next iteration in the history sketched in this chapter. Digital simulations represent a step forward in the treatment and description of form as a dynamic element subjected to forces, it also does appropriate the physical properties of matter which are translated into equations describing collisions between particles. Such morphing techniques resemble evermore closely the advancements in material sciences. We do not only refer to the phenomenal effects of such materials, but also to their performative qualities and their physical properties. Such transformation will push toward forms whose articulation and look will exceed any direct reference to natural ones. It is in fact interesting to notice that already at the time James Cameron was modeling his characters for *Terminator 2*, he chose mercury as a material for his T-1000 character, as "mercury doesn't look real in real life."[7]

Notes

1. An example of "dynamic contouring" occurs when the contour lines are parametrically linked to a surface so that when the surface is altered, contour lines are updated according to the new geometry.

2. In Lynn 1998, Footnote 8, pp. 57–60.
3. We are referring, for instance, to the "Curve from cross section profiles" in *Rhinoceros* in which given a minimum of three profiles (two would simply produce a line), the algorithm will automatically generate closed cross sections at desired points. "CSec." Online. Available at: http://docs.mcneel.com/rhino/5/help/en-us/commands/csec.htm (Accessed August 8, 2016).
4. Lofting takes its name from this ancient practice: CAD software simply adopted this convention and lofting commands can be found in all major 3D modelers.
5. Most 3D modelers not only have swiping functions, but they also allow to construct surfaces out of either one or two rails. A typical geometry obtained from swipe two-rail surfaces is *The Sage Gateshead* (1997–2004) completed by Foster + Partners in Newcastle.
6. The attribution of this fountain to Gian Lorenzo has been the object of several studies. It is beside the scope of this book to resolve this issue and it suffices to point out that (a) the official commission was to Pietro—Bernini's father—and also involved his brother and (b) the unique formal articulation of this work does signal the presence of a very original personality in the team, most likely that of the young Gian Lorenzo.
7. Quoted in Herzog (2015).

Chapter 3

Networks

Introduction

The notion of network—the physical or organizational system linking disparate elements—has perhaps become the key concept to understand the cultural and technological practices of the internet age. The penetration of digital devices in daily life has made it impossible to discuss networks as pure technological products detached from social considerations. Networks exchange, connect, and act in between objects—be them buildings, data, or people. As Keller Easterling suggested, this is a paradigm shift that has started from the hardware of cables, routers, etc., to eventually infect software. The emergence of BIM—a virtual platform to exchange information—has changed the workflow of digital designers, including communication tools within CAD environments. In general, networks—like databases—deal with structured information as a source of design: criteria such as hierarchy, form, and finiteness apply to both. As procedural elements they compute the territory: they survey it, mine it, returning a recoded image of it based on the very criteria (algorithms, in digital parlance) utilized. Networks are therefore mostly representational tools: they conjure up an image of a given territory resulting from the combination of cultural values and the very technology they operate with to connect. They can only be understood as generative in so far as they recombine existing elements of a territory or give rise to images of it which can elicit design innovation. Networks extend the considerations introduced first in the chapter on databases as they are here understood as significantly larger and, most importantly, resting on the notion of exchange making them more open, heterogeneous, and porous forms of organization.

If databases have fundamentally an internalized structure, networks have little intrinsic value if considered in isolation. Networks are embedded modes of organization, conduits facilitating exchange with other systems and networks. Specifically, we will investigate how networks mesh with the physical space of cities, countries, or even the whole planet, merging computational and geographical concerns. In delineating these introductory definitions it is perhaps useful to think of them along the lines of the brain/mind distinction in which the former is defined as an anatomically defined organ, whereas the latter—more akin to the notion of networks proposed here—refers to cognitive faculties which are not necessarily restricted to the brain. In terms of software, this conversation will take us into the world of Geographical Information Systems (GIS) whose penetration in the world of architectural and urban design has been steadily growing. Although this chapter will discuss older applications of digital tools to spatial information, the first successful GIS software to be accessible to the general public was completed in 1978: Map Overlay and Statistical System (MOSS) was both vector- and raster-based GIS developed by the US Department of the Interior to map environmental risks (Reed, no date).

Even earlier forms of spatial networks already show some of their recurrent characteristics: they are inherently able to routinize and distribute procedures within a given territory. For this reason, their origin is often military but their effect should not be solely bound to the development of the art of war: distribution of goods, agriculture, transportation, etc. all took advantage of and shaped networks.[1] This reciprocal relation will be central in our journey: spatial networks both *enable* a series of operations—mostly infrastructural—and *construct* a specific image of the territory they manage. Computation has had its peculiar way to intervene in this process; its abstract logic might appear alien to that of the natural features of a territory, but it has nevertheless engendered its own type of image which will be the focus of our discussion. The survey of examples will follow the trajectory of a particular image a type of network gave rise to: first the use of geometry to survey and manage territories, then that of topology, and finally the properly digital paradigm. In this trajectory, networks have steadily become more abstracted, widened their capacities to mesh together different objects, while moving toward more abstracted, more precise, granular representation and control of individual elements. The end point of this trajectory is the internet, the network par excellence embodying all these characteristics.

The geometrical paradigm

The first computational system to be applied to survey the land is geometry, as its etymology—defined as the art of measuring the earth—clearly suggests. Early signs of a land subdivision and surveying have been found in Babylonia and, in much greater quantity, in Egypt. Since AD 1300 after each flood, Egyptians retraced the boundaries of individual properties for the purpose of cultivation and taxation. The sizing of the plot followed some sort of algorithm which took into account the likelihood of the Nile to flood, and therefore fertilize, the characteristics of the land, the amount of taxes due, and the extent—if any—of damages caused by previous floods. The units for this heterogeneous system of measurement were based on parts of the body such as the cubit (forearm).The product returned by the "algorithm" was the census of all properties along the Nile. Though not triggered by military necessities, these surveys were not any less vital and, in fact, were carried out with great precision. From these very early examples it is possible to detect how the routinization of the territory through the superimposition of a spatial protocol allowed the consequent extrapolation of information from it, and the generation of an "image" in the form of parceling, grids, etc.

A decisive leap in these practices coincided with the introduction of surveying techniques by the Romans. Guided by pragmatic concerns, Roman *Agrimensores*, the "measurers of the land," followed troops and, upon conquering new territories, set up the military camp, and began subdividing and preparing the ground for an actual colony to grow. The whole process followed a sort of automatic protocol: once the starting point was chosen, they would first draw a line, a boundary, and then expand in four perpendicular directions roughly matching those of cardinal points to form squares of approximately 700 meters wide. The resulting square was called *centuriae* (century), as it should have contained about 100 holdings while the *centuriatio* (centurion) indicated the whole process. The computational tools applied in the process were those of the surveyors. Out of the many employed, two stood out for popularity and sophistication: the *gruma*—a wooden cross with weights attached at the four ends—was used to set out the grid, whereas the *dioptra*—a predecessor of the modern theodolite—could measure both horizontal and vertical angles (Dilke 1971, pp. 5–18). The surveyed land was eventually given to the colons to be cultivated. An inscription found in Osuna in Spain also stipulates that "no one shall bring a corpse inside the territory of a town or a colony" (Dilke 1971, p. 32). Though several instruments and practices were adapted from Greece and Egypt, the scale and precision of Roman surveyors were unprecedented: traces of *centuriae* are still very visible in the Po Valley in northern Italy and in Tunisia where—upon defeating Cartagae—the Roman Empire gridded about 15,000 square kilometers of land (Dilke 1971, p. 156). The scale of this network is also impressive, as *centuriae* can also be observed as far north as Lancashire in the UK and near the city of Haifa in Israel (at the time, the province of Syria). Its robustness is testified not only by its longevity—a more sophisticated method will only appear in the seventeenth century—but also by its pliability that allowed the

Romans to apply it not only to land surveys but also to town-planning, therefore using the system to both "encode" and "decode" territories.

In medieval times, castles would also be networked for defensive and military purposes. Through the use of mirrors or smoke signals, messages of either impending attacks or other matters could travel quicker than incoming troops. The nature of this "informatization" of the territory is not an open, extendible one, but it is rather organized in smaller clusters bound by their very topographical and geographical position. The length of each strut of the network coincides with that of human gaze and the resulting form—geometrically irregular—is completely dependent on topographical features: it is localized, specific rather than undifferentiated and infinite.

The statistical/topological paradigm

As mentioned, the role of the military in setting up networks should not be underplayed, but this narrative would not suffice to exhaustively comprehend the proliferation of spatial networks. For instance, the rise of bureaucracy in the nineteenth century has often been singled out as the birth of the contemporary, digital notion of network as a by-product of Industrial Revolution. Analytical charts first emerged in the beautiful drawings of William Playfair (1759–1823) and so did the spreadsheet to facilitate the ever-expanding network of trading. A new kind of objectivity based on numbers, and statistics, accompanied the introduction of these new technologies. The effects of these transformations exceeded the domains in which they had surfaced so much as that in the same period art historian Leopold von Ranke (1795–1886) advocated a type of art criticism in which he wanted to "as it were erase my own Self in order to let things speak" (1870, p. 103).

The implementation of the bureaucratic network to the space of nation-state eventually transformed to notion of the *res domesticae*, no longer a space shielded from bureaucracy but rather put to work to extrapolate information and, in turn, to redraw according to a specific algorithmic pattern. In Jean-François Lyotard's (1924–98) words, these transformations yield the emergence of the Metropolis, a new urban type: here we witness the transformation of the *domus*, the small monad animated by domestic "stories: the generations, the locality, the seasons, wisdom and madness" into the Megalopolis. The *domus* is also the place where "pleasure and work are divided space-time and are shared out amongst the bodies" (1988, p. 192), whereas the Megalopolis with its bureaucratic apparatus "stifles and reduces *res domesticae*, turns them over to tourism and vacation. It knows only residence [*domicile*]. It provides residences for the presidents of families, to the workforce and to another memory, the public archive, which is written, mechanographically operated, electronically" (1988, p. 193). In this transformation the territory was redrawn according to numerical parameters forming the archive Lyotard refers to: the quantifying logic of bureaucracy was the algorithm marching through it to turn into a datascape to extract and inject information. The tenets of such a project clearly rested on rationality and the ambition of creating an "objective" representation of cities and countryside. It was also the world in which Foucault detected an inversion of the relation between bodies and space, now biopolitically—to borrow Foucault's term—modulated. Foucault registered this inversion through the relation between the body and diseases: whereas the leper used to be expelled from the city, modern power inverted this practice. The plague was treated by constraining bodies to their domicile, while an army of doctors and soldiers parceled and routinely scanned the urban space counting the victims of the disease. The "algorithm" is internalized to redraw an image of the city based on statistical distribution (Foucault 2003, pp. 45–48).

If the library and, later on, the museum could be seen as the architectural types of the database, it is the post office to provide a first fully formed model for the network as we just defined it. The mail service rather than being made of individual artifacts—be it architecture or even cities—is a network embedded in the physical morphology of the very territory it serves. It is constituted of heterogeneous elements, including people, machines, furniture, and architecture, etc. which makes use of other existing networks (e.g., roads, railways, etc.). It is in fact in the development of postal service that we observe one of the first forms of computable spatial networks through the birth of postcodes. The modern postal service resulted from the reforms enacted in the 1840s in Britain to repair an increasingly unreliable service that also struggled to cope with the growth of some of its cities, such as London. These transformations should also be read as the precursor to the first integration of bureaucracy and computation, which will be realized in the 1890 U.S. Census, when punch-card computers will be employed to gather and process data. In London, these measures included both renaming some of London's streets and dividing its metropolitan area into districts so that "by the end of 1871 some 100,000 houses had been renumbered and 4,800 'areas' renamed."[2] The promoter of most of these radical changes was Sir Rowland Hill (1795–1879) who not only invented the stamp and prepaid postage, but also made plans to implement postcodes in London.[3] The final plan divided London into ten districts obtained by slicing an imaginary twelve-mile radius circle and locating a post office in each of the districts. In 1858, when the scheme was fully implemented, the first comprehensive, non-military, digital (based on digits), virtually computable network was in operation. The success of the system was immediate and quickly adopted by other major British cities.

In 1917 further subdivision through districts was introduced, but it was only after the end of the Second World War that the whole system was expanded to take the shape it still maintains today.[4] The key to the success of the UK postcode system was its precision in pinpointing physical locations. This colossal system allowed to identify, on average, no more than twelve households per code. Postcodes were utilized both as a list and as a geo-positioned series of coordinates; the former was a proper database that provided a description of the British Isle without any use of geographical coordinates (also a good indicator of density of settlements and business activities). Upon its implantation, it became quickly evident that the benefits of this system far exceeded its original aim and was quickly adopted as a tool for spatial analysis. A whole economy based on pure spatial information management grew in the UK, also thanks to the parallel development of computers which were able to handle these massive datasets. The development of GIS finally allowed to couple the advantages of database management with CAD; postcodes could thus be visualized as areas (as topological representations of the landscape constructed as Thiessen polygons used for the census or by the police), as lines (identifying, for instance, railway networks), and points (recording disparate data from house prices to pollution levels) (Raper, Rhind, and Sheperd 1992, pp. 131–40). Large information companies such as Acorn built whole sociological models based on the abstract geography of postcodes; their "Acorn User Guide" is a precise document portraying the British population and its cultural habits (Grima 2008). Again, the conflation of fast-evolving computers and accurate databases allowed gaining insights in the evolution of cities and the effects of urban planning. Los Angeles was the first among American cities to redraw its territories according to cluster analysis and cross-referencing them with census data. The city could be represented as a physical entity or reshuffled to bring together areas that were physically distant but shared common traits. Out of this exercise in data correlation, important observations were made: for instance, the birth weight of infants, sixth-grade reading scores, and age of housing became robust indicators of the poverty level of a particular cluster. We should note in passing that these initiatives were carried out by public agencies which immediately posited the issue of how to give agency to data by making recommendations to the appropriate authorities to affect the planning policies (Vallianatos 2015).

The results of these experiments revealed an image of the territory which would have not been possible to conjure up without the powerful mix of computers and management strategies. It also revealed the inadequacies of elementary, more stable images of the city based on the description of its physical properties alone: the abstraction inherent to computation helped to foreground more intangible and yet all too real elements of the city regardless of whether these computational analyses were employed for marketing analysis or town-planning. The abstract and topological description of territories conjured up by the powerful mix of computation and bureaucracy had collapsed previous binaries such as spatial regimes of inclusion and exclusions suggested by Foucault. Likewise the *domus* and the Megalopolis of Lyotard had merged: evermore detailed profiling individuates personal cultural and consuming habits eroding the distinction between public and private life.

The case of French departments

France has been divided into departments since 1665 when Marc-René d'Argenson's (1652–1721) plan was implemented for the purpose of managing roads and water networks. The end of the Ancien Règime brought about by the revolution not only called for a removal of any trace of the old system, but also sought methods of territorial subdivision that could directly respond to the new egalitarian principles. In July 1789 the Constitutional Committee—based on the work of geographer Mathias Robert de Hesseln (1733–80) sketched out a radical proposal which overlaid a regular grid over the French territory dividing it into provinces identical in size. The proposal, inspired by the work of Jefferson in the United States, was probably drafted in little time as a "working document" (several parts were left handwritten) showing imprecisions; however, it definitely did not lack ambition and political clarity. Final pattern was a checker grid of 81 cells, each 18 leagues wide (72 kilometers); alternate cells are colored in green, whereas all political features, including land use were removed from the map where only rivers still featured. Cities were marked by small dots, and no district was given a specific name with the only exception of the Île-de-France which was checkered in red and further subdivided presumably to account for its larger population. The grid "flattened" France providing a new, literally, egalitarian political ground for access and democratic reconstruction. It has been noticed how the revolutionary committee was not afraid to experiment and draw from the most advanced examples of technological innovation. Despite the strong iconicity of the final image, a more careful reading of the principles informing the grid suggested a topological rather than a geometrical principle at work; the width and length of each cell was marked such that "in the space of one day, the people furthest from the centre can get to the capital, do business for several hours and return home."[5]

In 1790 when the final map was approved, some of the ideas of de Hesseln's were still visible. The final version not only took into account geographical

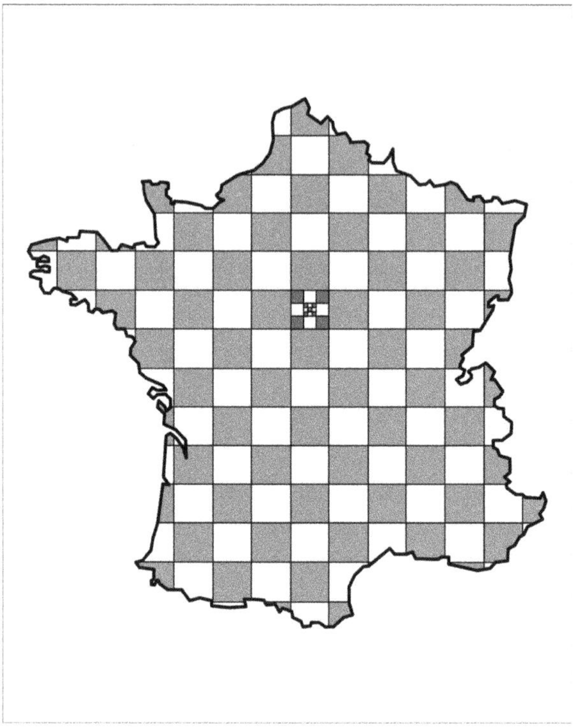

Figure 3.1 Diagram of the outline of the French departments as they were redrawn by the 1789 Constitutional Committee. Illustration by the author.

features, but it also shaped each department to be relatively similar in size. However, the more interesting element is that the subdivision was still based on topological principles constructed around ideas of proximity between administrative centers and the rest of the province (Kendall 1971, pp. 158–59). If drawn as a diagram, this quality becomes rather evident; in fact, the overall image generated is very similar to a Voronoi subdivision, which follows closely the positions of the points to integrate (Fig. 3.1).[6] Voronoi grids are a recurrent formal move utilized by architecture students, as some software such as *Grasshopper* already provide commands specifically designed for this purpose.

The digital paradigm: World game as a Planetary network

> We are going to set up a great computer program. We are going to introduce the many variables now known to be operative in the world around industrial

> economics. We will store all the basic data in the machine's memory bank; where and how much of each class of the physical resources; where are the people, where are the trendings and important needs of world man. (Fuller 1965)

Buckminster Fuller's philosophy had always been conceiving design almost as an exercise in resource management; however from the 1960s onwards the American polymath made a decisive attempt to systematize his work in this area. In designing his *World Game*, Fuller called upon the creation of an "anticipatory design science" to underpin a planning system able to manage world resources and fairly redistribute them at the scale of the whole planet. Fuller trusted the combination of design—rather than traditional political action—and technological innovations to be able to deliver fair access to natural resources and knowledge, two essential steps toward the ultimate aim of the game: world peace. His approach was warranted by the technological optimism springing out of the military innovations the American government had developed during the Second World War whose benefits were being passed onto the civil society. Particularly, the transition from crafts to industry gave rise to technologies that deeply impacted society—global air travel and networked communication systems, and, of course, the modern computer—which had laid out the material conditions for the success of the *World Game*.[7] Fuller set up a team at South Illinois University—where British artist John McHale (1922– 1978)[8] joined him—and set out two five-year plans to complete the project. Through annual interventions at the International Union of Architects (UIA), Fuller addressed schools of architecture around the world urging them to radically challenge the organization of the profession to redirect their efforts toward educating generations of architects to "deal with the design of the whole once more" (Fuller, McHale 1963, p. 72). This new kind of designer would have matched Fuller's description of the "world man" whose actions would have been informed by multi-scalar thinking and (proto-)ecological sensibility, equipped with access to data on earth's energy flows, necessary to maintain the overall energetic balance. Half a century after its introduction, *World Game* still remains one of the most radical and visionary proposals to have emerged in the field of urbanism to deal with environmental challenges. As these problems are all the more relevant now, the project's seduction and relevance still seem intact.

Fuller's plans branched into parallel fields—most notably, cybernetics and system theory—to craft the tools to implement his ambitious project. What interests us here are two specific moments in the history of the project. The first one coincided with its official beginning in 1963 when Fuller's team started publishing the first of two volumes on the project titled "Inventory of World

Resources Human Trends and Needs." These publications aimed at setting out the categories necessary to eventually compile the largest database possible on world's industrialization: in other words, the raw materials to play the game with. Mapping out the general lines of research underpinning the success of the *World Game*, the two tomes were largely dominated by graphically seductive charts covering disparate issues from the distribution of natural resources to the development of communication networks. Fuller's interest in data is well documented and deserves to be expanded here. If the information gathered in these two publications exhibits the "global" aspects of Fuller's visions, the *Dymaxion Chronofiles*, on the other hand, represented the more granular and detailed account of Fuller's life. Collected in a continuous scrapbook, the *Chronofiles* recorded Fuller's every activity in Warholian fifteen-minute intervals. Covering from 1917 to 1983, in June 1980 Fuller claimed that the entire collection amounted to "737 volumes, each containing 300–400 pages, or about 260,000 letters in all" (1981, p. 134). This collection—which made Fuller's passage on planet earth the most documented human life in history—contained not only personal notes, sketches, or even utility bills, but also numerous paper clippings of relevant articles, charts, etc., along with any article written by others on Fuller (approximately over 37,000 in 1980) (1981 p. 134). The result was a sort of private—because of the notebook format—*ante litteram* social media page, not unlike the one provided by Facebook. Organized in chronological order, the archive overlapped the micro- and the macro-scale showing ideas and phenomena in constant transformation. Fuller's emphasis on data gathering did anticipate the present interest in collecting and mining large datasets—generally referred to as Big Data. In 2012, British scientist Stephen Wolfram published an equally meticulous record of his life—albeit largely based on data gathered from electronic and digital devices (Wolfram 2012). Records of emails sent and received, key strokes, phones calls, travels, meeting schedules, etc. were gathered and synthetically visualized in a series of graphs—generated through Wolfram's own software *Mathematica*—showing an unprecedented level of detail in gathering and analyzing large datasets. As in Fuller's *Chronofiles*, Wolfram too saw in these exercises the possibility to uncover new insights on the content of the datasets analyzed. Through a continuous, chronologically organized logbook, Fuller designed his own analytical tool—not unlike the current software utilized to aggregate and mine large datasets—with which to observe his own life at a distance disentangling himself from the flow of events he was directly or indirectly involved in. For instance, Fuller noticed that looking back at the clippings collected in the *Chronofiles* between 1922 and 1927 made clear to him a trend of comprehensive "ephemeralization" of technology as well as of "accelerating acceleration"—that is, the growing efficiency that allowed to obtain more by doing less: both considerations had a lasting impact on his view on design. As such the *Chronofiles* have exceeded their personal value and rightly been considered alongside Fuller's other creative endeavors.[9]

In developing his *World Game*, Fuller intuited—in truly ecological fashion—that emerging technologies not only allowed to generate and analyze large datasets—obviously still a very small capacity for the computers of the 1960s—but also that the development of his anticipatory design science demanded a different mode of data retrieval and visualization. Exploiting the structural and aesthetic qualities of databases, the *Inventory* showed data at an unusually large scale, such as that of the entire planet and deep time frame often arching back to the beginning of human civilization. The management of this complex operation was, of course, to be eventually handled by computers.[10] The instrumental use of databases was implicitly calling for a different sensibility toward design whose essential prerequisites were now resting on the ability to synthetically grasp large datasets to widen the range of materials designers worked with to include energy itself. The game would unfold by players making "moves"—for example, implement a new infrastructure, develop an industrial center, set up a port, etc.—and input the decision back into the computer which, in turn, would have calculated the consequences of these acts against the global database and returned feedback. The first project Fuller developed through the game was to close the gaps in the electricity grid bringing electricity to all parts of the planet. Data was explicitly treated as a design material—like concrete or wood—and the computer was both the ideal tool to manipulate it and the platform to represent it. The detailed reports were only intended to be an initial draft for the world database which, eventually, would have become a growing, dynamic tool as schools scattered across all continents would regularly update it. It goes without saying that computation was essential to the success of the project not only because of the speed in data transmission, but also, most importantly in this discussion, because computers could form an image for such planetary network by aggregating, reconfiguring, and displaying data at a global scale, therefore opening up new design domains. Fuller saw this way of planning as the beginning of a truly global type of governance, one based on "de-sovereignty" (1981, p. 214). The capacity to handle data of the 1960s' computers would have never coped with the scale of this project and, anyway, no actual computer was really resourced. The game was only played in five consecutive workshops in New York in which participants sketched their notes directly on Dymaxion world maps. As a result, the *World Game* remained just an idea (Kenner 1973, p.224).[11]

Though it will only be with Stafford Beer's *Cybersyn* that we will witness a more decisive and integrated relation between data and planning, Fuller nevertheless proposed the construction of a series of designed objects to make data public, visualize networks, and share the knowledge contained in the databases. Some initial sketches appeared as early as 1928 but it was only in the 1950s that Fuller developed the *Geoscope* ("Mini-Earth") which was eventually presented in its definitive design in 1962 (Fig. 3.2). The *Geoscope* consisted of a 200-foot diameter sphere representing "Spaceship Earth" acting as a curved screen for data projections. The surface of the sphere was controlled by a computer and intended to be covered with ten million light bulbs of varying intensity which would have visualized data from the global datasets. *Geoscopes* should have been built in all the schools of architecture adhering to the project; however, the proposed location of the most important of these interactive spheres was the East River in Manhattan, right next to the UN headquarters. Eventually only a handful of much smaller *Geoscopes* were built: a twenty-foot one at Cornell University

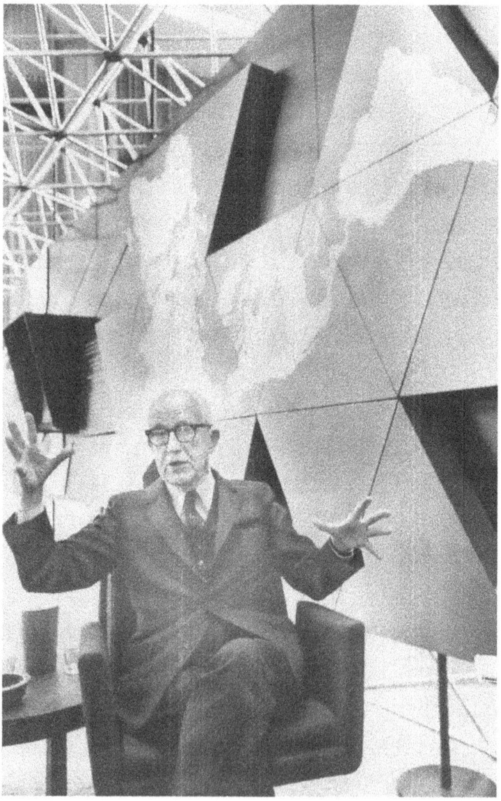

Figure 3.2 Model of Fuller's geodesign world map on display at the Ontario Science Museum. This type of map was the same used for the Geodomes. © Getty Images.

(1952), one at University of Minnesota (1954–56, partially completed), ten-foot diameter one at Princeton University (1955), fifty-foot diameter one within the Southern Illinois Campus (1970), one more at the University of Colorado (1964), and one in University of Nottingham, UK. None of the prototypes had millions of lights, and the Dymaxion Air-Ocean World map—in its 1943 formulation—was used instead. Their geodesic structure was constructed out of metal tubes and subdivided into flat triangular faces; each face could have also been displayed on a flat wall (an option implemented only for the structure built in Colorado). All panels also had a tagging system that would have allowed to coordinate them with the general database to facilitate their installation. The metal structure defining the sphere crucially ensured that multiple layers of information could have been stacked up on a single face in order to either show different types of data, their evolution over time, or simply allow users to sketch additional information. Each additional layer was oriented radially so as to give the sense of the earth expanding out into the cosmos, of "designing from the inside out," in line with Fuller's idea of a "world man." Finally, the complete structure had to be installed so that "all Geoscopes were oriented so that their polar axis, with latitude and longitude of the installed Geoscope's zenith point always corresponding exactly with the latitude and longitude of the critically located point on our real planet Earth at which the Geoscope is installed" (1981, p. 172). An invisible network was to guide the orientation of each object, relating it to the cosmos. The *Geoscope* continued the line of research started with *Chronofiles* that were developed to make immaterial phenomena visible to consequently include them in the design process. Projects such as the *Geoscope* or the *World Game* conflated computation, electronics, media, and data to shift phenomena previously undetectable by humans—because either too small, or large, or too fast or slow—within the range perceivable by our senses. It is in this sense that we have to understand the accelerated timelines displayed on *Geoscope*; as devices to lower the "threshold of perception" above which the phenomena previously invisible would become intelligible and, therefore, a matter of design.

The history of the *World Game* and the *Geoscope* should have crossed in 1967. Fuller had in fact been approached by the United States Information Agency to develop a design for the pavilion representing the United States at the coming world exposition in Montreal in 1967. The initial response by the American polymath was to combine the two projects by, respectively, employing the *Geoscope* to provide the form for the pavilion and the *World Game* for the content for the exhibition. Schematically, the initial proposal consisted of two geodesic domes of, respectively, 400 and 250 feet in diameter and placed one inside the other. The smaller sphere would effectively be a *Geoscope* covered in light bulbs on which data about world population, natural resources, climate, etc. would be displayed; while the outer structure would support the *Geoscope* giving the final appearance to the whole building. In the basement, below both structures, a large mainframe computer would have controlled the whole apparatus. The visitors would have approached this data spectacle through 36 radial ramps arrayed at 10-degree intervals that would have lifted them up from the ground and brought them onto a terrace closer to the *Geoscope* (Fuller 1981, pp. 165–69). The description of this proposal—which even in its verbal form already presented rather insurmountable difficulties—can be rightly considered as one of the first attempts to reconcile the immaterial nature of information and material reality of design. In this sense, Fuller opened up a line of design research and confronted issues which are still very much part of the concerns designers struggle with when working with digital data. Besides the technical and financial obstacles to overcome to implement such a vision, the design for the Expo 67 showcased a series of exemplary moves showing Fuller's ability to think at planetary level, straddling between scales, media, abstraction, and materiality. The *Geoscope* was in fact supposed to dynamically oscillate between a perfect sphere—the earth—and an icosahedron coinciding with the Dymaxion projection method Fuller had conceived. The whole structure would eventually resolve into a flat map of the earth (1:500,000 scale) composed of twenty equilateral triangles. Visitors to the pavilion would have witnessed this real-time metamorphosis of the terrestrial globe into a flat, uninterrupted surface. One final detail should not be overlooked in this description. Fuller carefully controlled the scale of the overall installation turning the *Geoscope* into an ideal canvas on which different media and information could converge and be overlaid. Fuller based the overall scale of the Expo 67 *Geoscope* on the size of the aerial photographs taken at the time by the US Army to produce world maps. One light bulb would represent the area covered by one aerial photo, thus not only creating the conditions for conflating new sets of data onto his moving sphere, but also showing once again his ability to conceive of the earth as a design object. Of this ambitious proposal only the large geodesic structure survived; the idea to dedicate the US pavilion to geopolitics was deemed too radical and contentious and was abandoned in favor of an art exhibition on American art.

Through the *World Game* Fuller created a comprehensive framework to think and plan at a planetary scale; perhaps the first resolute attempt to engage globalization through design. The digital management of the database not only was essential in this task but also meant, first and foremost, as a design tool rather than a mere representational one. The possibility to juxtapose heterogeneous datasets or varying the time frame from which to observe them—by varying the lights' intensity to speed up or slow down natural or artificial phenomena—allowed designers to develop a geopolitical and ecological sensibility toward scale, flow, and the political mechanisms governing them. In Fuller's view the "designer is a coordinator of information, less of a specialist [and more of a] comprehensive designers and 'system' and 'pattern' creator" (Fuller and McHale 1965, p. 74). Computation would allow "specialist information to be incorporated in the memory storage unit of a computer and called upon as required" (1965, p. 72). The formal expression of such database is celebrated through the *Geoscope* not only for its efficiency and plasticity, but also for its aesthetics. The ultimate geopolitical agenda implicit in the dynamics of the game was to encourage "de-sovereignty," seen by Fuller as the way to diminish national interests in favor of global outlook accounting for and planning redistribution of natural resources.

Fuller only devoted a couple of pages of his reports to the role computer software—not yet referred to as CAD—would have had in his project but had definitely considered this part of the project in detail (1965, p. 73). By employing the pioneering *Sketchpad* or other digital devices such as RAND Tablet[12] or *Calcomp*, users would have been able to digitally interact with the *World Game* by sketching on maps, made instantaneous use of large databases by overlaying them on the computer screen. The impact of digital tools on design disciplines was already clear in Fuller's mind: not only in terms of efficiency as information on building components could have been retrieved at the click of a button, but also in being germane to the emergence of a different design culture based on the design of bespoke rather than standardized architectural parts. In passing, we should also recall that explorations in digital database management lead to the formation of two design paradigms: BIM and mass-customization. As we will see in Nanni Balestrini's work, if artists and designers were already able to conceptualize and speculate the effects of mass-customized objects on the creative process, both the software development and the industrial sector could not materialize their visions yet. On the one hand, the standardized logic of the assembly line could not cope with demands of variation and uniqueness; on the other, the software packages available did not have tools to capitalize on the exponential growth of databases in which every item could have been defined by an ever-increasing number of variables.

Through the *Geoscope*, Fuller did, however, succeed in coupling large digital datasets with the iconic image of the earth to forge a powerful spatial narrative linking data, world resources, knowledge, and technological tools in a potentially ever-expanding loop. Software was seen as much a piece of infrastructure as a "new social instrument" (1965, p. 74), a conduit toward a new "electronically operative democracy" (Fuller 1981, p. 197). The physical image of the *Geoscope* was therefore as important as the information it displayed: it was both the structure and the media for a dynamic urbanism. If schools of architecture were the primary target for the diffusion of the *World Game*, the campus was perhaps the first urban type that could have been reinvented in the light of the introduction of computers. The new university campus was a distributed and immaterial one, more of an "educational service network" in which "'high frequency' technologies . . . may enable us to deploy education so that it may be more widely available to all men" (Fuller and McHale 1965, p. 93).

Cybersyn: A socialist network

Similar to Fuller, British cyberneticist Stafford Beer (1926–2002) dedicated many pages of his prolific writing activity to education, aiming to reduce the role of bureaucracies and proposing innovative pedagogies. The link between education and how information is gathered, circulated, and adapted would be a constant theme throughout his work. Stafford Beer's trajectory in regard to the topics discussed in this chapter could be seen as an unorthodox one by today's standards, but did not particularly stand out within the postwar circles of British cyberneticists. Beer did not complete his undergraduate studies—which he had started at the age of seventeen at University College London—as he was forced to join the army when the Second World War broke out. Nevertheless, by the age of thirty he had managed to secure a prestigious position as director of the Department of Operational Research and Cybernetics at United Steel—the largest steel manufacturer in Europe at the time. His leading work on computer simulations and management theories led him to set up his own consultancy and work for the International Publishing Corporation (IPC). In July 1971, he was unexpectedly contacted by Fernando Flores (1943–), an equally talented individual who, at the age of twenty-eight, was heading the rapidly growing Department of Nationalization of all Industries in Chile. Beer was invited to Chile to put his ideas to practice and develop a nationwide cybernetic system to manage the nation's transition to a socialist economy under the newly elected government led by Allende. Beer saw a link between the management theories he had been championing in books such as *The Brain of the Firm* (1972) and Chilean way to socialism. The project—succinctly named *Cybersyn* by conflating the terms cybernetics and synergy—spanned between 1970 and 1973 and still represents one of the most advanced and yet relatively unknown experiments to network data, geography, and politics constituting a clear precursor of the contemporary Smart City.

Beer's theories greatly appealed to Allende for at least two reasons. First, Chilean socialism sought to differentiate itself from that of the Soviet bloc by avoiding becoming a totalitarian regime by taking a more progressive approach. Secondly, the re-organization of the entire economic apparatus was still a colossal task made even more complex by the unique geography of Chile—4,300 kilometers in length with average width of 180 kilometers only—which made digital networks the only instrument to be conceivably able to accomplish such an ambitious project. The path to this radical transformation involved setting up a new management layer to keep a fluid relationship between centralized and de-centralized forms of control as well as between machines and humans. In a country that in 1970 could only count on fifty computers—most of which were already outdated—Beer conceived of this new layer as made up of four components: Cybernet, Cyberstride, Checo, and Opsroom (Medina 2006, p. 587). Cybernet was a nationwide network of 500 telefax machines that should have transmitted real-time data about productivity.[13] The second component—Cyberstride—was a purely digital intervention consisting of a suite of pieces of software to aggregate, analyze, and distribute data gathered. This mainly resulted in a series of analytical charts tracking economic trends. The team—split between Chile and London—utilized a Burroughs B3500 mainframe to run the Cyberstride layer, purging out "noise" data and passing on actionable information only.[14] Checo (Chilean Economy) would allow the government to plan and test future policies by running digital simulations on the information received from the lower levels. This was undoubtedly the most complex of tasks for programmers, as the design of *Cybersyn* coincided with a period in which large-scale simulation models had almost invariably failed. The team heavily relied on its British contingent to adapt *DYNAMO*; a compiler developed by Jay Forrester (1918–2016) at MIT whose work will also be discussed in the chapter on random. The last piece—the Opsroom—was an actual physical space acting as an interface between the other three elements of Cybersyn "modelled after a British WWII war room" (Medina 2006, p. 589) in which seven representatives of the government would sit on custom-designed armchairs arrayed in a circle and surrounded by screens and projections displaying the relevant information. Ideally, this was only a prototype for operation rooms to be built in every nationalized factory, thus giving a material form to both the recursive structure envisioned in *The Brain of The Firm* and the socialist values to empower workers. The general architecture of Opsroom came from the war room set up by the British army during the Second World War. No chair had any actual space for notepads; these were substituted by a series of large, iconic buttons. The buttons not only allowed interaction with the data displayed, but also cut out all potential intermediaries to make the conversation in the room as agile as possible (Medina 2006, pp. 589–90). Of the four components planned, only the first one was fully functioning and permanently utilized by the government. Despite all the difficulties a project of such ambition presented, Beer managed to blend cybernetics, education, and elements of Marxist theory to conjure up a nationwide dynamic planning system. The radical combination of elements was counter-balanced by feedback loops, cross-checking points to recognize the limits of the system itself and design regulatory mechanisms. The ultimate ambition was to put the workers at the center of the economy and empower them through digital networks closing the feedback loop between the government and "At last, *el pueblo*" (Beer 1972, p. 258).

At the center of Beer's implementation strategy was the computer, the machine able to respond to the growing demands of gathering, analyzing, and outputting large amounts of dynamic data. However, Beer did not subscribe to the technocratic use of computers as mere instruments to reinforce existing organizational structures. Computers, if "channelled" or programmed in the right way, were simply machines too powerful and complex to be devoted to reproducing the status quo; rather they should have promoted and orchestrated change or, in Beer's own words, "designing freedom" (Beer 1975 [1973]).

Beer's approach is essential to understand the potential of networking and planning with data. We should therefore consider Stafford Beer as a designer, a designer of systems and organizations rather than buildings or objects; a designer, nevertheless. His complex five-tier diagram describing any effective organization positioned information exchanges at all levels and flowing recursively as co-extensive of human capacities at the service of change. Once this major shift was declared, information could no longer be seen as static, or as an accessorial element to manage an organization. Perhaps due to his strong involvement with business rather than academic circles, Beer had always preferred focusing on operational research to drive action rather than the development of mathematical models of increasing complexity and exactitude. Beyond what Fuller had already imagined, Beer implemented more holistic techniques for data gathering and management which were conceived as design operations, essential to not only improve efficiency but also support the revolution of the social structures of Chile. Today, despite the undisputable advancements in computing power, most of the work on data in spatial planning still struggles to see itself as design and, most importantly, to understand that technological development should be seen as a nested component in larger cultural and societal systems and transformations. Beer was clear that change was the central characteristic of all systems, whether artificial or natural; their instability and dynamic behavior due to their constant adaptation to internal and/or external inputs was understood as their "default" condition rather than the exception. Conventional mathematics—which had privileged reductive approaches to complex phenomena—had successfully described static systems, but once time had been introduced as one of the variables to compute, it could have no longer coped with their overwhelming complexity. Beer's work was among the first to clearly break with that tradition and make computers the central instruments for this conceptual shift.

This is not just a theoretical quarrel. Breaking free of modernist thinking also meant abandoning "naïve, primitive and ridden ideas with an almost retributive idea of causality." Rather than framed by "a crude process of coercion" (Beer 1967, p. 17), design could concentrate on notions of adaptation and feedback. Computation—whose development had been tangled up in the paranoid world of Cold War skirmish—could be redeployed as an instrument at the service of "soft," open-ended processes of negotiation, decision-making, and, ultimately, empowerment.

The radical ambitions of *Cybersyn* become even clearer if we compare them to similar attempts carried out during the 1960s mostly in the United States. Cities as diverse as Los Angeles, San Francisco, Boston, and, perhaps most importantly, Pittsburgh developed computer models to simulate urban dynamics to plan for major infrastructural and housing projects. The Department of City Planning in Pittsburgh developed *TOMM* which stood out for its proto-dynamic qualities. These large efforts—the cost of an operational simulation model in 1970 was about $500,000—were all invariably abandoned or, at least, radically rethought. The experiments of the 1960s on urbanism and computers received their final blow when Douglass Lee unequivocally titled his review of these attempts "Requiem for Large-Scale Models" (1973). In constructing his argument, Lee pointed out how the limitations in data-gathering techniques, in designing adequate algorithms governing the models, and a lack of transparency in their logical underpinnings eventually made these projects fundamentally unreliable. Besides his telling description of the disputes within the various American agencies between "modelers" and "anti-modelers"—still embarrassingly applicable to today's discussions on the use of computers in design both in practice and academia—Lee clearly outlined that computer models were never neutral or objective constructs but rather always a reflection of the ideas conjured by the teams programming them. Beer understood better than most this apparently self-evident point and was always unambiguously declaring upfront the aims of his cybernetic models—an approach that was even clearer in the case of *Cybersyn*.[15] This point also reveals how much Fuller, first, and then more decisively, Beer progressed computation beyond a pure, linear, problem-solving tool to transform it into a more "open" instrument to test scenarios, stir conversations in parallel with other societal issues and institutions. Such a heuristic approach was defined by Beer as "a set of instructions for searching out an unknown goal by exploration, which continuously and repeatedly evaluates progress according to some known criterion" (Quoted in Scoates 2013, p. 299). Computers were part of a comprehensive approach to link information and planning: if applied to "segments" of systems rather than "wholes", any of the tools developed would have been immediately absorbed in the very technocratic ideology Beer was escaping from and had prompted Douglass Lee to write his critique. Fundamentally oppressive regimes such as Brazil and South Africa expressed their interest in adopting *Cybersyn* confirming to Beer the importance of considering the project as a whole.[16] These steps marked a shift in the way in which computation was discussed and applied as it moved away from the military and scientific domains. Computation was here developed within an economic and political framework, but also, most importantly in our discussion, networks were understood as designs linking information to territory and planning—the domains architects and urbanists operate in.

Despite the internal difficulties the project survived until 1973 when Allende's government was overturned by a military coup led by General Pinochet. The new military regime initially kept *Cybersyn* in the hope to reconvert it to the new political imperatives. After some fruitless attempts, Pinochet abandoned the project and destroyed it.

With the introduction of computers—whether actual or only imagined as in Fuller's game—networks became interactive for the first time. Beer introduced the "algedonic signal," an interactive system connected to, for instance, the TV set in order for Chilean workers to provide real-time feedback on the success—or lack of—policies managing the nationalization of the economy. If previous types of networks had conjured up evermore complex images of the territories they managed, such images were invariably only *overlaid* on to a territory which was conceptualized as a passive receiver of such innovations. The two-way systems enabled by networks and developed by both Beer and Fuller, allowed end users and technological apparatuses to co-create the image of the territory and evolve it.

Contemporary landscape

The development of ubiquitous computing and wearable technologies has radically changed the notion of network. The once-unprecedented precision of postcodes has been eclipsed overnight by smartphones; the data recorded by mobile devices are significantly more detailed than those recorded by devices from the pre-smartphone years, as they not only record the movements of bodies in the city, in the countryside, or even in the air and at sea, but also, and for the first time, are able to record their behavior over time. Computers too have leaped forward to develop both hardware and software that are able to cope with such deluge of data. The age of "Big Data"—as it is often termed—describes an area of both design and theoretical investigation exploring the possibilities engendered by this technological transformation. It is interesting to notice the emergence of new models for research and design that no longer rely on clear-cut distinctions between sciences and humanities; mapping—as both a technical and cultural activity—has consequently been receiving a lot of attention producing some important contributions to the management and planning of cities. Among the vast literature available in this field, the work of the Centre for Advanced Spatial Analysis (CASA) at The Bartlett-UCL led by Michael Batty,[17] MIT Senseable City Lab stirred by Carlo Ratti,[18] and Spatial Information Design Lab—Laura Kurgan[19] at Columbia University—stand out. Besides the stunning visual allure of the visualizations lies a more profound idea that digital technology allows to see cities differently, and therefore plan them differently. The analysis of the networks of trash in the United States by Senseable Lab or the correlation between planning and rates of incarceration by Kurgan reveal a politically charged image of the city in which citizen-led initiatives, mobile apps, satellite communication, and GIS software can be mobilized (Fig. 3.3). The conflation of digital technology and urban planning has also been championed by the so-called Smart City. Examples such as Masdar by Norman Foster and Partners in the United Arab Emirates, Songdo in South Korea are often cited by both those who welcome smart cities and their critics. But what remains of the image of the network whose metamorphosis we have been following in this chapter? In a recent report global engineering company ARUP in collaboration with the Royal Institute of British Architects (RIBA) candidly admitted that "the relationship between smart infrastructure and space is not yet fully understood" (2013); correctly pointing out a worrying gap between the depth of analysis and lack of innovation. While the penetration of digital networks has been giving rise to their own building type—the datacentre—more complex and more dubious integration of digital technologies in urban areas has also emerged for the purpose of controling public spaces. For instance, the organization of the G8 summits—a three-day event gathering the eight richest countries—presented a complex image of networks in which digital technologies, legal measures, spatial planning, and crowd-control tactics abruptly merged and equally rapidly dissolved to reconfigure the spaces of organizing cities. The qualities of this kind of spaces have often remained unexamined by architects and urbanists creating a gap between theory and practice (Bottazzi 2015). In bridging this hiatus, the promise is to change the role of the urban designer, a figure that will necessarily

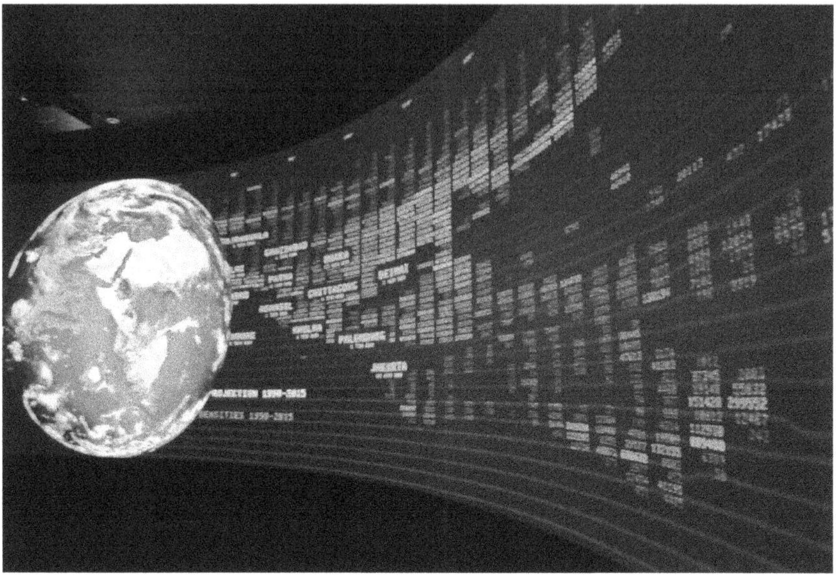

Figure 3.3 *Exit* 2008-2015. Scenario "Population Shifts: Cities". View of the exhibition *Native Land, Stop Eject*, 2008-2009 Collection Fondation Cartier pour l'art contemporain, Paris. © Diller Scofidio + Renfro, Mark Hansen, Laura Kurgan, and Ben Rubin, in collaboration with Robert Gerard Pietrusko and Stewart Smith.

need to straddle between physical and digital domains, and therefore change the very tools with which to design and manage cities.

In this post-perspectival space shaped by simultaneity and endless differentiation, the image of the digital network cannot any longer be associated with the modernist idea of legibility: the dynamics of spatial or purely digital interaction seem too complex, rapid, and distributed for designers to claim to be able to control them. However, as designers, spatial images—be it geometrical, statistical, or topological—will also play an important role in conceptualizing our thoughts and directing our efforts. The range of precedents listed here reminds us what is at stake in setting up networks: the balance between spatial, ecological, and political systems; the ability of designers to conceptualize networks in order to enable a larger set of actors to inhabit, appropriate, and transform them.

Notes

1. *MOSS* is a case in point as it was developed to support the work of wildlife biologists in monitoring species potentially endangered by the acceleration of mining activities in Rocky Mountain States in the middle of the 1970s (Reed, no date).
2. *Postcodes*. Available from: http://www.postalheritage.org.uk/explore/history/postcode (Accessed May 11, 2016).

3. Incidentally, it is worth mentioning in passing that among the many experts consulted to resolve the issue of postage costs Charles Babbage was also contacted in order to put his engines to work to devise a uniform postage rate (Goldstine 1972, p. 22).
4. The British postcode system is based on six digits divided into two groups of three characters each. The first three are called Outward code and are formed by a mix of letters—denoting one of the 124 areas present in 2016—and 1 or 2 numbers—to a total tally of 3,114 districts. The areas are identified geographically (for instance, NR for Norwich, YO for Yorkshire, etc.). The Inward code also mixes numbers and a letter to correct sector (12,381) and, finally, postcode. At the time of writing, there are 1,762,464 live postcodes in Britain, each containing on average 12 households. Though, some 190 countries have adopted this method, the UK system still stands out for its degree of detail. The system developed as a response to the introduction of mechanization in the sorting process after the end of the Second World War and the need to have a machine-readable code. The current postcode system was first tested with unsatisfactory results in Norwich in 1959 and then modified and rolled out on a national scale in 1974. From "Postcodes in the United Kingdom," *Wikipedia*. Available at: https://en.wikipedia.org/wiki/Postcodes_in_the_United_Kingdom (Accessed June 4, 2016).
5. "dans l'espace d'un jour, les citoyens les plus éloignés du centre puissent se rendre au chef-lieu, y traiter d'affaires pendant plusieurs heures et retourner chez eux." Translation by the author (Souchon and Antoine 2003).
6. A Voronoi subdivision—named after its inventor Georgy Voronoi (1868–1908)—is a popular one among digital designers. It can be performed both in 2D and 3D. In the simpler case of a plane, given a set of predetermined points such subdivision will divide the plane into cells in the form of convex polygons around each of the predetermined points. Any point inside the area determined by the call subdivision will be closer to the central point than any other one.
7. As for many other ideas, Fuller's notes indicate the first embryonic sketches on planetary planning date as far back as 1928.
8. John McHale was a British artist part of the Independent Group (along with Richard Hamilton, Reyner Banham, and Alison and Peter Smithson) which played a central role in blending mass culture and media and high culture, anticipating the pop art movement of the 1960s.
9. For instance, Hsiao-Yun Chu has described the *Chronofiles* as "a central phenomenon in Fuller's story, arguably the most important 'construction' of his career, and certainly the masterpiece of his life" (2009, pp. 6–22).
10. The *Inventories* contained a good overview of the digital tools necessary for the implementation of the *World Game*. Perhaps more interesting than the actual feasibility of the plans sketched out in the document are the more "visionary" parts of the text in which a greater coordination between resources, design, and construction almost sounds like an accurate description of mass-customization and BIM. "The direct design function which has also been reduced, in many cases, to the assembly

of standard parts out of manufacturers catalogues, is now renewed, even in large scale 'mass' production to the point where each item can be different and 'tailored' to the specification through computer aids." Also, in '1964 Fuller envisioned "...total buildings, jig assembled by computers...air delivered, ready for use in one helilift" (Fuller, McHale 1963, pp. 72–74).

11. Though Hugh's account is factually correct, it however omits a number of documents in which Fuller describes with great detail the actual computational architecture of the *World Game*. The hardware would be provided by a mainframe IBM 1620, whereas the programming language identified to read, convert, and plot various datasets was FORTRAN (compatible with the IBM 1620). The first document goes on to list the types of data to compute and what we now call the metadata hierarchy; that is, the numerical code the software would use to call up a particular dataset emphasizing both the informative but also pedagogical nature of these publications (Fuller, McHale 1965, p. 64).
12. Also discussed in the chapter on pixels.
13. Data, at best, was actually sent only once a day.
14. This was in line with Beer's motto: "Information without action is waste."
15. The socialist ideology constituting the context in which *Cybersyn* was implemented convinced Beer that the relation between theory and practice had to be explicitly declared in order to be involved workers in the project. For instance, copies of *The Brain of the Firm* circulated in factories.
16. Beer recognized that "an old system of government with new tools" could have produced results opposite to his intentions. In Beer, S (April 27, 1973). *On Decybernation: A Contribution to Current Debates*. Box 64, The Stafford Beer Collection, Liverpool John Moores University (Quoted in Medina 2006, p. 601).
17. http://www.bartlett.ucl.ac.uk/casa.
18. http://senseable.mit.edu.
19. http://www.spatialinformationdesignlab.org.

Chapter 4

Parametrics

Introduction

The notion of parametrics is perhaps the most popular among those discussed in this book. Of all the techniques explored, parametrics is in fact the one that has permeated the vocabulary of digital architects the most to the point of becoming a paradigmatic term for the whole digital turn in architecture. Patrik Schumacher (1961–)—whose *Parametricism as Style—Parametricist Manifesto* was launched in 2008—has been the most outspoken proponent of such reading by elevating parametric tools to the level of paradigms for a new type of architecture (Schumacher 2008). Not only is there a plethora of parametric software available to architects and designers, but also an extensive body of scholarly work analyzing the theoretical implications of parametrics both in design and culture in general (Bratton 2016; Sterling 2005; Poole and Shvartzberg 2015). Despite its straightforward computational definition,[1] parametrics has somehow become a victim of its success with the consequence of an evermore extended use of the term and an increasingly difficult stable definition to identify it with. The correspondence between grammarian James J. Kilpatrick (1920–2010) and R. E. Shipley well expressed the nature of the problem when they agreed that "with no apparent rationale, not even a hint of reasonable extension of its use in mathematics, *parameter* has been manifestly bastardized, or worse yet, wordnapped into having meanings of consideration, factor, variable, influence, interaction, amount, measurement, quantity, quality, property, cause, effect, modification, alteration, computation, etc., etc. The word has come to be endowed with 'multi-ambiguous non-specificity'" (Kilpatrick 1984, pp. 211–12. Cited in Davis 2013, p. 21).

Such success has led to a significant number of designers and theoreticians to go as far as to say that all design is inherently parametric as constraints dictated by site, materials, client's requests, budget, etc. all impact on the design output. As we will see throughout the chapter, we will resist such broad definitions and rather limit our survey to the relation between CAD tools and architectural design. In fact, within the realm of parametric CAD software, parametric relations must be explicitly stated in mathematical terms; therefore elements such as budget, site, etc. can only be understood in terms of correlations rather actual parametrics (Davis 2013, p. 24).

Despite its contemporary currency, the idea of designing with parameters is nothing new and has a very long history both in architecture and in mathematics which we will endeavor to sketch out. A parameter can be concisely defined as a variable whose value does not depend on any other part of the equation it is inserted in (the prefix *para-* is Greek for "beside or subsidiary," while *metron* means "measure") (Weisstein 1988). What is parametric design, then? First of all, parametric design envisions a design process in which a number of *parameters* control either parts or the totality of the object, building, or urban plan designed. Basically all CAD software used in design disciplines have parametricized procedures, which are made more or less explicit to users. By coupling definitions from design disciplines and mathematics, it is possible to delineate with greater precision what a parametric design model can be. From the field of mathematics, for instance, we realize that parametric models must possess two basic characteristics: (a) be based on equations containing a set of symbols—parameters—standing for a set of quantities, and (b) concatenate the different equations—and respective parameters—through "explicit functions" (Davis 2013, p. 21). When applied to CAD, this latter characteristic is often referred to as *associative*. We will also define as independent those parameters that can be edited by the user, and as dependent those resulting from mathematical operations and therefore not editable. If *Excel* does constitute the first popular piece of software allowing direct parametric operations, all CAD packages also allow different degrees of parametricization and interaction with variables. When we draw a circle in, for instance, *Rhinoceros*, we interact with a class composed by assignable variables and "closed" equations. The variables necessary for the equations to return values will determine the center and radius of the circle. If correctly inputted, the conditions stated in the equations will be satisfied and values will be returned. The types of parameters made editable are the *properties or attributes* of the object, whereas the inputs are called *values*.[2] A slightly more limited range of software also allows to track and edit properties and values as modeling progresses: we can imagine this property as recording the history of the model we are working on, therefore making values in the stored database permanently editable.[3] *Vectorworks*—again, to pick one out of the many CAD packages endowed with such features—stores the variable attributes of the each shape modeled in a separate window allowing users to alter them at any point during the modeling process. The ease with which changes can be made has actually affected designers' workflows by heavily relying on editing capacities: the right class of object—cube, circles, etc.—is first placed without paying attention to more detailed characteristics—such as its position or size—and adjusted later on.

However, this way of proceeding involves no concatenation of equations. Whenever multiple equations are linked to one another, we have a higher-level parametric model in which a greater connection between individual components and overall composition can be achieved. In such a model, some of the variables could still be editable, whereas others could be fixed as results of certain operations or software settings. A first-level concatenation is achieved through classes of object: these are groups of objects sharing the same attributes which can be potentially edited all at once. Any change to the attributes propagates through the class updating all the objects included. Operating this way, it is even possible to derive an entire programming language by simply scripting the properties of objects—endowed with data—and actions—described through equations. Alan Kay (1940–)—a key pioneer of digital design—did exactly that in the 1970s, coining object-oriented programming, a powerful computing paradigm which facilitated association between different objects and, consequently, interactivity.[4] This "deeper" notion of parametrics challenges designers to conceive their design in a more systematic fashion by shifting their focus away from any single object toward the relations governing the overall design as well as the sequence of steps to take to attain the desired result. On the other hand, the potential is to gain greater understanding of the logic behind the objects developed, work in a more adaptable fashion, and generate versions of the same design rather than a singular solution (See SHoP 2002). This way of operating has acquired cultural significance beyond its obvious pragmatic advantages: the ease with which models can change has altered the meaning of error and conversely created an environment conducive to experimentation leading some technology commentators to term this way of working as "Versioning" and "Beta-version culture" emphasizing the permanent state of incompleteness and variation of any object in a software environment (Lunenfeld 2011). CAD programs able to parametricize design can however look rather different from each other: *Grasshopper*, for instance, utilizes a visual interface, whereas *Processing* is a text-based scripting software in which values, classes, and functions are typed in. Finally, parametric elements are also nested in software packages primarily addressing the animation or simulation of physical environments, such as *Autodesk Maya* and *RealFlow*.

By operating associatively, parametric systems operate according to the logic of variation rather than that of mere variety as, in the former, objects are different from each other and yet their differentiation results from a common, overarching logic. Within this definition variables can be arbitrarily changed by attributing different values to symbols: for instance, in many scripting languages variables can be declared at the beginning of the script, their value assigned by the operator who can also change them at any point he or she wishes. These variables are precise values which are in themselves static. Variables can have inherently more dynamic qualities, as their variation can be coordinated: this can happen through the definition of domains within which to choose variables (e.g., *Grasshopper* provides users with number sliders to select a value within a predetermined range, like numerical gradients) or through the very concatenation of equations—earlier termed as indirect. Finally, variables could be imported as external inputs. For instance, a sensor linked to an *Arduino* circuit board could record the environmental temperature and use it as a variable to control a property of the objects designed in CAD (e.g., the size of the openings in a perforated wall).

To highlight the cultural significance of these procedures is not a trivial point, as it marks an important watershed in our discussion on parametrics in design. The possibility to make coordinated changes to a digital model is undoubtedly important, but it is not a sufficient condition to elicit more profound conversations on the nature of the digital-design process and its cultural and architectural relevance. The advantages of such fluid workflow are in fact often celebrated by software manufacturers not for their generative capabilities, but rather as tools to speed up and make more efficient a design process which fundamentally remains unvaried in terms of its cultural references or ambitions. Echoes of these considerations are also present in the current debate on the role of BIM packages such as *Revit Autodesk* (mostly tailored toward the construction industry and exchange of information) and other CAD programs more deliberately geared toward design. Rather than mere change, we will identify a more peculiar characteristic of parametric modeling in the notion of variation which not only implies a rigorous part-to-whole relationship in the design process—often conducive to greater spatial continuity—but also engenders the possibility to generate multiple outputs from a single parametric model. Through these categories, we will be able to not only detect early predecessors of contemporary parametric digital modeling, but also foreground more culturally charged values which have affected design beyond measurable efficiency.

From mathematics to CAD

To survey how the notion of parameter has been penetrating the realm of design, we will first have to understand how this notion emerged in mathematics in the work of Diophantus (around AD 300) to identify unknown elements in mathematical operations. In Diophantus' work there was only one valid number that could replace the symbol utilized and satisfy the logic of the calculations. This definition of parameter remained fundamentally unchanged until the fifteenth century as the works of al-Khwarizmi—who used it in his astronomical calculations in the ninth century—as well as Italian algebraists demonstrate (Goldestine 1972, p. 5). Muhammad ibn Musa al-Khwarizmi (c.780–c.850) should also be mentioned here as the first mathematician to write an algorithm—from which the very word derives—and also to develop a system of symbols that eventually would lay the foundations of algebra as a discipline (Goldestine 1972, p. 5). In these latter examples, parameters could identify multiple rather than singular numbers; in other words, they could *vary*, a feature that would eventually have far-reaching consequences for design too. This aspect marks the most important difference between this chapter and that on databases: we will define the latter as essentially static organizations of data, whereas the former as a dynamic one that has an inherent ability to change. This characteristic—which finds its first expression in the thirteenth century—is still very much at the core of parametric software be it CAD or others.

If Diophantus already employed symbolic notation, this was appropriated and greatly expanded by Ramon Llull—the object of lengthy discussions in the chapter on databases—as his *Ars Magna* extensively used variables to propose the first use of parameters as varying values. Contrary to the tradition established by Aristotle—according to which the logical relations between subjects and predicates was unary—Llull repeatedly swapped subjects' and predicates' positions, implicitly opening up the possibility for varying relations. His *Ars Magna* is "the art by which the logician finds the natural conjunction between subject and predicate."[5] Though the idea of interchanging the two main elements of a statement would not find a proper mathematical definition until the seventeenth century, in Llull's *Tables* we already find ternary groups of relations. It was in these precise steps that computer scientists detected the first examples of parametric thinking, which also presented some elements of associative concatenations. It was in the light of these considerations that Frances Yates (1966, p. 178) famously commented that "finally, and this is probably the most significant aspect of Lullism in the history of thought, Lull introduces movement into memory." Movement has to do less with the invention of machines consisting of concentric circles, but rather to the very idea of variation made possible by binary and ternary combinations.

We would have to wait until the end of the sixteenth century in the work of Francesco Maurolico (1494–1575) to find a formulation of variables similar to the one we use today, whereas the complete mathematical treatment would take place with the publication of *Artem Analyticien Isagoge* (1591) by François

Viète (1540–1603).[6] All these innovations would be extensively used by Leibniz—who was also familiar with Llull's work. Leibniz's oeuvre has been discussed in the database chapter, however it is important to mention here that in his work the notion of variation acquires a much more significant role thanks to the introduction of calculus. Leibniz defined it not only mathematically through derivatives and integrals, but also, and more importantly for digital architects, geometrically by providing a coherent and reliable method to compute curves.

These developments would eventually converge with that of modern computers forming the core of CAD software since its inception in 1962. *Sketchpad*—designed by Ivan Sutherland (1938–) as part of his PhD at MIT—not only marked the invention of specific computer programs for drafting, but also revealed how the design process could be augmented by digital tools. Similar to the contemporary discussion on parametric design, in Sutherland's description (Quoted in Wardrip-Fruin 2003, p. 109) of the software we also find an emphasis on efficiency and ease of operation as design objects "can be manipulated, constrained, instantiated, represented ironically, copied, and recursively operated upon, even recursively merged." However, more interestingly for our discussion, we also find that even while developing the software, Sutherland was already clear that designing with computers was not merely about replicating hand-drawing techniques. By constraining design moves through a set of relations, *Sketchpad* could not only guarantee higher levels of precision, but also enable a series of operations that could have not been performed by human hands: for instance, the software could automatically draw a line parallel to one drafted, lines could be constrained to be perpendicular to each other, or more complex procedures could recursively generate multiple copies of an object or sequentially delete parts of the overall drawing.[7] The development of *Sketchpad* is paradigmatic for the narrative of this book, as it shows how new tools are often introduced to address direct and pragmatic issues to eventually raise more profound, conceptual questions on the nature of design and its potential outcomes.

Regardless of several definitions and experiments scattered throughout the history of architecture, the first fully fledged parametric CAD software would only emerge in 1987 when Parametric Technology Corporation will first demonstrate its *Pro/ENGINEER*. Though this software was not aimed at enhancing designers' creative process, it, however, brought together a number of important features which we had introduced and worked independently up to that moment. *Pro/ENGINNER* allowed for both solid-based and non-uniform rational basis spline (NURBS) modeling geometries to be employed and—not unlike *Grasshopper* or *Photoshop*, for instance—had a dedicated "history" window. Any change in the database structure would propagate through the entire model updating it. The "assembly" function—one of the ten unique set ups provided by the software—allowed to model parts of the design individually and then merge them, again automatically updating the overall model as well as the shop drawings. The structure of the software implicitly dictated the design workflow: an object would be first drafted by determining its profile curves which would be individually manipulated, a series of three-dimensional tools would then turn the curves into surfaces and volumes; a method which also echoes Greg Lynn's description of his *Embryological House* (Weisberg 2008). The goal of the project was "to create a system that would be flexible enough to encourage the engineer to easily consider a variety of designs. And the cost of making design changes ought to be as close to zero as possible" (Teresko 1993). Beyond the initial emphasis on cost and speed, one can begin to sense the more profound effects that parametric modeling would eventually have on design: the shift away from focusing on the single object toward the concepts of series, manifold, concatenations, etc. as well as the possibility to mass-customize production by coupling parametric software with robotic production.

Early parametric design

To some extent systems of geometrical proportions governing the size and relation of different architectural elements could be seen as the first manifestations of some sort of parametric thinking in architecture. The Golden Section—which could be applied both parametrically and recursively—is definitely the most well known but by no means the only proportioning system employed by architects since antiquity. However, as Mario Carpo (2001) eloquently pointed out in his work on this subject, the emergence of a proto-parametric thinking in architecture emerged out of necessity rather than cultural sensibility. The impossibility to include drawings in their publications because of the lack of adequate reproduction techniques forced architects to devise vicarious notational systems resting on natural language rather than abstract symbolism. This method could not rely on measurements and visual documentation—both of which could not be reproduced precisely—to focus on the mathematical and geometrical relations between different parts of the building instead. As early as in Vitruvius' treatise—written between 30 and 15 BC—architectural orders were communicated through verbal description portraying how each element of a column could be obtained by subdividing an initial, modular quantity. Often such a modular dimension was provided by the diameter of the column which could be recursively divided by different values to size all its essential parts. Conceived through the articulation of parameters, this method guaranteed that columns could be built to comply with the formal requirements of a certain classical order (Carpo 2013). If this process was to be replicated in a parametric software, we would speak of columns as a class of objects whose shared attributes would include, among others, its diameter.

Both the elements of parametric modeling are present here: explicit functions relate independent variables—for example, column's diameter—to dependent ones, which are eventually concatenated to one another. This meant that all columns built out of Vitruvius' instructions could be all different while being all faithful "descendants" of the same "genetic" proportioning system. The effects of such notational system—and the philosophical ideas underpinning it—have resurfaced several times throughout the history of architecture and are still applicable criteria to understand the relation between CAD systems and design. For instance, in the enlightenment, Quatremère de Quincy's (1755–1849) definition of architectural type did remind of some of the characters of parametrics discussed thus far. Quatremère affirmed (1825) that "the word 'type' represents not so much the image of the thing to be copied or perfectly imitated as the idea of an element that must itself serve as a rule for the model. . . . The model understood in terms of the practical execution of art, is an object that must be repeated such as it is; type, on the contrary, is an object according to which one can conceive works that do not resemble one another at all." Surveying pre-digital architecture through parametric modelers has not only unveiled important scholarly knowledge, but also provided a deeper, richer context for digital architects. Among the many examples in this area we would like to mention the work of William J. Mitchell (1990) on the typologies illustrated by J. N. L. Durand's (1760–1834) *Prècis des Leçons d'Architecture* (1802–05) as well as on Andrea Palladio's (1508–80) *Villa Malcontenta* (1558–60), and John Frazer' and Peter Graham's (1990) studies on variation of the Tuscan order based on the rules James Gibbs described in 1772.

Baroque: Variation and parametric trigonometry

Perhaps the first accomplished exemplification of parametric thinking in architecture coincided with the emergence of baroque architecture in Rome in the first part of the seventeenth century. Baroque production has not always enjoyed the most positive critical appraisal, as it had often been perceived as gratuitous formal exuberance lacking rigor and method.[8] More accurate and positive analyses of this architectural period emerged only in the nineteenth century, although these were still largely avoiding a rigorous survey of the geometries and design methods informing the period's more iconic architectures. At the core of these architectures there is a design methodology which articulated spaces through the attribution and variation of parameters to basic geometries as well as established relational links between different forms so that the variation in one of these forms would result in a subsequent variation in all the other geometries related to it. It is in these terms that in baroque architecture we observe the potential of parametric articulation as a driver for design: this manifested in a new sense of wholeness often based on complex relations between different forms subjected to geometrical transformation, if not actual formal metamorphosis. At the core of these innovations are both mutating cultural values and a methodical exploitation of the very tools architects had at their disposal to set out geometrical compositions. Cords and rulers were employed to draft plans and elevations: this meant that all main geometrical forms were generated from the basic geometry of the circle through a process of topological transformation regulated by the variation of a series of parameters. As the drawing equipment allowed architects to compute and draw much more complex curves, trigonometry could also be applied to practical problems: for instance, manipulating the geometry of the circle to extract triangles or squares implies making use of the properties of sines and cosines (See Kline 1972, pp. 119–20). The kind of computation engendered by drafting tools was analogical—rather than discrete as in modern computers—and was evaluated both from the point of view of its internal proportions and transformations and for its perceptual effects onto the viewer.

The first, and perhaps still best, examples of baroque architecture are those produced in Rome at the beginning of the seventeenth century, whose deviations from the canon can only be detected when read against the backdrop of Mannerist production. For baroque architects the classical repertoire was not a hefty formal heritage to abandon; on the contrary, it constituted the basic formal vocabulary on which the logic of variation could be applied. True freedom lay within, and not outside, the canon, as it was the canon itself to be the invariant element, warranting legitimacy to any novel experiment. Rather than retracing the history of a complex international movement which affected almost all fields of knowledge, we will selectively be looking at some key instances of baroque architecture, examining them through the lenses of contemporary digital design. Since its emergence in Rome in the 1620s, baroque architecture was invested with a large societal mandate to exemplify the counter-reformist politics of the Roman Catholic Church aiming at reestablishing its cultural and political centrality after the Council of Trent. Two architects in Rome came to embody this new spirit, Francesco Borromini (1599–1667) and Gian Lorenzo Bernini (1598–1680) whose personalities sharply contrasted and resulted in one of the bitterest rivalries in the history of architecture. Despite the differences in the production of these two architects may not stand out to the untrained eye, Bernini's work was decisively more theatrical and exuberant in line with the personality of its creator, who managed to thrive in the Roman society of the time; Borromini, on the other hand, arrived at his virtuosic formal manipulation through a more controlled—proto-parametric, we will claim—process which largely borrowed from the tradition and more in tune with his complex and introverted personality.

The first of these examples is *S. Carlino alle Quattro Fontane* which represents both the first and last major piece of architecture built by Borromini. The commission came in 1624 after a series of minor works—including some ornamental apparatuses in Saint Peter working side by side with Bernini—whereas the façade was only completed in 1682. Upon completing the small cloisters, Borromini concentrated on the design of the main church. Within the highly constrained space—the whole of *S. Carlino* would fit inside one of Saint Peter's pilasters—Borromini managed to position a distorted octagon—with differing sides—obtained through a series of successive subdivisions based on an oval shape. The actual profile of the octagon is, however, not legible, as each of the four "short" sides has been further manipulated through the insertion of concave spaces: three of them contain altars, while the forth is occupied by the entrance. The long sides of the octagon are further articulated into three parts in which concave and convex curves alternate giving an undulating, "rippling" overall spatial effect. The overall module for the entire setout is the diameter of the columns which are positioned to punctuate the rhythm of alternating concave and convex surfaces. The elevation of the church is no less intriguing: three types of geometrical, and symbolic, forms are stacked on top of each other: the bottom third can be approximated as an extrusion of the plan figure. The middle third not only acts as a connection between the other two elements, but also alludes to a traditional cruciform plans through a series of reliefs constructed as false perspectives. The internal elevation is then concluded by the dome based on an oval geometry whose ornamentation—based on an alternating pattern of crosses, octagons, and hexagons—gradually reduced in size to enhance visual depth. Each third is clearly separated by continuous horizontal elements giving legibility to an otherwise very intricate composition. Only two openings let light in: the lantern which concludes the dome and the small opening window placed right above the entrance and now partially occluded by the addition of the organ in the nineteenth century. Though completed much later, the façade beautifully echoes the geometries of the interior: the concave-convex-concave tripartite rhythm of the lower order is inverted at the upper level; likewise the convex surface on which the entrance is placed finds its counterpoint in the concavity of the main altar. Finally, the edges of the façades are not framed by columns conveying a sense of further dynamism and drama to the overall composition which appears unfinished. In describing his ambitions for the façade, Borromini wanted it to "seem to be made out a single continuous slab"[9] emphasizing the importance of continuity and seamless relation between individual motives and overall effect.

Rather than reading *S. Carlino* against the canons of the history of architecture as many other scholars have done, it is useful here to point out how Borromini's process anticipates the design sensibility now engendered by parametric modelers. As Paolo Portoghesi (1964) suggested, *S. Carlino* departed from the traditional cruciform plan in which four main focal points were located at the end of each arm of the cross and made to coincide with altars and entrance, leaving the areas in between to act as transitional or preparatory spaces. *S. Carlino* provided no such "resting" spaces: the entrance, the altar, and the chapels were put in close relationship with one another both perceptually and formally in order to merge them into a continuous, dynamic experience. Whereas Renaissance and Mannerist churches conceived space as an aggregation of modular elements often based on cubical or rectangular modules, Borromini—who at the time of his appointment was twenty-five—subverted these principles by adopting recursive subdivisions and articulation of a space whose totality was given from the outset. The sense of wholeness is still one of the first elements to stand out in this impressively complicated composition also emphasized by the homogeneous treatment of the internal surfaces, all rendered in white in which only chiaroscuro provides three-dimensional depth.

The close part-to-whole relationship as well as the idea of varying the relation between different geometries was the result of the conflation of emerging cultural values and drafting tools available. To understand recursive subdivision and continuity, we have to consider that the setting out geometry of the small church had been computed and plotted with a pantograph, which had the properties of both rulers and cords. A masterful use of this tool would allow to generate flowing curves with varying tangents; recent studies by George L. Hersey (1927–2007) and Andrew Saunders demonstrated—albeit through different media—the presence of nested epicycle figures in the ruling geometries of *S. Carlino* (Hersey 2000, pp. 191–94; Saunders 2013) (Fig. 4.1). From the point of view of contemporary CAD this can be described as a parametric system, as we have invariant equations regulating the form of ruling curves and their internal relationship and varying parameters governing the variation of curves. Epicycles are "dynamic" geometries, not because they literally move, but because they are generated by imagining one geometry spinning along the path of another one; the procedures followed to plot them are dynamic rather than their final appearance. In computational terms this is a recursive function in which the same step in a script

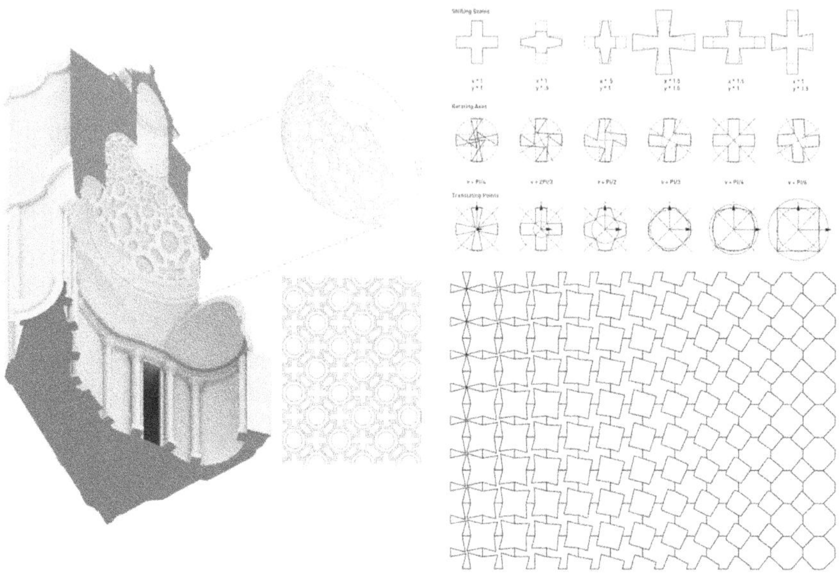

Figure 4.1 Work produced in Re-interpreting the Baroque: RPI Rome Studio coordinated by Andrew Saunders with Cinzia Abbate. Scripting Consultant: Jess Maertter. Students: Andrew Diehl, Erica Voss, Andy Zheng and Morgan Wahl. Courtesy of Andrew Saunders.

is repeated albeit by incrementing the controlling parameters by a small quantity until they satisfy an overall stopping condition. The interplay between sines and cosines—which Borromini could play with through cords and pantographs—not only was at the base of this variating logic but also can be easily replicated through text-based scripting languages (Bellini 2004). It is perhaps not a coincidence then that Sanders and his students utilized *Rhinoceros*—in combination with one the supported scripting languages, *RhinoScript*—to retrace the process followed by Borromini: first by scripting the various equations describing the epicycles, and then by employing *Grasshopper* to concatenate the different parts. This digital construct can easily be turned from an analytical tool into a generative one: the variation of the independent parameters allows the users not only to understand the logic of Borromini's work in greater depth, but also to experiment with it.

The associative qualities of the forms employed for *S. Carlino* are also legible in the dialectic relation between concave and convex geometries: both in plan and elevation these two geometries are continuously counterbalanced by its opposite pair. The observer's visual experience is restless and disorientating at first, as the eye is guided from curve to curve emphasizing the spatial dynamism and tension of the overall composition. Alternating convexities in CAD would require to invert the cord of each arc: an operation can could be carried out either geometrically—by inverting the vector in the center point of each arch—or mathematically by playing with sine and cosine values. Similar proto-CAD techniques are also employed in the decoration of the intrados of the dome in which the alternation between crosses and diamond shapes gradually shrinks toward the lantern. Whereas the alternation between concave and convex curves is mathematically abrupt—by shifting values from positive to negative—in the dome we see a gradual transition based which can be achieved by combining a numerical series to a given geometry.[10] Although numerical series had been long utilized in architecture for the purpose of proportioning different parts—for example, the abovementioned Golden Section—baroque architects understood them as systems able to spatially articulate both the infinitely large and the infinitely small.

The issue of the articulation of scale in baroque architecture would deserve greater attention, but we should mention in passing that the first half of the seventeenth century was also marked by great advancements in the field of optics which led to the invention of the telescope and microscope, respectively, allowing new forays in the domains of the infinitesimally large and small. Borromini's treatments of numerical series are not only used to refer to a different spatial sensibility toward matter but also distort perceptual qualities of space—in the case of *S. Carlino*'s dome to accentuate depth of the otherwise small volume. It is, however, the figure of the spiral that best exemplifies the mutated sensibility toward scale as it literally presents an infinite development both emanating outward endlessly and converging toward a point in equal infinite fashion. The spiral began to feature in many baroque architectures though Borromini did not employ it in *S. Carlino* but rather in *S. Ivo alla Sapienza* (1642–60)—his other major architectural work—to sculpt the lantern topping the dome. In the spiral we find several themes of baroque and parametric architecture: the variation of the curve is continuous; primitive shapes are distorted as in the case of the ellipse which can be interpreted as a skewed, variating circle; finally it spatializes the problem of the infinitesimal as the spiral converges to a point. This problem would find a decisive mathematical definition around the same the time in the work of Gottfried Leibniz, and Isaac Newton (1642–1727), whose contribution to calculus provided a more precise and reliable method to compute and plot curves. More precisely, differential calculus concerned itself with rates of infinitesimal variation in curves computed through derivatives. Obviously, none of these notions feature in the calculations Borromini carried out to set out his buildings; however these almost contemporary examples formed the rather consistent image constituting a large part of the cultural heritage of the baroque.

To appreciate the impact of calculus on design, we should compare the algebraic and calculus-based description of, for instance, a surface. While algebraic definitions would seek out the overarching equations defining the surface, calculus provide a more "flexible" method in which points describing the surface are only defined in relation to the neighboring ones. The rate of variation—that is, the varying angle of the tangents of two successive points—is then required to identify the profile of the surface. The idea of an overarching equation describing the whole geometry is substituted by a more localized one; besides the mathematical implications, one can intuitively grasp the efficiency introduced by calculus to describe, and therefore, construct, complex curves and surfaces. The implications of these variations had been known since Leibniz but architects have always had limited tools to employ them as generative tools in their designs. In the 1980s the adoption of *CATIA* by Frank Gehry marked a very significant shift as it allowed the Canadian architect to represent, and fabricate its intricate, irregular geometries by computing them through a calculus-based approach. Used for the first time for the *Peix Olimpico* (1989–92) in Barcelona, these tools found their best expression in the paradigmatic *Guggenheim Museum Bilbao* (1991–97).[11] Parallel to these design investigations, in 1988 Gilles Deleuze published *The Fold* (1992), a study on Leibniz's philosophy and mathematics. The logic of variation found in Deleuze a new impulse delineated by the notion of the *Objectile*, which describes an object in a state of modulation, inflection; therefore it is given in multiples, as a manifold. The influence of this book on a young generation of architects cannot be overstated and proved to be particularly important for architects such as Bernard Cache (1958–)—principal of *Objectile* and once Deleuze's assistant—who employed parametric tools to design manifolds of objects rather singular ones. Greg Lynn (1964–) coupled philosophical insights on the nature of form with the advancements in animation software—such as *Alias Wavefront* and *Maya*—that allowed him to manage complex curves and surfaces in three dimensions. The most important outcome of these experiments was the *Embryological House* (1997–2001), a theoretical project for a mass-customized housing unit designed by controlling the variation in the tangent vectors of its ruling curves which were eventually blended together to form a continuous, highly articulated surface. The *Embryological House* did not result in an individual object but in a series of houses, all different and yet all stemming from a single, and therefore, consistent series—which Lynn defined as a "primitive"—of geometrical principles and relations.

Finally, a very early version of the blending techniques employed in the *Embryological House* can be observed in *S. Carlino.* Borromini had the arduous problem of connecting the distorted octagonal profile of the plan to the oval volume of the dome. The middle third of the elevation resulted in a rather complicated form not really reducible to any basic primitive that found its raison d'être in its ability to blend the outline of the bottom and the top third of the elevation.[12] In today's digital parlance we would call this a lofted surface resulting from the interpolation of its start—distorted octagon—and end—ellipse—curve. As we saw in the chapter on contouring and fields, lofting was also at the core of morphing techniques in which several different shapes can be continuously joined.

Physical computation and parametrics

As we have seen in the case of baroque architecture, parametric modeling often involves formalizing physical phenomena in mathematical language such as the movement described by the sliding of a cord along a moveable wooden rod to draft spirals and parabolas. The role of drawings here slightly changes from their traditional one as they are not used to prefigure the effects of a physical artefact that will be built at a later stage; rather they survey, in fact, encrypt the actions performed by a physical phenomenon acting as an analogue computer—in our examples represented by cords or pantographs. Parametric modeling here finds a mathematical expression to the various forms and relations established through the physical modeling, which will also eventually affect the realm of digital simulations.[13]

As for other digital tools analyzed in this book, the exact origins of this practice are hard to pinpoint, as the idea of moving from the empirical domain to the representational one is perhaps as old as the definition of design itself. However, one paradigmatic example of this practice is the famous model completed by Antoni Gaudi (1852–1926) prior to the construction of the *Sagrada Familia* (1882–) in Barcelona. This physical model not only shows an elegant and intricate way of solving the distribution of loads in a structure, but also exhibits characteristics which have been absorbed by digital-design tools. The model was famously constructed upside down in order to take advantage of gravity to act as a force simulating the condition of compression the cathedral would have to eventually stand. It was made of a series of strings representing the center line of the arches structuring the vaulting system of the building; attached to key joints in the structure were small sachets filled with sand that tensioned the wires into a state of equilibrium determined by a balance between force and material. The final configuration was then surveyed, turned back on its intended orientation, and built. From the point of view of parametric modeling each strand was a catenary curve which could have been computed by an equation containing four independent variables: the length of the string, the weight attached to it, and the coordinates of the two end points of the curve. This equation could have been iteratively applied to all segments in the model leaving the four parametric variables open to adjustment. By coupling material properties and mathematical equations this project is one of the finest and earliest examples of topological modeling; that is, of geometrical elements—be it lines or surfaces—subjected to a system of external (gravity) and internal (strings and weights) physical properties. The outstanding work recently done by Mark Burry (1957–) to complete Gaudi's project made an extensive use of computational tools not only to manage the complexity of the original design, but also to formalize—through parametric associations—the spirit of the original catenary model. Incidentally, it is interesting to notice that many CAD packages offer default tools to control catenary curves. Though seldom utilized for generative purposes, *Rhinoceros*, for instance, has a weight command allowing to control the "strength" of each control point in a curve.

The case of the *Sagrada Familia Basilica* presents an exemplary use of physical and digital parametric modeling; however such design methods have been even more popular in other fields where geometrical concerns are often subservient to performative ones. Both aeronautical and nautical design relied on similar abilities to compute and draft precise curves to provide the best penetration coefficients. For instance, the curves describing the profile of an airplane wing were drawn at 1:1 scale directly on the floor of the design office by using long wooden rods to which weights—called "ducks"—could be "hooked" to in order to subject the wood to a temporary deformation resulting from the precise distribution of forces. The resulting curve—called spline—was obtained through parametrically controlled physical computation, represented by the material constraints of the drafting instruments employed were integrally contributing to. Though not always very practical, this practice had a long tradition in design going as far back as the eleventh century when it was first introduced to shape the ribbing structure of hulls (Booker 1963, pp. 68–78).

The formalization of these relations found a renewed interest in the 1950s when two French engineers—Pierre Bézier (1910–99) and Paul de Casteljau (1930–) respectively working for car manufacturers Renault and Citroën—simultaneously looked for a reliable mathematical method to compute, and therefore fabricate complex, continuously variating curves. Before venturing into more detailed discussions of the methods invented and their impact on digital design it is worth describing the context within which their work took place. Car design at the time relied on the construction of 1:1 mock models of cars—either in wood or clay—generated from outline sections of the car's body take at approximately 100 millimeter intervals. Once these were cut out and assembled a rough outline of the car was obtained and then perfected to produce an accurate, life-size model of the whole car. Additional measurements to produce construction drawings to manufacture individual parts could then be directly measured from the 1:1 model. This method was prone to potential errors in taking and transferring measurements and heavily relied on immaculately preserving the physical model from which all information would come. The treatment of complex curves was also made more complicated by a workflow which moved between different media before manufacturing the final pieces. Most importantly, the 1950s also saw the emergence of computational hardware able to machine 3D shapes; these machines were operated by a computer, and an adequate software to translate geometrical information into machine language was required. Before delineating the architecture of such software, a mathematical—and therefore machine-compatible—description of splines was required.

Both engineers sought a more reliable method that would not be fully reliant on physical models and whose mathematics would be divorced from the physical task to sculpt and manipulate curves. The result of such research was the Bézier curve, a notational system that greatly facilitated plotting complex, smooth curves. Despite its name, the notational system was not Bézier's invention—though he also attained similar results—but rather de Casteljau's who presented his method to Citroën managers in 1959. While Citroën's board immediately realized the importance of methods introduced and demanded Casteljau's equations to be protected as industrial secret, Bézier did not encounter a similar reception and was allowed to publish his work claiming these results first.[14] The fundamental innovation consisted in computing the overall shape of a curve by only determining the position of its control points (often represented by many CAD software as small editable handles). Prior to the introduction of the Bézier method to draft a complex curve would have involved to formalize a mathematical equation describing the curve, resolving the equation for a high number of values in order to find out the coordinates of points on the line which would then be plotted and joined. Plotting control points only divorced mathematics from drafting. While the previous method identified points on the actual curve to eventually connect, Bézier's method was plotting the position of control points which can be imaged as sort of strings "tensioning" the actual curve to shape. The result is that to plot a complex curve we may only need to determine the position of 3–4 points leaving to the de Casteljau algorithm to recursively compute the position of all points on the final curve.

The Bézier notational method found an immediate success in CAD programs and is still at the core of digital modeling of complex curves. All CAD packages, architects, and designers normally use these parametric algorithms. The user chooses the degree of the curve to construct and place the minimum number of control points for the algorithm to be computed: incidentally, the number chosen for the degree of the curve also determines the minimum number of control points necessary to visualize the desired curve.[15] Nowadays the combination of computational power and robotic fabrication is making these conversations less relevant, but it was not too long ago that designers had to make careful choices regarding curve degrees, negotiating between the aesthetic effect sought—the higher the degree of the curve, the smoother is the surface—and its computational and economic viability. The use of material computation as a driver for design innovation is, however, a strand of design research far from being exhausted, as it still represents one of the most debated and fruitful topics in digital design (Menges 2012). Among the many works that have emerged, Achim Menges' (1975–) *Hygroscope* (2012)—first exhibited at the Pompidou Centre—not only merges digital and material computation, but also creates a fluid, intricate surface of great elegance.

Luigi Moretti: *Architettura Parametrica*

Regardless of the various genealogies of parametric modeling sketched out thus far, it is architect and urbanist Luigi Moretti (1907–73) who must be credited for first coining the term *Architettura Parametrica* (Parametric Architecture). The formula emerged at the beginning of the 1940s—though Moretti claimed he had been thinking about it since 1939—as *Architettura Parametrica* called for a new design research and methodology which drew from the advancements made in mathematics and, in particular, statistics. A more precise formulation of this agenda and its implications on architecture came some years later in an article titled "Structure as Form" (Moretti 1951)—published in *Spazio*, the magazine Moretti had funded and directed—in which he affirmed that "a work is architecture when one of the possible *n* structures (in a constructive sense) coincides with a form that satisfies a group of required functions and with a form that adheres to a determined expressive course 'of a soul of the human place' that is taken by the architect." Before discussing the details of his new methodology, it is useful to point out that Moretti was one of the most formally gifted Italian architects of the twentieth century, whose fluent, almost baroque, language could not have been more distant from the apparent positivistic, somehow "cold," prose of passage quoted. Moretti in fact did not see the adoption of scientific methods and theories as a treat to his individual creativity, but rather as an admission of the limitations of purely formal or empirical thinking, which required an injection of rigor to keep up with societal changes; a sentiment surely still shared by many digital designers.

Rather than solely focusing on declaring its theoretical principles, Moretti wanted to implement *Architettura Parametrica* and forged a series of collaborations leading to the foundation of Institute for Operational Mathematics Research in Mathematics Applied to Urbanism (IRMOU) in 1957.[16] Among the collaborators, mathematician Bruno De Finetti (1906–85) stood out not only because he brought advanced mathematical thinking and procedures to the group, but also because he introduced the IBM 610 to put to test the ambition of the institute marking—perhaps for the first time in Italy—the use of computers in architecture. The institute conceived the introduction of parametric thinking through three clear steps to be iteratively evolved: (1) definition of a theme (Moretti mostly concentrated on sport facilities as illustrative of the urban potential of his method), (2) definition of parameters to articulate all the different components of the theme (for sport complexes, those involved viewing angles, etc.), and (3) definition of analytical relations between dimensions dependent on the various parameters (Moretti 1971). In Moretti's mind, *Architettura Parametrica* was a response to the fast-changing Italian society of the postwar years: a new scientifically inspired computational method in which urbanists, foremost, and then architects could respond to the challenges of reconstruction. Such transformations were too broad and their effect still too uncertain to warrant the use of traditional methods: the IRMOU aimed to use mathematical and statistical methods to grasp both quantitatively and qualitatively the nature of Italian modernity.

The results of the application of these tools to architecture featured for the first time at the 12th Triennale in Milan in 1960. The four designs proposed—a football stadium, a swimming pool, a tennis arena, and a cinema theater—did not fail to attract the attention of the press both for the novelty of the process followed and for the daring forms proposed (Fig. 4.2). The theme of the sport arena provided Moretti with clear, measureable sets of parameters, quantifying viewing angles, and "visual information" values related the activities taking place. The design of the football stadium deserves particular attention as the final proposal—presented through large plaster models—not only was very elegant, but also showed more clearly the inner workings of *Architettura Parametrica*. The combination of various parameters determined two main criteria—visual desirability and visual information—to evaluate the various design options. Moretti was often accused of inconsistency between methods and results: the design of the stadium presented in Milan did not substantially differ from the architectures he had been designing since the 1930s. A more detailed analysis of the process followed would have resolved this apparent contradiction and opened up a useful conversation on the relation between process and outcomes in digitally driven design. The data input in the IBM mainframe did not return a fully fledged three-dimensional model or even a generic spatial design, rather the computer

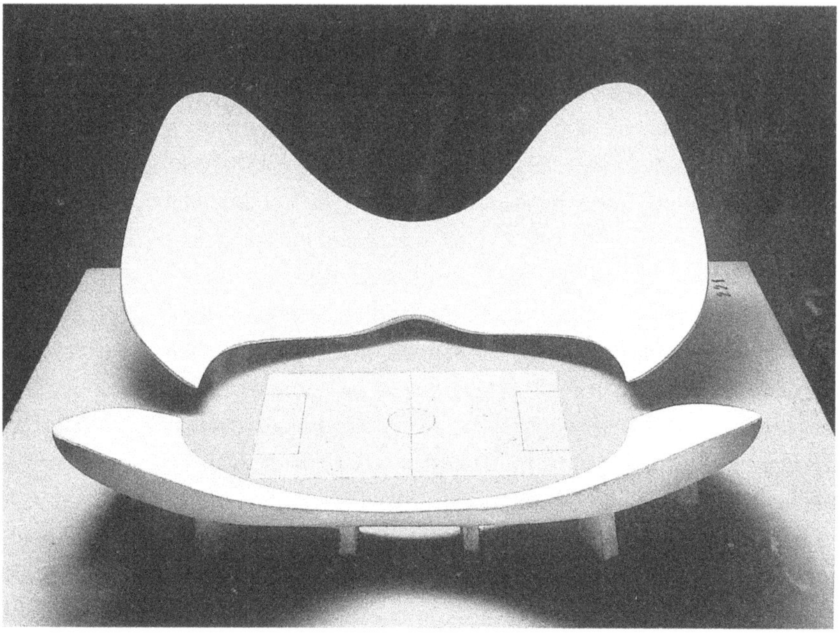

Figure 4.2 L. Moretti and IRMOU. Design for a stadium presented as part of the exhibition 'Architettura Parametrica' at the XIII Milan Triennale (1960). © Archivio Centrale dello Stato.

produced bi-dimensional diagrams showing contour lines wrapping around the rectangular shape of the football pitch. These diagrams remind of pressure maps in weather forecast, as they only showed the distribution of design criteria in 2D; the work of the designer was to interpret them as "spatial brief"—Moretti referred to them as "methodological schemes"—which could have not been attained without the support of computers. The tension between parametric modeling conceived as a purely procedural activity and as an instigator of a new formal language was never resolved by Moretti and, to some extent, is still present in today's debate. Critics of Patrik Schumacher's Parametricism still identify similar inconsistencies, as this new movement is presented both as a new aesthetic language—Parametricism as a style, a Morettian expression of new societal problems—and a new method for design and research. The tension here lies in the fact that parametric modeling is not inherently biased toward any particular group of forms: both a curvaceous and a rectilinear design can be generated parametrically and yet most of the parametric production concentrates on organic forms (Frazer 2016, pp. 18–23).

Though more scholarly research is needed in this area, we know that Moretti applied his methodological innovations to two projects: the *Watergate residential complex* in Washington, DC, (1960–65) and the unbuilt *Project for a stadium and*

Olympic complex in Tehran (1966). Though the large hotel complex in Washington is now better remembered for its political rather than architectural vicissitudes, Moretti did make use of a computer program to control the distribution and layout of the hotel rooms (*Washington Post* 1965). A more extensive use of parametric modeling was employed in the large urban complex proposed as part of Tehern's bid to host the Olympic Games. The overall urban plan distributed the major sport arenas along rectilinear boulevards; the organic shapes of all the major buildings proposed not only provided a counterpoint to the more rigid urban pattern but was also generated parametrically. The Aquatic center proposed the same overall organization already hypothesized for the swimming pool presented at the 1960 Triennale, while the center piece of the plan—a stadium for 100,000 people—differed from previous designs to provide a novel application of parametric techniques. Still based on the criteria of visual desirability and information, the overall plan consisted of two tiers of seats shaped to follow the perimeter of the racing track, while the higher tiers were skewed to increase capacity along the rectilinear sides of the track. Moretti also varied the overall section to follow a parabolic profile to guarantee good visibility for the higher seats. Other parameters included in the analysis made the overall organization asymmetrical as press areas, etc. were grouped together. The final effect is unmistakably Morettian for its elegant and sculptural quality (Santuccio 1986, pp. 157–58).

The domain of investigation of the IRMOU greatly exceeded that of architecture to venture into urban, infrastructural, and organizational proposals, such as transportation hubs, zoning, and urban management. Moretti had already advocated the introduction of cybernetics in urban design in 1939—it is worth noting in passing that the first modern computer, the ENIAC, was only completed in 1946—claiming that urban studies should have taken into consideration the developments in the fields of electronics, psychology, and sociology, as well as all disciplines that cyberneticists concerned themselves with (Guarnone 2008). As mentioned earlier, Moretti saw in *Architettura Parametrica* not only a chance to align urbanism with the latest advancements in scientific disciplines, but also a rigorous method to respond to the increasing complexity of cities. Moving from architectural to urban issues significantly increased the number of variables to consider: the design process had to move beyond causal relations to embrace multi-factor modeling. In this context the use of computer was a matter of necessity rather than choice. IRMOU worked on various themes including a proposal for the reorganization of the land registry office in Rome, projections for migratory fluxes as well as a study for a parametric urban model to relate road layout to the distribution of institutions (also presented at the 1960 Triennale). In 1963, the group produced perhaps the most important piece of research: a study of the distribution, and potential future projection, of real estate prices in Rome. The topic undertaken presented much more explicit political and social challenges which the group worked through to eventually present the outcomes of the research to representatives of the Italian government with the ambition to advise future policies to control the speed and extent of the large reconstruction program initiated after the end of the Second World War. We should immediately point out that the resolution and rigor of these urban studies was rather approximate and showed clear intentions rather than convincing results. The group—particularly de Finetti— not only began to set up the various routines to gather data, efficiently aggregate them and mine them, but also made a proposal for the institutional framework necessary for a successful implementation of their programs. The relevance of these operations—which remained at a level of speculations and never really applied—does resonate with some of the attempts to simulate urban environments developed in the 1960s and described in the "Network" and "Random" chapters.

The contemporary landscape

The pervasive diffusion of parametric modelers in all aspect of architectural production from conception to fabrication has not only challenged previous forms of practice, but also brought along the promise of a greater integration and synthesis between organizational and aesthetic disciplinary concerns. Perhaps, such quest for coordination and variety within repetition are not only a reflection of the very strengths of parametric software, but also a further indication of a profound cultural shift which digital design is trying to respond to. To limit the discussion to architecture, contemporary production has been integrating parametric modeling in three types of projects which broadly map three areas of future research in this field. The first can be understood as a "historical" project as parametric tools allow us to reevaluate or, in fact, discover the deeper principles informing the design of key architectures of the past. This includes not only scholarly research such as that carried out by Andrew Saunders, but also the impressive work undertook by Mark Burry and his team at *Sagrada Familia* to both dissect Gaudi's blueprints and complete the cathedral. At a larger scale, parametric modeling was also essential to appraise some of the experiments in computational planning of the 1960s to update and expand them.[17] We are here referring, for instance, to UNStudio's *Deep Planning* (1999) tool to masterplan large, complex areas (UNStudio 2002, pp. 38–58).

A second type of integration is taking issues with the current division of labor in architecture and the divide between producers and consumers. Here, it is the coupling of parametric software and computer-aided manufacturing (CAM) to bring about a paradigm shift: it is easy to imagine a future situation in which architects will not simply design objects but rather systems to generate potentially infinite series of objects all based on the same parametric model—the *Objectile* in Deleuze's words. Consumers could manipulate the variables themselves to fit their desires and preferences to customize the final object. This phenomenon—a sort of "cultural parametrics"—already exists for certain products such as trainer shoes or cars and since the 1990s has been broadly referred to as mass-customization (Pine 1993). Such scenario had already been anticipated by French engineer Abraham Mole (1920–92) who, in his writings on aesthetics and computation, talked of Permutational Art as a "systematic exploration of a field of possibilities" based on algorithmic variation. Mole intuited that the effects of this shift were in no way limited to technology, rather they were cultural as they allowed to conflate two previously distinct domains: art whose architectural container was the museum and commerce represented by the supermarket. The promise of changing the relation between production and consumption was that "each patterned formica table-top sold at every chain store in every town could be distinguished by being different from all the others" (Mole 1971, pp. 66–67). The instances anticipated in the 1960s now find renewed traction propelled by a far more effective series of tools to control design process, fabrication, and distributions of objects and architectures. Carlo Ratti has explored the design implications of this paradigm in his *Open Source Architecture* (2015), whereas Mario Carpo (2013b) has questioned the role of designers and authorship for such co-designed objects.

Mole's observation also gives rise to a more radical type of research seeking to do away with the mediation of professional figures in the design process. This "participatory parametrics" found its origins in the experiments carried out in the 1960s by the likes of the *Architecture Machine Group* led by Nicholas Negroponte at MIT and Yona Friedman (1923–) which respectively stood out for their experimentation and political stance. In 1971 Friedman (1975) presented his *FLATWRITER*, a concept for CAD software to allow nonprofessionals to design their own spaces. In eight steps any person with a computer and Friedman's software could shape their environment: a series of icons (fifty-three in the first interaction) would allow users to express their desires, be shown all the possible configurations fulfilling their inputs, and calculate the effects of their unit once placed into a three-dimensional grid. "Auto-planification," as Friedman called it, combined parametric associations and graph theory allowing to include qualitative inputs (e.g., by "weighting" user's lifestyle by inserting the number of times a space in the house was likely to be used, therefore determining possible adjacencies or size). By taking advantage of the tools developed by the gaming industry, architects such as Jose Sanchez—author of *block'hood*—are expanding on this tradition.

A final strand of research has been seeking a more continuous relation between parametric tools, practical applications, and theory. Patrik Schumacher (1961–) has led the charge in this field by coining the term "parametricism" to identify such undertaking. Parametricism positions itself as "a new style within contemporary avant-garde architecture" developed through the work at Zaha Hadid Associates and various publications (Schumacher 2010, 2012). In its latest iteration in 2016, Parametricism 2.0 is proposed as the adequate style to address the material, social, environmental issues of contemporary society (Schumacher 2016). parametricism claims a direct connection between "low-level" tools of a discipline—in this case, parametric modeling in architecture—and the "high-level" thinking to produce a potentially new field of research of production.

The impact of this integration is legible in the works of a variety of architects. Among the most original ones, marcosandmarjan—led by Marcos Cruz (1970–) and Marjan Colletti (1972–)—have been producing architectures conflating several of the strands mentioned above. Their *Algae-Cellunoi* (2013) (Fig. 4.3) presented at the *9th ArchiLab: Naturalizing Architecture* in Orleans utilized parametric modeling to bring together robotic fabrication, ornamentation, and

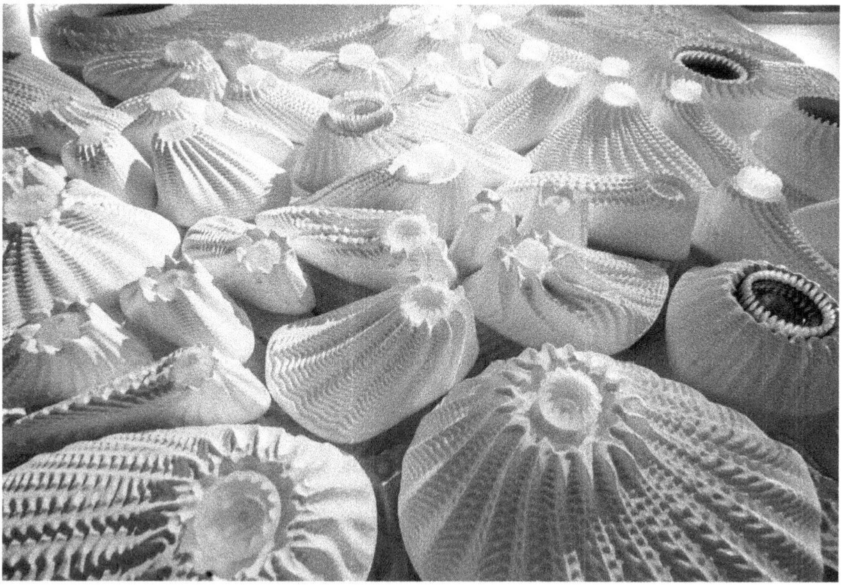

Figure 4.3 marcosandmarjan. Algae-Cellunoi (2013). Exhibited at the 2013 ArchiLAB Naturalizing Architecture. © marcosandmarjan.

applied research. The installation consisted of an ornamented wall subdivided into cells, all made of foam. A Voronoi pattern parametrically controlled the overall subdivision, whereas each cell was seeded with terrestrial algae which grew over time contributing to overall ornamentation of the piece. The choice of foam as material was particularly interesting, as it allowed to apply parametric design to a rather neglected and yet ever-present material in the construction industry. Mostly utilized for insulating buildings, *marcosandmarjan* showed with this piece how complex techniques and ideas are mature enough to take on standard architecture issues. It is in this process of integration that parametric modeling promises to more profoundly impact architectural design and fabrication.

Notes

1. "Parameter is information about a data item being supplied to a function or procedure when it is called. With a high-level language the parameters are generally enclosed in brackets after the procedure or function name. The data can be a constant or the contents of a variable" (BCS Academy Glossary Working Party 2013, p. 282).
2. Using *C++* scripting language as an example, values can be "public" or "protected," to signal the degree of accessibility to a certain parameter. For instance, a value anticipated by the keyword "public" can be accessed from outside the class, allowing, for instance, value to be input by mouse-clicking or keyboard. *C++ Classes and Objects*. Available at: https://www.tutorialspoint.com/cplusplus/cpp_classes_objects.htm (Accessed July 5, 2016).
3. It is therefore not a coincidence that the first version of the scripting plug-in *Grasshopper* was in fact named *Explicit History*.
4. In the early 1970s a group of researchers from Xerox PARC led by Alan Kay developed *Smalltalk*, which marks the first complete piece of software based on object-oriented programming (See Kay 1993).
5. "A man is composed of a soul and a body. For this reason he can be studied using principle and rules in two ways: namely in a spiritual way and in a physical way. And he is defined thus: man is a man-making animal" (Crossley 1995, pp. 41–43).
6. The rediscovery of Diophantus' work in 1588 prompted Viète to pursue a new research to bring together the algebraic and the geometrical strands of mathematics to prove their isomorphism. In order to do so, he had conceived a "neutral" language that could work for both domains: substituting numbers with letters provided such abstract notational language. Viète called it "specious logistic" as he understood symbols as species "representing different geometrical and arithmetical magnitudes" (Taton 1958, pp. 202–03).
7. Sutherland's work is also important as it will indirectly influence the development of scripting language applied to visual art and design and in the emphasis on interactivity between end users and machine. An example of the former can be

identified with object-oriented programming developed by Alan Kay—as already mentioned—which also led to the design of *Dynabook* project (1972), the progenitor of the personal and laptop computer. The more interactive aspect of Sutherland's project was later picked up by the likes of D. C. Smith's *Pygmalion* (1975) whose software allowed direct interaction with the monitor screen and whose logic ended up influencing the window-based interface commercialized by Macintosh and Windows (See Sutherland 1963).

8. For instance, Claude Perrault (1676) spoke of an "unproductive deviation"; while Marc-Antoine Laugier (1775) dismissed Borromini's work as too extravagant, not functional.
9. "Apparisse composta di una sola lastra continua." Translation by the author (Borromini 1725).
10. Series components in parametric software such as *Grasshopper* contain a predetermined number of value each at certain interval between each other. In regard to the actual application of these tools to retrospectively understand Borromini's work, Andrew Saunders is again mentioned here as his scripting exercises were able to reconstruct the logic of variation with which the two figures used in the dome morph.
11. These very same projects were also discussed in the chapter on scanning technologies. The two discussions should be seen as complementary to each other.
12. See chapter on morphing.
13. We shall refer to the chapter on simulation to expand this specific aspect of the design process.
14. Incidentally, this managerial choice helped Citroën to produce a series of iconic cars; the DS19 manufactured from 1955 to 1975 perhaps represents the best example of Bézier curves applied to car design.
15. Some pieces of software have a clear didactic approach to controlling degree of curves: in *Maya* this value is clearly visible when the curve command is selected and no curve will appear on screen until the minimum number of points has been input. See Degree of NURBS Curve and Surfaces. *Autodesk Knowledge Network*, [online]. Available at: https://knowledge.autodesk.com/support/maya-lt/learn-explore/caas/CloudHelp/cloudhelp/2015/ENU/MayaLT/files/NURBS-overview-Degree-of-NURBS-curves-and-surfaces-htm.html (Accessed July 12, 2016).
16. Instituto per la Ricerca Matematica e Operative in Urbanistica.
17. See chapter on networks.

Chapter 5

Pixel

Introduction

By discussing the role of pixels in digital design we once again move out of the strictly computational tools to discuss the role that peripherals have; as we have seen in the introduction, input and output peripherals do not strictly compute.[1] Pixels—a term that has by now far exceeded its technical origins to become part of everyday language—are the core technology of digital visualization, as they are in fact defined as "the smallest element of the display for programming purposes, made up of a number of dots forming a rectangular pattern" (BCS Academy Glossary Working Party 2013, p. 90). Pixels are basically the digital equivalent of a piece of mosaic; they are arrayed in a grid each containing information regarding its position and color (expressed as a combination of either three colors—red, green, and blue [RGB]—or four—cyan, magenta, yellow, and black [CMYK] numbers). Like mosaics their definition is independent of the notion of scale: that is, pixels do not have a specific size, however they differ as pixels are electronic devices that allow the information displayed to be updated and refreshed at regular intervals—often referred to as refresh rate. Pixels can be used to either visualize information coming from external devices, such as digital cameras or scanners, or information generated within the computer itself—creating digital images, such as digital paintings or the reconstruction of perspectival views. Pixels are not tools specific to CAD software, as they are a common feature of many digital output devices. Their function is therefore strictly representational rather than generative: we are in the domain of raster rather than vector images.

However, more advanced three-dimensional modelers are endowed with a series of tools that take the logic of pixels; that is, the type of information encoded in them and use it to sculpt objects. Here color information is not utilized to construct a particular image on screen but rather to manage the distribution of the parameters controlling a modeling tool. For instance, *Maya* and *Blender* provide users with paint tools to either apply textures to objects or sculpt them directly, utilizing information contained in pixels to construct or deform three-dimensional objects. These tools best exploited the characteristics of pixels to merge the intuitive nature of familiar techniques such as painting with the more complex process of three-dimensional modeling. Recently pieces of software such as *Monolith* have expanded the range of pixel applications allowing to model a whole three-dimensional field, de facto blending pixel information within a voxelized field—termed by the software designers as "voxel image."[2]

Among the first images to appear on a computer screen at the beginning of the 1950s were the draughts board of Christopher Strachey's (1916–75) software and Ben F. Laposky's (1914–2000) *Oscillons: Electronic Abstractions*, the first graphic interface for general-purpose computers (Fig. 5.1). The *Oscillons*—which represents one of the first examples of Computer Art—displayed a series of Lissajous curves simulating the movement of a pendulum on a cathode ray oscilloscope (CRO). The process followed to generate the seductive images of wandering dots and lines would deserve deeper analysis, as it does resonate with other architectural examples mentioned elsewhere in the book such as Karl Chu's *Chaos Machine* or early baroque architecture in which similar methods to construct forms were also employed. However, for the purpose of our study, it is

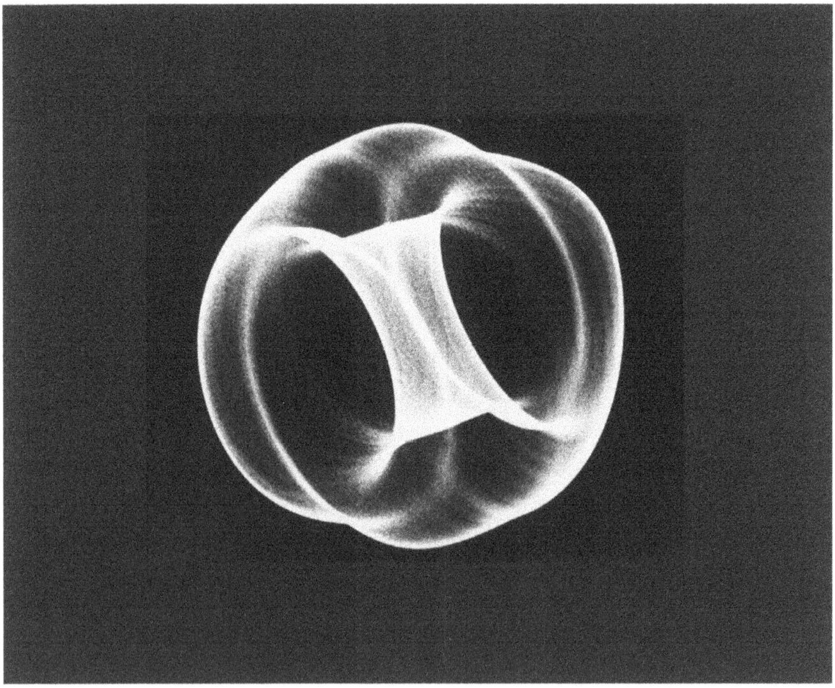

Figure 5.1 *Ben Laposky. Oscillon 40 (1952)*. Victoria and Albert Museum Collection, no. E.958-2008. © Victoria and Albert Museum.

the nature of the medium displaying the final images to be of interest. This is not only because the use of the screen has been largely overlooked in other studies, but also because this example began to shine some light on what opportunities for spatial representation such medium would give rise to. Laposky actually utilized a cathode ray tube (CRT) screen which formed images by refreshing 512 horizontal lines on the screen; this technology will be eventually absorbed in the technology of the pixel. Contrary to paper drawings, the CRO offered Laposky the possibility to directly represent the dynamic qualities of a pendulum. The refresh rate of the CRT gave a sense of depth and ephemerality much closer to the natural phenomenon Laposky set out to study. These new opportunities implied aesthetic choices as much as technical ones as it was even more evident in the few colored versions of the *Oscillons* in which the chromatic gradient applied to the varying curves enhances the spatial depth of the bi-dimensional projection.[3] It was the high-contrast visual quality of the screen that prompted Laposky to recognize in the array of rapidly changing pixels' architectural qualities when he affirmed that they looked like "moving masses suspended in space (1969, pp. 345–54)."

The images generated by Laposky were raster images, different from those of CAD software often which operate through vector-based geometries. The distinction between these two types of visualization is not just a technical one and deserves some further explanation. Raster images are generated according to the definition of pixel provided at the beginning of the chapter: they are fields of individually colored dots which, when assembled in the correct order, recreate the desired images on the screen. Vector-based images are constituted by polygons which are defined mathematically; for instance, a black line in a vector-based image is the result of a mathematical function which is satisfied once the values for the start and end points are inserted, whereas a pixel-based image of the same line will be displayed by coloring in black all the pixels coinciding with its path. Strictly speaking, CAD software utilizes vector-based images, though all images displayed on a computer monitor are eventually translated into pixels regardless of their nature. Perhaps more crucially in our analysis, vector-based images presuppose the presence of a semantic structure to discriminate between classes of objects and accordingly determine which properties to store and process. In other words, vector-based visualizations fit the formal logic of CAD software, as they presuppose a hierarchical organization associating information, structure, and algorithm, not unlike the way in which this information is linked in a parametric model.

As we shall see later, this problem was elegantly resolved in the 1960s through the work of Steven A. Coons (1912–1979) and Larry G. Roberts[4] (1937–) by constructing an algorithm that would automatically "flatten" the coordinates of all the vector elements in a three-dimensional scene into pairs of numbers to visualize as a raster image. It is worth remarking in passing that this algorithm—as for so many other innovations in the history of computers—was the result of the rather unorthodox conflation of knowledge gathered from nineteenth-century Gestalt studies in Germany and literature on mathematical matrices (Roberts 1963, pp. 11–14). It is also curious to note that Roberts's work compelled William Mitchell (1992, p. 118) to compare these momentous innovations to Brunelleschi's demonstration of geometrical perspective in Florence in the early fifteenth century as they marked a major step forward in the development of CAD—which Roberts himself referred to as "computational geometry" (In Cardoso Llach 2012, p. 45). In fact, Roberts' work not only streamlined the process making the visualization of three-dimensional forms easier and more reliable, but also inspired the very architecture of navigation of three-dimensional modelers we still utilize. He devised a mathematical matrix for each type of transformation—for example, rotation, zoom, pan, etc.—that allowed not only to change the point of view, but also to move between orthographic and perspectival views.[5]

Larry Roberts was also involved in the construction of the "hidden line" algorithm which he completed in 1963.[6] This method not only is crucial to the development of visualization techniques in CAD, but also shows the variety of applications computational innovations gave rise to. Roberts' method in fact—often referred to as "Roberts crosses"—was based on 2*2 pixel square to be analyzed through image recognition algorithms. This application could not have happened without the parallel studies on digital scanning carried out at the National Bureau of Standards. These researches—described in greater detail in the chapter on scanning—in turn utilized Alberti's model of the *graticola* which reduced an image into a series of cells to analyze individually. Russell Kirsch was explicit in citing Alberti as one of the sources of inspiration for the work of the bureau to which he also added mosaic, a finer-grain, controlled technique to subdivide and construct images that they utilized to design the first digital scanner (Woodward 2007).

Some of the innovations found a direct application at Boeing in the design of aircrafts. William Fetter (1928–2002) not only got credited for inventing the formula "computer graphics" in 1960, but he also managed to combine these algorithms to create CAD workflow to assist the design of airplane parts.

Throughout the 1960s computer visualizations quickly improved laying the ground for the now-ubiquitous computer rendering. Key centers were at University of Utah and Xerox PARC in Palo Alto, California where the first computer-generated images were created. The first implementation of a shading algorithm was accomplished by General Electric while working on a commission from NASA to simulate the space expeditions allowing real-time display of a space capsule on a television screen (Gouraud 1971, p. 3). Both companies worked on a prototype software developed by Peter Kamnitzer (1921–1998) called *Cityscape*, which could visualize a designed city-scape on a CRT. The user had two joysticks to control the direction of movement and eye-head movement, whereas a knob would determine the speed of what could very well have been the first digital fly-through (Kamnitzer 1969). The architectures of this virtual city were modeled utilizing *SuperPaint*, the first software to enable pixel manipulation designed by Richard Shoup (1943–2015) with a team of experts that included Alvy Ray Smith (1943–) who would go on to be one of the co-founders of world-famous computer animation film studio PIXAR. This software could rightly be seen as the predecessor of software packages such as *Adobe Photoshop* or *Adobe Premiere*. However, the algorithms to compute light reflections and refractions were mostly developed at the University of Utah under the guidance of Ivan Sutherland. To trace the history of these algorithms it would suffice to open the rendering editor of the one of the software digital designers daily use and scroll down the rendering options menu: we would encounter all the most important computer designers as algorithms were normally named after their inventors. French computer graphic expert Henry Gouraud (1944–) devised the first algorithm to smooth en the faces of curved surfaces, a feature that was repeatedly improved respectively by Edwin Catmull (1945–), James Blinn (1949–)—who also invented "bump mapping" giving the visual impression of having a rough, irregular surface—and finally Vietnamese student Bui-Tuong Phong (1942–1975) whose algorithm developed in 1973 as part of his Ph.D. research produced particularly smooth and shiny surfaces.

All these different types of rendering algorithms were invariably tested on the same object: the Utah teapot. This object has become an icon of computer imaging—a digital and physical copy are on display at the Computer History Museum in Mountain View, California—and is still one of the default volume primitives provided by *Autodesk 3DSMax* to test materials and lighting effects. The combination of concave and convex surfaces as well as saddle points made it an ideal benchmark object to test the effect of light on materials before applying them to a desired object or composition. Sutherland had used a digitized V. W. Beetle before Martin Newell sketched out the elevation of the teapot and then modeled it by combining Bézier and revolution surfaces. The final dataset—still available online—consisted of 32 patch surfaces determined through 306 world coordinate vertices.

The University of Utah was also at the forefront in embedding pixels within the fabric of our daily life by projecting computer-generated images in a three-dimensional space; a technology that would eventually give rise to Augmented Reality (AR). In 1968 Ivan Sutherland presented the work his team had done on the *Head Mounted Display*. As mentioned, this device pioneered the development of AR technology—that is, the possibility to overlay a digital image onto a real scene via special head-mounted devices or glasses. The device consisted of a special pair of spectacles containing two miniature CRTs attached to the user's head. A pivoting metal shaft connected the head-mounted device to the ceiling of the room recording its every rotation or movement. The coordinates recorded were processed through a series of mathematical matrices that recalculated the perspectival view, elegantly eliminated any superfluous calculation (through an algorithm called "clipping divider," a feature still found in most three-dimensional modelers) and, finally, sent the updated view back to the CRT screens, in the form of a wireframe image. Compared to previous experiments, the device did not offer a static view, but rather a dynamic one continuously updating as the user navigated in space. In this experiment, we have the first software-based experiment successfully "turning" the screen by 180 degrees—so to speak. Rather than be seen as a surface onto which to input data, CRT screens are here both inputting and outputting data in a constant dialogue with the end user. Sutherland saw the introduction of digital computers in the design not as a mere passive translation of ordinary drafting tools into computer language, but rather as an active process in which the very qualities of the architecture of computation demanded a different way to conceive design. Sutherland had already sought these opportunities when designing *Sketchpad* and saw in the *Head Mounted Display* the possibility to interact with virtual spaces (Fig. 5.2). He noticed how users should not have simply looked at pixels on screen but interacted with them by either moving in space—to alter their relation to the objects displayed—or by engendering them with editing capacities to change the objects in the virtual model (Sutherland 1968).

This latter point not only is central to our discussion but also informs the range of case studies that we are about to explore. The image of a window so central in Alberti's description of perspective is no longer sufficient to understand the role of pixels and screen in digital design. Digital tools allow to "turn" the metaphor of the window by 180 degrees, transforming the screen into a device able to both receive and project information. The development of graphic interfaces for CAD was in fact motivated by the desire of making computers "more approachable," easier to relate to, and, therefore, learn (Sutherland 2003, p. 31). Rather than a passive screen, it was an interface able to let information flow in both directions that was sought. Digital screens have since developed to project abstract information or images into the real world through a variety of media at scales that affect the design of buildings and public spaces, which will be the object of the discussion in this chapter. For the digital architect, it is therefore more fruitful to speak of pixels as the elementary part of the digital interfaces conjuring up a better metaphor to understand how pixels have influenced generative work in architecture and urbanism. Hidden-line drawings, renderings, AR, and

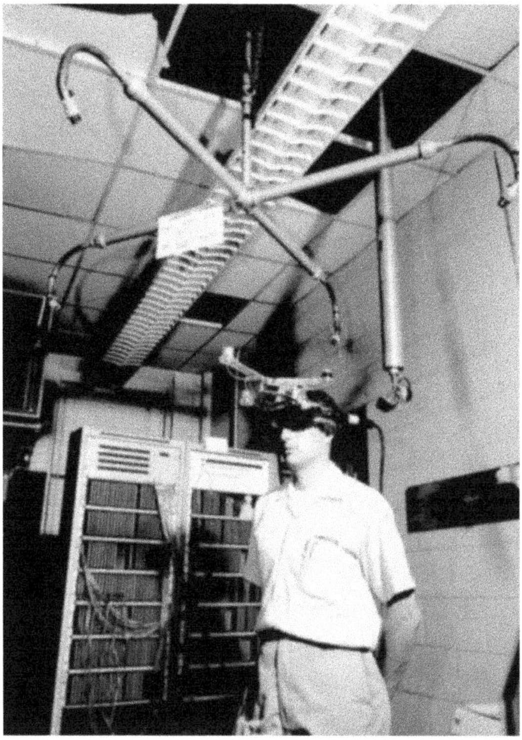

Figure 5.2 Head-Mounted device developed by Ivan Sutherland at University of Utah (1968).

digital projections have found increasing traction among designers perhaps because they have allowed them to look with renewed interest at symbolic, communicative, narrative elements of architecture.

Since its inception the surfaces of pyramids, churches, and temples have been designed not only to perform some function but also to carry messages. The study of ornaments has been a constant interest of architects as well as of scholarly research which has focused on dissecting its narrative, formal, and structural principles. The relation between pixels and architecture should be read within this very field of studies; however, some important caveats should be drawn out to better understand what is unique about pixels and how they can be conceptualized in the design process. There are in fact two elements of the design process that pixels have contributed to strengthen. The first regards the pictorial qualities of design; the introduction of color not only in digital representation, but also in modeling as exemplified by software like *Maya* or *Blender*. Secondly, pixels since Laposky's experiments possess dynamic qualities due their capacity to rapidly change to project moving images and allow real-time interactivity. Beyond technical features though, the possibilities enabled by these innovations have allowed designers to imagine buildings and spaces as ephemeral constructions. Both elements will act as a guide in our foray into the history of architecture.

Sfondato: Beyond physical space

Robert Venturi's (1925–) and Denise Scott-Brown's (1931–) description of pyramids as the "billboards of the Proto-Information Age" (2004, p. 24) is perhaps one of the first known architectural examples charged of highly communicational values. However, the first example of construction of an architectural image generated by simply controlling its smallest elements emerged with the invention of mosaic in which small pieces of glass, stones, or other materials were arrayed together to depict a scene. Whereas more recent techniques deviated from the use of only regular shapes, most of the historical examples almost invariably stuck to regular, square tiles. Mosaics have a central place in the history of art, as they can be found as early as 3000 BC in Mesopotamia, in Greece, and under the Byzantine Empire, in which they reached the highest level of sophistication.

What characterizes mosaics as proto-pixel communication devices is their bi-dimensional spatial quality; they do not have a sculptural, volumetric presence and are reduced to a surface. As such, their presence in the history of architecture is rather intermittent and an interesting precedent in this regard is the Western façade of Lincoln Cathedral probably completed between and twelfth and thirteenth centuries (Fig. 5.3). A wide and shallow porch was placed in front of the actual body of the main church forming its façade. More than 50 meters wide and entirely made of yellow limestone, this unusual structure was effectively a large, in fact massive for the time, screen acting at the urban scale. The rhythmic division of the screen through small arches in relief not only breaks its overall mass down, but also generates a suggestive interplay between light and shadow, which adds vibrancy to the whole composition. (Caspary 2009)

However, we will still have to wait for another century to find the first systematic description of a method to work with a pixel-like or raster-type image. In 1435, in the first treatise on art—*De pictura*—authored by Leon Battista Alberti, the Renaissance artist provided a famous account of the methods to draw a geometrical perspectival view. Alberti described the picture plane—plane on which the image to paint is captured—as a veil that would intercept the light rays connecting the eyes of the viewer to the object he is observing. As we shall see in the chapter on scanning, the metaphor of the veil was a powerful one but technologically unachievable. More apt to our discussion is Alberti's mention of the *graticola*, literally, a grill—a rectangular grid to subdivide the picture plane

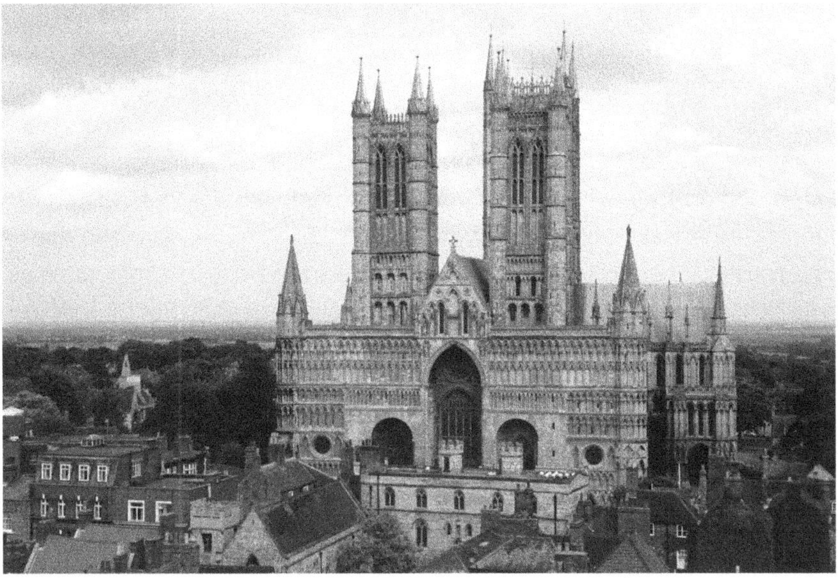

Figure 5.3 West entrance of Lincoln Cathedral, XIth century. © Getty Images.

into smaller, more manageable cells. According to this method, the work of the painter would consist in recording on paper the content of each cell by gridding the canvas to be homologous to the *graticola*. As Mario Carpo noticed, this is perhaps the first description on how to draw a raster-based image based on pixels. We could imagine that the computer screen is nothing but a massively denser *graticola* in which each cell is so small it can only be represented by a dot. By reducing the size of each cell reduces the information describing to just a color, a dot in fact without any geometrical feature. Once abstracted to pure color, the process of digitization would take care of translating this piece of information into a different, non-visual domain; that is, into a numerical field of RGB values in which each triple univocally pinpoints a color (Carpo 2008, pp. 52–56).

As the practice of perspective rapidly diffused based on the precise mathematical methods developed by painters and architects,[7] so did its application to architecture. In the baroque the perceptual effects of architecture onto the viewer became a central tool to convey the new type of architecture in which both the canons of the classical tradition and the position of the human subject were questioned. The impact on artistic production was tumultuous: a dynamic, immersive, vibe shook both art and architecture. The artistic production was characterized by drama and dynamism which also impacted on how the baroque city was conceived. It is therefore not a coincidence that the central element of baroque urban design was water made present either in grandiose terms through large sculptural pieces or in more modest fountains for daily use. Water was a perfect substance to encapsulate the spirit of the movement and the transformation agitating the baroque. The emphasis on dynamism and ephemerality extended to interior spaces too, as we witness through the emergence of a new pictorial style called *sfondato*[8] in which architectural scenes are painted on the walls and domes of churches and palaces in order to "push through"—the literal translation of the original Italian expression—the spatial boundaries of the architecture to give the illusion of being in larger, at times, even infinite spaces. The construction of such frescoes was rigorously based on geometrical perspective, often a central one, which also meant that the optical illusion could only be appreciated from a single point or axis. Perhaps one's anticipation of this virtuoso technique is the *Santa Maria presso San Satiro* by Donato Bramante (1444–1514), completed in 1482 in Milan. The plans for the expansion of the Romanesque church had to confront the extremely limited site, which was physically preventing Bramante from completing the four-arm symmetrical layout he had conjured up. The space of the choir—which should have occupied one of the arms—was painted over an extremely shallow relief, beautifully blending architecture and painting. Though not technically a *sfondato*, *San Satiro* represents one of the first examples of a technique that will find its highest expression in the seventeenth and eighteenth centuries. Out of the intense production, the dramatic ceiling of the central salon of Palazzo Barberini stands out: 28 meters in length it was completed by Pietro da Cortona (1596–1669) between 1633 and 1639.

Finally in the work of the Bibiena brothers we perhaps see the most accomplished works within the technique of the *sfondato*. Spanning over several generations, they developed a sophisticated method that also allowed them to deviate from central perspective to create more complex views—for example, portraying virtual architectures at an angle. This work would inevitably merge ephemeral and static architectures concentrating on scenography and resulting in the design of theaters such as the *Opernahus* in Bayreuth by Giovanni Galli da Bibiena (1696–1757).

The eighteenth century would also mark the first comprehensive theorization of architecture as a vehicle for communication. French architects such as Claude Nicolas Ledoux (1736–1806) and Étienne Louis Boullée (1728–99) would introduce through drawings and texts a new type of architecture whose role in society was to be symbolically manifested in its form and ornamentation. Though highly communicative, these imaginary projects did not have the dynamic, ephemeral qualities of baroque architecture which, in fact, they often criticized.

The electric screen

The use of dynamic images in the urban realm would only emerge with the Industrial Revolution in England, and then, even more decisively, with the rise of modernity in the United States toward the very end of the nineteenth century. These transformations were anticipated by the growing importance of billboards in terms of both their number and size. An interesting architectural precedent for this urban type was the Panorama, which provided an immersive simulation of reality. Robert Barker (1739–1806) had moved from Edinburgh to London bringing with him his reputation as a painter of panoramas, which he had invented in 1787. Panoramas captured large urban or rural views in a single gaze through the manipulation of perspectival rules, which Barker elegantly distorted to obtain cylindrical projections to be observed from its center. Besides the content of each image, what is interesting for our discussion is the relation between images and architecture. Upon relocating to London, Barker managed to build the first bespoke building to contain his panorama. Located just to the north of Leicester Square in London—where it still exists—the Rotunda was completed in 1801 by architect Robert Mitchell in the shape of a torus. The building was divided into two levels to house two panoramas and surmounted by a glass roof which controlled the amount of natural light washing down onto the two images wrapping the walls. Visitors would enter the building and reach its central column on which a terrace was cantilevering off. The visual and spatial qualities of the *sfondato* acquired a stronger, more spatial integration in the panorama. The aim was to trigger an immersive experience by turning architecture into a three-dimensional canvas for projections; however, compared to the *sfondato*, the panorama could only play with a much more limited formal repertoire: it could only avail of images to suggest sensations, whereas its form of the rotunda was completely dictated by the requirements of panoramas.

Toward the 1870s electricity would become an urban technology and the electrified billboards would constitute an important precedent in the integration of raster-type imagery and design. This would first happen through magic lantern projections, which may have been used to illuminate Parisian public monuments since the 1840s and then in Boston to project text and images (Huhtamo 2009, p. 24). Electricity would inaugurate the possibility of night life to extend the role of architecture beyond its daily use: commercial activities and shop windows would be among the first beneficiaries of the new technology, which would scale up rather quickly to attain a more substantial urban presence. The first electric billboards were in fact conceived as computer screens: each "pixel" was represented by a light bulb variedly colored—a static property, though—that could have been animated by choreographing which light bulbs were switched on and off. The ephemeral effects of electricity on urban environments also found their natural predecessor in fireworks often fitted on temporary and yet richly ornate pieces of architecture.[9]

The effects of the "electricization" on architecture could be increasingly measured through its erosion. Built forms found themselves competing and, as we shall see, often been defeated by the ephemeral, dynamic, experiential qualities electricity endowed space with. Though this process had started in the eighteenth century, when electricity made its entrance in the urban scene, its implications would only begin to be fully realized in the architectural production of the avant-garde, which would decisively first question and then do away with traditional means of architectural communication relying upon solid materials and clear geometries. The possibility enabled by electricity well met other political changes, which called for a radically new architecture. It was in the Soviet Union that this new type of architecture was conjured up to put new media to the service of the new communist ideology marking a sharp departure from previous historical models. The *Radio-Orator* stands by Gustav Klucis (1895–1938) combined audio and acoustic media reducing architecture to just a frame. Only the dynamic parts of the object were visible; if constructed, this project would have resulted in a flickering, colorful de-materialized piece of architecture. In 1922 Klucis also designed a series of propaganda kiosk emphatically titled "Agit-prop for Communism of the Proletariat of the World" and "Down with Art, Long live Agitational Propaganda" merging new technologies, architecture, and political messages (Tsimourdagkas 2012, p. 64). In the same years, De Stijl movement in the Netherlands managed to materialize some of these visions by building the *Café De Unie* in Rotterdam. The project—designed by Jacobus Johannes Pieter Oud (1890–1963)—marks an important point in the integration of text and pictorial motifs in architecture, one that was once again only meant to be temporary.[10] In 1924 Herbert Bayer (1900–1985) also worked on some temporary pavilions which had a deliberate commercial and ephemeral quality. They were intended to be installed in trade fairs to advertise new products, such as cigarettes or, tellingly, electrical products.

The insertion of messages on architectures was a prerogative of many avant-garde movements of the time. While Russian artists were promoting the communist ideology, Futurists in Italy celebrated speed and the recent emergence of the fastest form of communication of all: advertising. Fortunato Depero (1892–1960) had already stated (1931) that "the art of the future will be largely advertising." Beyond differences in content, these experiments shared the use of language not for its denotative qualities, but rather for its symbolic power. As Franco "Bifo" Berardi (1949–) noted (2011), the emergence of symbolism in art and literature had already changed the relation between language and creativity. Rather than representing things, symbolism tried to state what they meant; symbolism provided a formal and conceptual repertoire for new things to emerge by solely alluding to their qualities: the art of evoking had substituted that of representation. On the one hand, these new means of communication competed with and eventually eroded traditional modes of architectural communication based on brick and mortar; on the other, they began to show the effectiveness of a type of communication whose qualities would only be fully exploited by the new emerging media. The ephemerality of symbolic communication not only served well the agenda of the historical avant-gardes, but would also perfectly exploit the affordances provided by electronic screens and, many decades later, the emergence of virtual space through the internet.

What remained consistent in all examples showed was the erosion of traditional architecture by the introduction of more ephemeral, dynamic elements. The intricacy of the forms employed receded to give ground to the colorful, flashing, graphic elements. Particularly, Klucis' kiosks looked like rather basic scaffolding propping up propaganda messages: their urban presence would have been significantly different when not in use. This agenda—but certainty not the same political motivations—would inform the postwar years in which electricity would pervade all aspects of life and shape entire urban environments.

In fact the full absorption of electronic billboards in the city would not happen under the politically loaded action of European avant-garde groups, but rather in the optimistic, capitalist landscape of the United States. The most extreme effects were undoubtedly visible in Las Vegas, which would become the subject of one of the most important urban studies since the Second World War. In *Learning from Las Vegas* Robert Venturi, Denise Scott-Brown, and Charles Izenour (1912–2007) methodically analyzed the architecture of strip with its casinos and gigantic neon lights, which they saw as a spatial "communication system" (Venturi, Scott-Brown, and Izenour 1972, p. 8). This landscape was—and still is—dramatically designed by the dynamic elements: on the one hand, electricity radically differentiated its day and night appearance, and, on the other, cars acting as moving vectors from which the city was meant to be experienced. Through their famous definition of architecture as a "decorated shed," the three architects once again reaffirmed the growing importance of ephemeral spatial qualities over more permanent ones: the formal complexity of architecture of the strip had been reduced to its most basic shape: a box. Even before publishing their study on Las Vegas, Venturi and Scott-Brown had already started employing screens and billboards in their projects. Their proposal for the

National College Football Hall of Fame (1967) in New Brunswick, USA is perhaps the first project by high-profile architects to employ a large electronic screen. The design was made up by two distinct parts: the main volume of the building containing the actual museum and a massive screen placed next to it to form its public face. Despite not housing any program, it was the screen to constitute the central element of the design: it acted as a backdrop for the open space in front of the building and displayed constantly changing messages which radically redefined the façade. Robert Venturi referred to the project as a "bill(ding)board" celebrating the fertile confusion between different media and functions.

The steady "corrosion" of traditional architectural elements through the insertion of more dynamic media would eventually reach a critical point and give rise to a new spatial type: the disco club. Here spatial effects were solely created by artificial projections and sound, traditional architecture was nothing but a container which only revealed its basic articulation once projections were switched off.

Italian and Austrian radical architects such as Gruppo 9999 and Archizoom concentrated on this particular type of space with the aim of dissolving any residual element of traditional design.[11] Particularly interesting is the *Space Electronic* designed by Gruppo 9999 in 1969, inspired by the *Electric Circus* in New York in which the dissolution of tectonic organization of shape in favor of an electronic experience had already been developed since the early 1960s.

Contemporary landscape

"What will be the relationship between man and space in the new digital paradigm? Can architecture sustain its role as a cultural metaphor? What does the introduction of the computer mean for the role of architect and for typological traditions?" (Bouman 1996, p. 6). These were only some of the most representative questions asked by Ole Bouman (1960–) in introducing the Dutch entry to the 21st Milan Triennale in 1996. The installation proposed by Bouman placed itself within the rich and long tradition conflating architecture and other media with a major difference: the recent development of cyberspace had not only introduced a new powerful media but also disturbed the relation between old ones whose significance had been called into question. The solution proposed conflated images—both still and moving, architecture, and furniture design embracing the rise of new media and proposing a fundamentally different way to design and experience space. Surely the development of digital media has since massively moved on and so have the critical studies reflecting on possibilities and drawbacks engendered by new media; however, these questions are as timely today as they were at the time Bouman's writings. Similar conversations must have accompanied any insertion of new media in architecture: from the ceilings of Palazzo Barberini to the agit-prop structures proposed for new, communist Soviet Union. It is therefore unlikely that these issues will be settled here and a certain unease about the relation between architecture and more ephemeral media still invariably triggers controversies despite any shopping district in any major global city is abundantly furnished with urban screens and billboards. What we find interesting in contemporary examples is the increasing use of the screen as an interface allowing for an exchange between technology and the public domain calling on both to play an active role in the making of public space.

The architects accompanying Bouman in his project were from UNStudio—Ben van Berkel (1957–) and Caroline Bos (1959–)—an office that has consistently pioneered the introduction of digital technologies in architecture. UNStudio distinguishes itself for both its theoretical and design work in this that which resulted in several completed buildings in which the treatment of surfaces—both interior and exterior—has been thought of as images charged with communicative and aesthetic qualities. In the *Galleria Centercity Façade* in Cheonan, Korea (2008–10), UNStudio utilized color and images not to reinforce the commercial function of the building but rather to enhance its spatial qualities through optical illusion. In these projects UNStudio put to the test their "after image" approach in which techniques and iconography of electronic, popular culture are employed and resisted in an attempt to engage the user in different ways than through bombardment of commercial messages (van Berkel 2006).

A similar attempt was also completed by another Dutch architect: Lars Spuybroek (1959–)—leader of NOX—authored the *H_2O Water Experience Pavilion* (1993–97), which was intended to trigger awareness not through displaying exhibits but rather through atmosphere suggested by sound and light. Here light and sound effects took a more volumetric quality—not unlike some of the ideas that Frederick Kiesler also pursued—despite no real electronic screen was actually employed. The organic shape of the pavilion finally enhanced the effect of total immersion in a "fluid," electronic environment.

Finally, we have projects aiming at reversing the relation between pixels/architecture, turning architecture into a broadcasting device. A good example of such designs is the *Kunsthaus* in Graz completed by Peter Cook (1936–) and Colin Fournier (1944–) in 2003. The media façade was, however, designed by the Berlin-based studio realities: united which cladded the organic shape of the museum with 920 BIX (an abbreviation for big pixels). Each of these elements could be individually calibrated almost instantaneously making possible the projection of moving images. Perhaps even more important in this context was that the already vague, organic shape of the building hovering above the ground was further dematerialized by its electronic skin pulsating, fading, and blurring the edges of the physical architecture. Here pixels and architecture are merged not so much as to give rise to novel forms as to signal a different social role for cultural institutions; once again reaffirming how the urban interfaces—electronic or not—have the potential to change how architecture is designed and perceived.

Notes

1. Other important peripherals are: the mouse—an input device invented by Douglas Engelbart (1925–2013) in 1968—and printers as output devices.
2. *Monolith* will also be discussed in the chapter on voxels and maxels. See *Autodesk: Project Monolith*. online documentation. Available at: https://static1.squarespace.com/static/54450658e4b015161cd030cd/t/56ae214afd5d08a9013c99c0/1454252370968/Monolith_UserGuide.pdf (Accessed June 14, 2016).
3. It is worth remarking in passing that all material exhibited at various museums internationally consisted of photographic reproductions of the original experiments.
4. Larry Roberts is an important figure in the history of the internet too. His work on ARPANET—internet predecessor—concentrated on packet switching, an algorithm that allows to break large datasets in order to transmit over the network.
5. These notions have also been discussed in the chapter on scanning. Roberts' innovation will also play an important role in the development of computer-generated images through renderings.
6. The "hidden lines removal problem" occurs every time an edge or a vertex or an object is covered by either itself or other object. When constructing an opaque view of the model, the algorithm works out the position of the objects in order to remove from its calculations all the vertices and edges that are completely or partially covered.
7. See the discussion of perspective machines in the "Scanning" chapter.
8. *Sfondato* and *Quadratura* are two slightly different styles which are very similar; perhaps more useful is to distinguish *Sfondato* from *Trompe-l'oeil*, also a technique to create optical illusions based on perspective. However *Sfondato* cannot be detached from the very architecture inside which it is executed: the perspectival construction is based on the proportions of the room or space in which it is contained; this implies that the final image must be observed from a specific point. Sometimes even the themes portrayed in the *Sfondato* can be seen as an augmentation of those of spaces around it.
9. Fireworks also played a central role in Bernard Tschumi's work in placing the notion of events at the core of architecture and urbanism (See Plimpton 1984).
10. The café was destined to be demolished ten years after completion; however, *Café De Unie* not only still exists, but it was also recently restored.
11. Both Archizoom and Gruppo 9999 formed in Florence respectively in 1966 and 1967. Members of Gruppo 9999 were Giorgio Birelli, Carlo Caldini, Fabrizio Fiumi, and Paolo Galli; whereas Archizoom included Andrea Branzi, Gilberto Corretti, Paolo Deganello, and Massimo Morozzi. Two years later Dario Bartolini and Lucia Bartolini joined the group.

Chapter 6

Random

Introduction

The study of randomness in digital design will take us to the edges of this discipline—to the very limits of what can be computed—perhaps more than any other subject discussed in this book. Randomness should be seen here as a "dangerous" element of design. Such danger does not emerge from the risks arising from its arbitrariness, commonly perceived as a lack of logic. Though working with random mathematics challenges distinctions between what is rational and irrational, we are rather referring to its historical origins as an "anti-natural," artificial concept. As we will see, the presence or even allusion to random elements in governing natural processes conjured up an image of nature that was anything but perfect, implying that God, its creator, was therefore susceptible to errors. At times in which secular power was often indistinct from religious one, the consequences of such syllogism could have been fatal—as in the case of Giordano Bruno (1548–1600). Far from re-igniting religious disputes, this chapter will follow the metamorphosis of the notion of randomness from its philosophical foundations to its impact on digital simulations; an increasingly more central tool in the work of digital designers. Of the eight elements of digital design discussed in the book, random is the most theoretical subject, straddling between philosophy and mathematics. This chapter frames randomness as the result of the introduction of formal logic as an underlying syntax of algorithms. It is in this sense that we shall speak of purely computational architecture: that is, of design tools and ideas born out of calculations.

Though randomness does not refer to pure aleatory or arbitrary methods for design, these have nevertheless played an important role in the history of art—for example, Dada—and architecture—as in the case of Coop Himmelb(l)au's blindfolded sketches for the *Open House* in Malibu in 1983 (Coop Himmelb(l)au 1983). In computational terms, randomness, however, refers to the lack of discernible patterns in numbers preventing any further simplification; in other words, it has to do with complexity, with its limits determining what is computable.

In *Algorithmic Information Theory* (Chaitin 1987) this concept is effectively summarized as "comprehension is compression" (Chaitin 2006), as the efficacy of computer algorithms is directly proportional to their ability to compress the highest number of outputs into the shortest number of strings of code. The presence of random numbers puts a limit to compressing numbers into simpler, shorter algorithms: transferred into design this condition demarcates the limits of what can be computed, simulated, or generated. Computational randomness is not—at least in its conception—connected to any particular empirical phenomenon but rather a purely computational fact, born out of the abstract logic of the architecture of computers.[1] For this reason discussions on randomness within the field of information theory often also involve questioning the role of Artificial Intelligence (AI), as the use of random numbers also affects what can be thought by machines—that is, the presence and quality of nonhuman thought. As we will more clearly see toward the end of the chapter, the relation between nonhuman thought, design, and the ecological crisis will have radical implications for design.

If databases were treated as organizational structures, spanning in scale from the biological to the cosmological, parametrics added the notion of dynamics and time to databases through the logic of variation. Randomness complicates this picture once more by trying to compute the infinite, the unpredictable. We are here referring to a second—apparently more benign—type of risk associated with randomness involving conversations about the limits of our knowledge and, consequently, its foundations. In short, the mathematical paradigms underpinning design have moved from algebraic (database), to calculus (parametrics), and finally to stochastic (random).

If on the one hand, the integration of random numbers in computer algorithms has occurred at a deeper level, often distant from end users' experience, on the other, it has also provided designers with more rigorous and defensible methods to design in conditions of uncertainty. It is the very notion of uncertainty in design methods to take the center stage in this chapter to be dissected from the point of view of different design disciplines. Randomness, therefore, wholly plays a generative role in design; in computer-generative simulations, for instance, it largely acts as a way to dislodge previous assumptions to learn about complex phenomena as it happens in various fields, such as engineering, biology, and climate studies.

Before starting our survey it is useful to clarify some issues and applications of random algorithms in design. All CAD software packages extensively utilize random procedures; these are essential to generate, for instance, complex textures to render materials. Far rarer are tools explicitly allowing end users to generate either numbers or shapes through random procedures. Even those that do have a "random" command—like, for instances, *Grasshopper* or *Processing*—actually adopt pseudo-random procedures. These are generated according to a scripted algorithm in a deterministic logic which, paradoxically, will keep producing the same list of numbers if repeated.[2] Only more specialized pieces of software utilize more genuine aleatory processes in which true random events such as the time lapse between two successive key strokes or the value recording atmospheric noise are used as "seeds" to generate lists of random numbers.[3] In computer simulations too randomness is often the result of a complex concatenation of deterministic equations rather than truly random events; the overall visual outcome is nevertheless too complex and intricate to discern any pattern in it giving the impression of "true" randomness. The emergence of quantum computing promises to deliver truly random numbers by generating them not at the level of software as in all mentioned examples but hardware (See Gruska 1999).

The limits of reason: Random numbers in history

Our journey starts from a precedent already dissected in the "Database" chapter. Ramon Llull's wheels and their aleatory numerical combinations represented one of the first uses of random generative procedures. We saw how Llull was only partially interested in actual randomized processes, as its overarching religious ambitions compelled him to curtail the range of possible combinations achievable. The use of similar methods—but not similar devices—can also be found in the work of Giovanni Pico della Mirandola (1463–1494). Perhaps influenced by Llull, the Italian philosopher certainly differed from his Spanish colleagues as he tasked randomized procedures with the search of potentially new, unforeseen combinations and knowledge. Its combinatorial games were therefore played to their most adventurous and irrational conclusions giving rise to a labyrinth of anagrams and word permutations that at time puzzles the reader. His *Heptaplus* (1489) in which the combinations of both individual letters and syllables gave rise to a free play of signifiers with apparently no discernible meaning. Randomization was here an essential method to dislodge existing notions, to rationally venture into the unknown, the apparently irrational. The reward for taking such risks was to free man from the laws of cosmos, to affirm a humanist project in which mankind could be grasped and altered the very laws governing its existence (Eco 2014, p. 414).

Random methods diffused beyond the purely intellectual domain in the fifteenth century to find actual applications in encrypting and protecting military communications. The study of cryptography found its foundation in Johannes Trithemius' (1462–1516) *Steganographia* (written in 1499 but published only in 1606). Trithemuis utilized combinatorial wheels—although Llull was never mentioned—to encode and decode messages. Detached from the issue of meaning—religious or otherwise—Trithemuis could better exploit the possibilities of random combinations by generating the highest number of sequences possible. This logic inverted Llull's as the emergence of an improbable or "irrational" combination was actually preferred; random processes were utilized to substitute (encrypted) symbols with other symbols in order to protect military messages. Decoding had to be made too complex for the human intellect to discern, always needing an external device to compute it. In 1624 Gustavus Selenus (Augustus the Younger, Duke of Brunswick-Lünenberg, 1579–1666) would construct his treatise on cryptography on a Llullian machine consisting of twenty-nine concentric rings, each divided into twenty-four segments: the combinatorial power of this device was immense, as it could generate some 30,000 three-letter combinations all diligently listed in charts (Selenus 1624).

The use of random processes was never considered as an end in itself but rather as an instrument to generate new knowledge: it dislodged established notions, injected dynamism and new potential to move knowledge onward. This condition was true in the sixteenth century as much as it is today, as the insertion of random algorithms in, for instance, simulation software packages allows to expand designers' formal repertoire by being able to accurately reconstruct, test, and interact with physical phenomena. For this reason we should not be surprised to notice that early experiments in cryptography did not result in the proliferation of random methods but rather in the development of more advanced logics to control and interpret results borne out of random combinations. If on the one hand, the philosophers and scientists of the seventeenth century prepared the ground to study reality bereft of theological dogmas, as a fundamentally unknown reality, on the other, the dynamics of power were taking a very different direction as the counter-reformed Catholic Church—challenged by Martin Luther's split—had launched an ambitious plan to reaffirm its centrality. The personal vicissitudes of Giordano Bruno are testament to the risks associated with publically professing such views; his unbridled imagination, fearlessly communicated in several books, eventually caught the attention of the Tribunal of the Sacred Inquisition, which condemned and executed him as a heretic. It is, however, in this period that we can trace the passage from pure random sequences to the birth of formal logic, started by Leibniz and brought to its full maturity in the work of George Boole and Claude Shannon (discussed later in the chapter). Randomness was here introduced to bridge the gap between empirical reality of phenomena and their mathematical representation. The importance of logic for computational design cannot be overstated: not only because it would eventually form the basis of computer coding, but also because it would forge a cross-disciplinary field straddling between sciences—more precisely, algebra—and humanities—that is, linguistics.[4]

Despite the difficulties in ascertaining with incontrovertible precision the birth of these ideas, one document allows to clearly fix the first instance in which random, unpredictable events were subjected to mathematical treatment. In his letter to Pierre de Fermat (1601–65) written on July 29, 1654, Blaise Pascal—philosopher and inventor of the first mechanical calculating machine—utilized a method based on statistical probability to evaluate the odds of winning at a particular game. Pascal stated that he could not analyze the nature of randomness but admitted its existence.[5] In his *Ethics* (1675), Baruch Spinoza (1632–77) defined the nature of randomness as the intersection of two deterministic trajectories beginning to pave the way for a mathematical understanding of randomness (Longo, 2013). A turning point in the history of random procedures occurred in 1686 when Leibniz stated in *Discourse on Metaphysics*, section VI, that a mathematical law could not be more complex than the phenomenon it attempted to explain: "comprehension is compression. The implications of this law are of great importance for computation too, as it sets the limits of what can be calculated—whether by a computer or by any other device—and will become the subject of British mathematician Alan M. Turing's (1912–1954) research on the limits of computability and the possibility for the existence of a universal computing machine (Turing 1936).

Random processes in fact lay at the core of the architecture of the modern computer. The integration of random mathematics into computation is generally made to coincide with the publication of *A Mathematical Theory of Information* (1948) by Claude Shannon (1916–2001) while working at the legendary Bell Labs in New Jersey. Shannon's true achievements could best be described not as the invention of a theory ex nihilo, but rather as the combination of elements already known at the time of his research. To better understand it, we should take a couple steps back to focus on how digital computers operate. Precisely, we have to return to the discussion on formal logic we surveyed in the database chapter. After a long period of stagnation, studies in formal logics found renewed interest, thanks to the invaluable contribution made by George Boole (1815–64). Though probably not aware of the work already carried out by Leibniz, Boole developed an algebraic approach to logic which allowed him to describe arithmetical operations through the parallel language of logic.[6] Among the many important notions introduced, there also was the use of binary code to discriminate between true statements (marked by the number 1) and false ones (0). Despite the many improvements and revisions that mathematicians added between the nineteenth and the early twentieth centuries, Boole's system constituted the first rigorous step to merge semantics and algebra. Succinctly, the conflation of these two domains allowed to construct logical propositions using algebraic syntax—virtually making possible the inscribe forms of intelligence in a mechanical process. One of the key steps in this direction—at the root of AI—is the possibility to write conditional and recursive statements: the first characterized by "if . . . then . . ." structure and the latter forcing computer scripts to repeat the same series of logical steps until a certain condition is satisfied. It was philosopher Charles (1839–1914) in 1886 who noted that Boolean algebra neatly matched the mechanics of electrical circuits but did not make any work to further elaborate this intuition. Shannon's Master's thesis at MIT deposited in 1938 systematically applied Boolean algebra to circuit engineering: the system made a true statement to correspond to an open circuit, whereas the opposite condition was denoted by the number zero. Again, Shannon was not alone in developing this type of research, as similar works on logics were also emerging in the fields of biology, telecommunication, etc. It was also at this point that randomization began to play a central role as the transmission of information through electric circuits as transferring data always involves some "noise," that is, partially corrupted information. The tendency for systems to dissipate information (entropy) had already been stipulated by the second law of thermodynamics as early as 1824 by Nicolas Carnot (1796–1832). Similarly randomization was instrumental in the development of cryptography, a field in which messages are decoded in order to eliminate "noise." It is this third element—then much expanded and sophisticated due to the advancements in statistical studies—which Shannon added to conjure up a series of mathematical formulae to successfully encode a message in spite of the presence of noise. In this trajectory we can also detect a more profound and paradigmatic shift: if energy had been the key scientific image of the eighteenth century in the study of thermodynamic systems, information became the central element of the age of the modern computer and its cultural metaphor.

These fundamental decisions on the architecture of the modern computer unavoidably ended up influencing the type of tools and the opportunities made available to the end users, including digital architects. As we will see in the various case studies selected, artists and architects have been consistently trying to exploit the possibilities endowed by random numbers as they are understood as intrinsic qualities of modern computation.

Michael A. Noll's *Gaussian Quadratics*

A variety of artistic disciplines played with random numbers for creative purposes. Iannis Xenakis (1922–2001) composed stochastic music with the help of an IBM 7090—the results of which were performed for the first time in Paris in 1962—whereas one year later, A. Michael Noll (1949–)—a mathematician by training—applied random procedures to visual art. Noll's drawings were not originally produced for the benefits of the art community, and yet they attracted sufficient interest to be exhibited alongside other scientists and artists in a major exhibition at the Howard Wise Gallery in New York in 1965. Noll presented his *Gaussian Quadratics* in 1963 consisting of a series of vertical zig-zagging lines printed by a plotter on a letter-size sheet of paper: "The end points of the line segments have a Gaussian or normal curve distributions: the vertical positions increase quadratically until they reach the top, except that when any vertical position measured is greater than the constant height, then the constant height is subtracted. The result is a line that starts at the bottom of the drawing and randomly zigzags to the top in continually increasing steps. At the top, the line is translated to the bottom to once again continue its rises" (Noll 1969, p. 74). Random numbers are here mixed with more ordered ones and were intended to "surprise" the author of the work, to produce combinations and patterns that exceeded one's imagination; in other words, they were devices to elicit a creative conversation between humans and computers. It is therefore not surprising to notice that Noll always considered the piece of software scripted to produce the work to be his creative output, rather than the drawings themselves (Goodman 1987, pp. 23–24).

Nanni Balestrini: #109,027,350,432,000 love stories

At first glance Nanni Balestrini's (1935–) digital poems may appear to be quite distant from the type of case studies considered so far. Poet, writer, artist, and political activist, Balestrini's experiments are actually central to this discussion not so much for his use of the computer in the creative process, but rather for his ability to clearly sense the larger effects of digital culture on artistic production, its societal impact in terms of both content and distribution, which anticipated post-Fordist culture.[7] His experiments also invested database management and aleatory procedures with aesthetic implications.

In 1961 Nanni Balestrini—who would soon join the nascent avant-garde literary collective *Gruppo 63*—became interested in the relation between computers and literature. In an attempt to update the language of poetry to the emerging lifestyle of the fast-changing Italian society of the postwar years, Balestrini conceived a series of poems eventually published under the title *Tape Mark I*. In the spirit of Llull's medieval wheels, Giulio Camillo's theatre, Dada poems, Mallarmé's or William Burroughs' novels—to name only a few—Balestrini recombined passages from existing poems. However he did so by employing a computer programmed by IBM engineer Dr. Alberto Nobis: the two wrote a script able to select passages from three given texts, recombine them according to aleatory patterns, and recompose them all into new poems sharing the structure of the original compositions. Working at night on the mainframe computers a famous Milanese bank[8] (IBM 7070 with 14 729/II magnetic tapes for memory and two IBM 1401, one of the three computers in Milan at the time) Balestrini was not so much interested in employing combinatorial logic to imitate human creativity, but rather to explore a new kind of creative process exploiting the very "inhuman" capacity of modern computers: speed. By executing a large number of simple codified procedures, computers could return an unprecedented quantity of data (3,000 poems every six minutes); quantity was an essential ingredient of computational aesthetics, moving the work of art away from the unique, finished object toward an ever-changing, potentially infinite series of outputs. The three poems chosen—*Hiroshima Diary* by Michihiko Hachiya, *The Mystery of the Elevator* by Paul Goldwin, and *Tao te King* by Laotse—were thematically different but similar vis-à-vis their metrics which allowed to combine them according to the scripted logic (Balestrini 1963, p. 209). Each segment of text was given a "head" and a "end" code to control how verses were linked one another. Four rules determined their combination:

1. "Make combinations of ten elements out of the given fifteen, without permutations or repetitions.
2. Construct chain of elements taking account of the head-codes and end-codes.
3. Avoid juxtaposing elements drawn from the same extract.
4. Subdivide the chains of ten elements into six of the four metrical units each" (Balestrini, 1969, p. 55).

Finally, the poems generated were edited by the author who checked grammar and added punctuation. Tellingly, when Balestrini published the results of his experiment, he gave great space not only to the sets of technical instructions designed, but also to both some of the lines of code—out of the 1,200 scripted lines translated into 322 punch cards (Balestrini 1963, p. 209)—and machine instruction language generated by the code written, implicitly claiming aesthetic value for documents recording the manipulations of the database. The shift in emphasis from the finished product to the process should be read in the context of the mutations traversing Italian culture in the 1960s. Several Italian intellectuals and artists at the time—for instance, the literary magazine *Il Verri* or Umberto Eco's *Open Work* (1962)—promoted a new poetics encouraging artists to seek potential sources of creativity in other disciplines, including the sciences. The modus operandi of this new artistic production—labeled *Arte Programmata*[9]—was based on a rigorous and systematic series of transformations of an elementary configuration, such as a platonic solid, a single beam of light, or a basic geometric composition. The introduction of the computer in this debate allowed not only to foreground and formalize such ideas, but also to explore the application of aleatory principles to static databases. At the end of their experiment, Balestrini and Nobis had approximately 3,000 poems of varying artistic merit; most importantly though, they no longer had a finite object but an ever-varying series of objects. The conceptual character of the experiment exceeded the quality of the individual outputs, changing the notion of creativity and role of the artist.

In 1966 these initial experiments were expanded into a full novel: *Tristano* (1966). The creative process utilized for *Tristano* is a mix between the one employed for the *Type Mark I* poems and those developed for *Type Mark II* (1963) in which Balestrini operated on a longer text and developed the idea of randomly selecting the final verses out of a larger pool. Contrary to *Type Mark I*, this latter series of algorithmically generated poems were not edited; both ideas also featured in *Tristano*. Although the sophistication of 1960s' computers would not match Balestrini's ambition, he managed to complete a whole novel structured in ten chapters each containing fifteen paragraphs. These paragraphs were randomly selected and re-ordered out of a database of twenty paragraphs all written by the author himself. Though generative rules were few and simple, no two novels would be identical, as the combinatorial logic of the algorithm allowed for 109,027,350,432,000[10] different combinations. The result was a rather impenetrable novel, obviously fragmentary and deliberately difficult to read. However, traditional literary criticism would not grasp the importance of this experiment whose ambition was rather to challenge what a work of art could be and what role computation could play in it. Balestrini's poetics also aimed to renew its language by exploiting the technology of its time, the computer became an essential instrument to destabilize received formats—such as that of the novel—rejecting "any possibility to interpret reality semantically" (Comai 1985, p. 76),[11] and substituting it with the combinatory logic of algorithms. In anticipating both such kind of artistic production and the criticisms that it would predictably attract, Umberto Eco had already warned that "the idea of such kind of text is much more significant and important than the text itself."[12] Computation must be understood as part of a more radical transformation of the work of art as a result of its interaction with technology. Several years after its publication Roberto Esposito critically appraised this experiment affirming that "without over-emphasising the meaning of a rather circumscribed operation, in terms of its formal results and the modest objective to scandalise, we are confronted by one of the highest and most encompassing moments of the experimental ideology [of those years]. Such ideology is not only and no longer limited to innovating and generating new theoretical and formal content, but it is also interested in the more complex issue of how such content can be produced. . . . What the market requires is the definition of a repeatable model and a patent ensuring its reproducibility. Serial production substitutes artisanal craft, computer scripting penetrates the until-then insurmountable levees of the temple of spirit" (Esposito 1976, pp. 154–58).[13] However, rather than the logic of industrial production, Balestrini was already prefiguring the paradigms of post-Fordist production in which advancements in manufacturing allows to abandon the logic of serialization in favor of potentially endless differentiation. As Eco remarked in his analysis of these experiments, "The validity of the work generated by the computer—be it on a purely experimental and polemical level—consists in the fact that there are 3,000 poems and we have to read them all. The work of art is in its variations, better, in its variability. The computer made an attempt of 'open work'" (Eco 1961, p. 176).[14] *Gruppo 63* and Balestrini in particular stood out in the Italian cultural landscape for their new, "entrepreneurial" attitude toward publishing and mass media in general. This was not so much to seek immediate exposure and popularity, but rather to be part of a broader intellectual project which considered mass-media part of a nascent technological landscape open to political critique and aesthetic experimentation. Confronted with "the stiff determinism of Gutenbergian mechanical typography"[15] based on the industrial logic of standardization and repetition, Balestrini had to eventually pick which version to publish; an unnatural choice given the process followed.

The vicissitudes of these early experiments with computers closely echo that of early digital generation of architects in 1990s. Balestrini's radical critique and appropriation of the latest technology available in the 1960s' Italy eventually challenged what a novel was and how it had to be produced and distributed. This project was one of the earliest examples of what later in the 1990s would become known as mass-customization; the idea that computer-controlled machines were no longer bound to the logic of serialization and could produce endlessly different objects without—theoretically—additional cost. Mass-customized objects can be tailored to fit specific needs or personal taste and require a greater degree of coordination between design and manufacturing (Pine 1993). The popularization of computer numerical control machines such as Computer Numerical Control (CNC) and 3D printing since the 1990s has spurred some of the most interesting developments in digital architecture which find a very fruitful precedent in the work developed by the literary Italian neo-avant-garde in the 1960s. Although Balestrini's production moved on from these experiments, his interest in computers and, in general, technology was not episodic. In 2013 the poet completed a video installation *Tristan Oil*[16] in which 150 video clips related to oil and global exploitation of natural resources were randomly combined. The found materials from TV news, documentaries, TV series such as *Dallas*, etc. eventually formed an infinite and yet never-repeating video. The viewing at dOCUMENTA (13) lasted 7,608 hours.

The recent introduction of digital printing and consequent radical transformation of the publishing industry finally allowed Balestrini to complete his original project; since 2007 Italian publisher *Derive&Approdi* and *Verso*—since 2014—have both been publishing unique versions of *Tristano*'s 109,027,350,432,000[17] possible combinations so that no two identical versions of the novel are available.

Karl Chu's catastrophe machine

"This is non-computable stuff!"[18] The trigger of such burst of enthusiasm in structural engineer and mathematician Cecil Balmond (1943–) was caused by seeing one of Karl Chu's (1950–) *Catastrophe Machines* in action. Toward the end of the 1980s Chu had already built three of these machines all in Los Angeles (two at Sci-ARC and one at UCLA). The machines were a more complex version of Christopher Zeeman's (1925–2016) devices consisting of a system of pulleys connected through rubber controls to move a pen mounted onto a metal arm. Though based on analogue rather than discrete computing principles, the machines could combine in a complex fashion, a series of rather simple and deterministic movements regulated by each pulley to generate unexpected results. In scientific terms, the *Catastrophe Machine* made creative use of nonlinear phenomena in which small adjustments in the initial conditions of the individual components eventually produce overall variations that cannot be anticipated.

The importance of these early experiments is manifold. First, Chu went on to become an important architect and educator in the field of digital design; parallel to constructing analogue machines, he also carried out similar experiments with computers by testing the design possibilities inherent to mathematical systems such as Cellular Automata (CA) and L-Systems. Although largely debated in the field of sciences, architects had rarely made use of random mathematical algorithms to design, a deeply rooted habit that Chu broke. Finally, the *Catastrophe Machine* (1987) also represents one of the few design experiments in which the notion of randomness was understood beyond the superficial idea of arbitrariness and explored to test the limits of computation, knowledge, and, consequently, design. In line with the narrative presented in this chapter, Chu's machines straddle between design and philosophy or, rather, they explore the possibility to employ randomness to think of design as philosophy—a point well captured by Balmond's reaction.

Chu's involvement with CA deserves greater attention as he was one of the first architects to develop genuine computational architecture; that is, designs that no longer derived their formal inspiration from other formal systems—for example, biology, human body, plants, etc.—but rather were directly shaped by code and binary logic as generators of potential new worlds. CA not only provided a computational logic complex enough to warrant novel formal results, but also exhibited potential to simulate random processes of growth or evolution. Though based on simple, deterministic rules, certain combinations can—over a certain number of iterations—give rise to unpredictable, non-periodic patterns. British mathematician Stephen Wolfram (1959–) explored such possibilities leading him to state the Principle of Computational Equivalence according to which every physical phenomenon can eventually be computed and therefore setting the basis for a new understanding of the universe and science (Wolfram 2002). Design research in this area is far from being a historical fact and very much alive: the paradigmatic exhibition *Non-Standard Architecture* (2003) curated by Frédéric Migayrou at the Centre Pompidou and, more recently, designers such as Alisa Andrasek—Biothing, Philippe Morel, Gilles Retsin, and Manuel Jimenez not only represent some of the best work in this area showing the timely nature of these conversations.

Applied randomness: Designing through computer simulations

The Second World War acted as an impressive catalyst for the development of modern computers as different strands of scientific research combined giving a great energy to both the development of modern computing and digital simulations of physical phenomena. The definition of what constitutes a computer simulation and, more importantly, how it can act as a valid surrogate for empirical testing is a complex issue that goes beyond the remit of this study (see Winsberg 2010). It suffices a superficial reading of key titles to appreciate the intricacy and richness of this debate; as early as 1979 Alan Pritsker already managed to gather twenty-one different definitions of computer simulations.[19] More recently, Tuncer Ören increased this number to one hundred and then to four hundred incontrovertibly demonstrating how far we are from a general consensus in this field (Ören 2011a,b). The use of computer simulations for military purposes found some key applications worth discussing, as they have relevance in today's digital design: the development of the atomic bomb, weather forecasting, and the foundation of modern cybernetics.

Despite computer simulations were being utilized to predict the behavior of a particular system—for example, particles' propagation in an atomic explosion—it soon became clear that the epistemological issues raised by artificial simulations were deeper and potentially more radical than simply predicting behavior. Rather than prediction it was experimentation that computers aided; computer simulations augmented the range of explorations possible, allowing designers to explore uncertainty endowed with robust conceptual and methodological tools. It is this particular use of computer simulations that we would like to explore and promote here as it shows the possibility for paradigmatic shift in design disciplines, one which was already latent in our discussion on random numbers. Framed this way, it is easy to see the relation between computer simulation and design, as they are both exploratory and yet rigorous activities looking for some forms of novelty and emergence. French epistemologist Franck Varenne (2001) sees such endeavor resulting in three possible uses for simulations: a kind of experiment, an intellectual tool, or as a real and new means of learning. Simulations can be understood as either deterministic or stochastic depending to the mathematics supporting them. Deterministic simulations are equation based when implement equations derived from theoretical discoveries to the whole model. Agent-based simulations, on the other hand, only script the behavior of single particles without any global, overarching equation controlling the environment of interaction.

The use of computer simulations to study urban environments finds its origin in the notion of metabolism as first put forward by Karl Marx (1818–83) in the nineteenth century (Marx 1964). The dynamics of the human body were utilized as metaphors for the relation between cities and nature; more precisely, to explain the exchange of energy occurring between the extraction of natural resources and their industrial transformation into commodities. This was also the model adopted by Abel Wolman (1892–1989) whose article in the *American Scientific* in 1965 marked the first decisive attempt to model urban flows with scientific tools (Wolman 1965).[20]

One of the first applications of metabolic thinking to real problems took place at Guinness brewery in Dublin around 1906–07 where W. S. Gosset (1876–1937), started investigating how mathematical thinking could be applied to model the relations between the yield selection and production. In the process Gosset—whose work had to be published under the pseudonym of Student—began to make use of randomized and statistical methods to refine his simulations.[21]

The introduction of feedback loops and information-based techniques in urban design coincided with the rise of the modern movement and, particularly, the International Urbanism Congress in 1924. This approach to urban planning favored "scientific" methods based on demographic analysis and statistical projection for both physical and social data. Dutch architect Cornelis van Eesteren (1897–1988) not only promoted this approach but was also one of the first to put it to practice. In 1925 he joined forces with French colleague George Pineau (1898–1987) to draft out the competition entry for the new traffic plan of Paris. Pineau was a young graduate, fresh from his studies at the groundbreaking École des Haute Études Urbaines. Students coming out of this course could boast not only to be among the few to hold a specialization in town planning, but also to have mastered systematic and analytic tools to organize and visualize information on cities. While Pineau's role in the team was to gather and analyze traffic data, van Eesteren was the lead designer in charge of translating the initial insights into a spatial proposal. The entry—titled "Continuité"—was not successful but did have a lasting impact on van Eesteren's views as he began to realize that this more systematic way of proceeding was calling for a new architectural language unencumbered by reference to the historical city (van Rossen 1997, pp. 19–23). These ideas were eventually also at the core of the Amsterdam General Expansion Plan drafted in 1934–35 by van Eesteren this time in collaboration with Theo van Lohuizen (1890–1956). van Lohuizen's role was not dissimilar to Pineau's; he was, however, a much more established personality in the Netherlands at the time having carried out cartographic surveys on Dutch population distribution and growth prior to working on the Amsterdam Plan. Adherent to the motto "survey before plan," the team made extensive use of some of the scientific precepts by gathering data from various disciplines and employing statistical forecasting to plan population distribution—until the year 2000—and transport, clustering functions in the city, prioritizing access to light and air, and promoting standardization and prefabrication (Mumford 2000, pp. 59–66).

Though the Amsterdam Plan marked the introduction of statistical methods in planning, it also revealed a substantial distance to the parallel advancements in the contemporary discourse in the sciences. The use of simulations to test out planning options was not explicitly included in the design tools, and had a peripheral role. The type of simulations applied here was still strictly deterministic and did not include aleatory techniques. Rather it was the prevalent modernist discourse to take the center stage: the promise of industrialization also brought about efficiency, standardization, and the political promise of a more equitable distribution of wealth, all values that somehow "coherently" suited the deterministic logic of these methods. Though relevant to understand how more scientific approaches penetrated architectural and urban design disciplines, the general position explored in this chapter rather emphasizes the use of computer simulation techniques to expand the range of variables considered, to "complexify" the nature of the problems tackled, and scope out solutions that would have not been available otherwise: all values only latent in the Amsterdam Plan.

We will have to wait until the 1940s to see the emergence of the first computer simulations as a result of the work carried out by a series of scientists at Los Alamos National Laboratory to develop the first nuclear weapon. The Manhattan Project—as it was classified by the US government—could not have been developed through trail and error not only because of the devastating power of a nuclear detonation, but also because of the complex set of calculations to describe the possible states particles could arrange into and propagate. Again, confronted with a degree of complexity which could not be reduced or anticipated, scientists began to adopt a combination of randomized and probabilistic methods. The result of these experiments was the invention of the Monte Carlo method, which allowed to resolve a set of deterministic equations by repeatedly computing them by inserting random values as variables and then analyzing the results statistically. Mathematician Stanislaw Ulam (1909–84) is credited for the development of this statistical method, whereas John von Neumann (1903–57) contributed to translating it into computer code by employing the first modern computer—the ENIAC. The method is perhaps best explained by Ulam himself:

> The first thoughts and attempts I made to practice [the Monte Carlo Method] were suggested by a question which occurred to me in 1946 as I was convalescing from an illness and playing solitaires. The question was what are the chances that a Canfield solitaire laid out with 52 cards will come out successfully? After spending a lot of time trying to estimate them by pure combinatorial calculations, I wondered whether a more practical method than "abstract thinking" might not be to lay it out say one hundred times and simply observe and count the number of successful plays. This was already possible to envisage with the beginning of the new era of fast computers, and I immediately thought of problems of neutron diffusion and other questions of mathematical physics, and more generally how to change processes described by certain differential equations into an equivalent form interpretable

as a succession of random operations. Later [in 1946], I described the idea to John von Neumann, and we began to plan actual calculations. (Eckhardt 1987, p. 131)

Rather than expanding on the implications and use of these methods in the sciences, the Monte Carlo method has had important consequences on design methodologies. In fact this method reverts the traditional design process: rather than defining an "abstract" model listing all constraints, opportunities, etc., out of which the designer will generate an optimal solution in a linear fashion, the Monte Carlo method attempts at statistically inferring a pattern based on a series of random outcomes. Obviously, such a method can only effectively be implemented with the aid of a computer not only because of the large quantity of data to be handled, but also because random combinations of numbers could describe conditions which are unlikely or altogether impossible to recreate in reality. The adoption of these design methods is, for instance, at the core of Big Data—a much more recent discipline—which also promises to deeply revolutionize methods of scientific inquiry.[22] Whereas architects and urbanists have very rarely utilized such methods, other design disciplines have more actively engaged with them: for instance, videogame designers—especially for first-person shooter (FPS) games—often develop initial versions by letting the computer play out all the possible scenarios in the game and then selecting and reiterating only those that have proved to be more successful or unexpected.

Monte Carlo method for design could be described as a more radical version of "What if?" scenario planning: a method that enters spatial design through the field of Landscape Design and has been finding increasing traction among architects since the 1990s. In the work of the Dutch firm MVRDV/The Why Factory or OMA this method has often been tested, however, only for specific sets of conditions (e.g., mean values, or extreme ones) rather than all possible ones within the domain of inquiry. If "What if?" scenarios can still be computed and played by individuals, Monte Carlo-like methods are rather "inhuman," as they can only be calculated by computers. Finally, though these methods require an advanced knowledge of scripting, simplified tools have been inserted in CAD packages. For instance, *Grasshopper* offers "Galapagos," an evolutionary tool testing very large sets of numbers in different combinations to return the numerical or geometrical combination best fulfilling the fitness criteria set.[23] As pointed out by Varenne, the role of computer simulations in the design is to experiment, to tease out qualities that would have otherwise been inaccessible, and to augment designer's imagination and skills.

Computer simulations' role is fluidly moving between that of laboratories for experimentations and learning tools.

Jay W. Forrester: *DYNAMO* and the limits of growth

Since the 1960s computers were increasingly utilized to simulate the evolution of a piece of design or an urban phenomenon. The work of Luigi Moretti and Bruno de Finetti at IRMOU in Rome in the 1950s—discussed in Chapter 4 on parametrics—was one of the first experiments on design simulation directly involving an architect. However these experiments were episodic and it was only in the 1960s that several American municipalities embraced computer models despite the prohibitive investment necessary to set the system up.[24] The promise of computer simulation models was to "complexify" urban studies by not only interrelating discrete factors but also showing the nonlinear nature of cities as complex systems: they could monitor how the alteration of a parameter could lead to secondary and unforeseen consequences. Despite the investments, the criticism against the use of computer models for planning purpose was vehement. The critique blended together issues of different origins: some were material in nature, as they concerned the limited capacity provided by computers in the 1960s or the scattered access to data; whereas others pointed at inconsistencies in the theoretical models informing the actual programming. Regardless, these critiques eroded the credibility of these methods whose popularity eventually faded in the 1970s and 1980s (Douglass Lee 1973).

A key figure in this field both in terms of theory and actual practical applications was is Jay W. Forrester (1918–2016). He was an active participant in the pioneering Macy conferences in which the field of cybernetics found its first definition. Forrester also derived his approach from studying industrial cycles—his beer game is still played at the Sloan School of Management at MIT where he first launched it—to eventually model world dynamics (Forrester 1961, 1969, 1971). Central to Forrester's work were not so much the political and philosophical implications of simulations, but rather their implementation through computers; *DYNAMO* was the software Forrester developed with his team at MIT to manage databases and simulate their potential evolution (Pugh 1970). We have already encountered this scripting language in several occasions: Buckminster Fuller mentions it as the scripting language of choice for his *World Game*, whereas Stafford Beer's *Cybersyn* was actually built on a variation of the *DYNAMO* system. However, the most well-known use of the software was the simulations of world resources developed for the Club of Rome in their pioneering study: *The Limits of Growth* (Meadows 1972). The Club of Rome was a private group formed by seventy-five individuals acting as a think tank stirring public debate. The report marked an important step in environmental thinking, as it was the first document addressed to the broad public discussing the environmental crisis, and resource scarcity. Supported by the Volkswagen Foundation, the predictions announced by the report resulted from the application of Forrester's models to world dynamics. The results were nothing less than shocking bringing unprecedented popularity to such kind of exercises as they unequivocally showed that the current process of industrialization was on a collision course with the earth's ecosystem,[25] a phenomenon we have come to identify as climate change. We will return to the cultural and design consequences of this realization, though not before having looked more closely at the role of computers in the preparation of the report. Forrester's main tenet was that all dynamic systems presented common basic characteristics which always reoccurred and could therefore be identified as invariants: all natural systems were looping ones, based on stock-and-flow, etc. (Forrester, 2009). It was not the idea of remapping biological systems onto a simulation software and society that drew the more vociferous criticisms; after all this was a well-trotted precept of cybernetics. It was rather the emphasis on invariants that troubled observers and made them doubt the veracity of the results obtained: the thrust of the architecture of the software was on individual equations and their relations rather than empirical data which were deemed as "secondary" in this exercise. Rather than a model however we should speak of models nested into each other: this allowed specific areas to be studied independently and be successively aggregated. To some the combination of these assumptions implied that the results of the simulations were independent of empirical data, repeating mistakes that had been known since T. R. Malthus' (1817) predictions in his *Essay on the Principle of Population* in 1798.

Besides the technical discussion on the validity of Forrester's models, these experiments marked an important step forward in utilizing computer simulations as generative tools in the design process. The outputs of the simulation cycles were to be considered either as scenarios—hypothetical yet plausible future situations that designers had to evaluate, adapt to, or reject—or learning tools charting out the nature of the problem to tackle. Forrester's impact went well beyond the field in which it first emerged. For instance, the basic algorithmic architecture of *DYNAMO* later on became the engine of the popular videogame *SimCity* (first released in 1989) in which players design and manage a virtual city. Here too we encounter the issue of random numbers: randomization in metabolic systems helps in modeling the inherent disorder regulating any exchange, the entropic evolution of all systems.

An interesting synthesis of some of the different strands of research mentioned here ranging from videogames, planning, and academic subjects such as game theory and evolutionary thinking is represented by the digital platforms designed by the MVRDV. Among these projects, the *SpaceFighter* (2005–07) stands out not only as perhaps the more mature of these experiments encompassing great levels of complexity operating at several scales (from the globe to buildings represented as pixels), but also because it conflates some of the most radical precedents in this field injecting renewed energy in the much-debased practice of computational planning.[26] This tool is presented in the form of a videogame in which multiple players co-create urban environments interacting with a database containing data on transport, demographics, and environmental risks to test hypotheses at various scales. The game clearly deviates from the precedents already discussed, as it employs complex, more randomized algorithmic elements allowing for a more sophisticated treatment of functions: whereas van Lohuizen concentrated function to form homogeneous compounds, MVDRV encourages understanding urban programs as both influencing and influenced by other factors. The emphasis of the *SpaceFighter* is human oriented; the aim of the game is to foster participation through a supporting digital platform. For this reason, the project belongs to the category of the "What if?" scenarios rather than a proper Monte Carlo-like computer interaction which rather inverts the relation between humans and machines.

Contemporary landscape

The use of computer simulations in design has radically evolved. The increased ability to sense and gather data have made "equation-heavy"models such as the DYNAMO obsolete and promised to extend or even exceed human thought. In philosophy this movement has broadly been termed as posthumanism, framing a large body of work questioning the foundations and centrality of human thoughts and cognitive abilities. The increasing capacity to gather accurate data about the environment and simulate them through more complex algorithms finds here a fertile ground to align philosophical and design agendas to speculate what role random procedures might have in design.

The limits explored through computational randomness broadly trace those of our limited knowledge of ecological processes regulating planet earth. Repositioning architecture and urbanism vis-à-vis large ecological issues will demand us to confront the impressive scales and timeframes of engagement posed by climatic transformations such as global warming: received notion of site, type, and material all will need re-thinking. As architecture and urbanism become increasingly tangled up in large-scale, slow, and uncertain phenomena, computer simulations will play an increasingly central role not only as devices making such phenomena visible, but also as crucial instruments for speculation and testing—that is, to design in uncertain conditions.

Climate change is perhaps the clearest and most powerful example of what Timothy Morton calls *Hyperobjects* (2013); objects whose dimensions are finite—global warming is roughly matching the scale of the earth—and yet whose size, temporality, and scale radically exceeds what your minds can grasp (Morton fixes the "birth" of the hyperobject climate change with that of the steam engine and projects its effects to last for the next couple of millennia). How to study them? Hyperobjects do not exist without computation. Computers are responsible for vast consumption of energy and raw materials while having given us an access to the very phenomena they contribute to cause; we would not really have debates on climate change without a substantial and prolonged computational effort to understand and simulate the climate of the planet. As for the limits of computation first delineated by Alan Turing, environmental processes also exhibit a similar "incompressible" behavior which cannot be engaged without computers. The extension in space and time of global weather systems influences and is influenced by a whole plethora of other cultural, economic, etc. factors. Beyond catastrophism, the mirage of easy solutions, or technocratic promises often masked behind sustainable architecture, computer simulations should be located at the center of a renewed agenda for design operating across much wider time and spatial scales.

This experimental and urgent agenda for design has been embraced by several academics and practitioners—including me—who have been testing the use of computer simulations as both representational devices and generative ones.[27] The work of Bradley Cantrell (1975–) (Cantrell and Holzman, 2015) or *EcoLogic Studio*—Claudia Pasquero and Marco Poletto—elegantly merge environmental concerns, computer simulations to straddle between a range of scales unusual to architects and urbanists (Poletto and Pasquero 2012). The kind of design proposed operates as an evolving and self-regulating system in which distinctions between natural and artificial systems have been erased. Here we witness an "inversion" of the traditional scientific method: not so much "the end of theory" hypothesized by employing Big Data methods, but rather the use of broad theoretical frameworks to tease out empirical evidence. John von Neumann again comes to mind here as he introduced the use of computers in physics to simulate theoretical conditions impossible to empirically reconstruct. Once again, the advantages of computation can only be exploited if an equally theoretical and political agenda reinforce each other.

Notes

1. Some of these themes have been analyzed and expanded in Luciana Parisi's work (2013).
2. This is, for instance, the case of *Grasshopper* in which, unless "seed" values are changed, the same list of values keeps being outputted by the random command.
3. See www.random.org (Accessed August 12, 2015). Recently, Rob Seward has developed Z1FFER, an open-source True Random Number Generator (TRNG) "for Arduino that harnesses thermal noise in a Modular Entropy Multiplication architecture to provide a robust random bitstream for research and experimentation." *Z1FFER—A True Random Number Generator for Arduino (and the post-Snowden era)*. Available at: http://www.creativeapplications.net/arduino-2/z1ffer/ (Accessed February 11, 2017).
4. See Leibniz in the chapter on databases.
5. Pascal (1654).
6. For an accessible and yet enticing overview of Boole's work see Martin (2001), pp. 17–34. Boole's research introduced many important new notions, some of which were further developed by Gottlob Frege (1848–1925) to apply formal logics to semantics, virtually opening up systematic studies on language, one of the most important fields of studies of the twentieth century. His essay "On Sense and Reference" (1892) presents an embryonic distinction between denotation and connotation, which will find a decisive expansion in the *Course of General Linguistics* taught by Ferdinand de Saussure at the University of Geneva (Geach and Black 1952, pp. 36–56). Another example—albeit more experimental in nature—bridging between semiotics and morphogenetics is represented by René Thom's work (1923–2002), Thom (1989).
7. Almost every component of Balestrini's work had already been anticipated by others by the time he started working on his computerized poems. The originality of Balestrini's work can therefore only be grasped if his work is analyzed holistically rather than in fragmentary fashion. Many creative ideas developed in other artistic fields conflated in Balestrini's work. As early as 1953 Christophe Strachey (1916–75)—who had studied mathematics with Alan Turing in Cambridge—had already managed to write a computer program—called "Love-letters"—to write one-sentence long poems. The program would randomly select words from a dictionary, allocate them to a predetermined position within a sentence structure according to their syntactical value. The program did not consider punctuation. By only considering syntactic but no sematic restrictions, "Love-letters" could generate up to 318 billion poems. See Strachey (1954). 1961, the year in which Balestrini started his experiments on computer poetry, was also the year marking the first explorations on computerized stochastic music by Greek composer and engineer Iannis Xenakis (1922–2001). Working with IBM-France on a 7090, Xenakis scripted a series of rules and restrictions, which were played out by the computer to return a piece of music perhaps appropriately titled ST/10-1,080262. On May 24, 1962, the Ensemble Instrumental de Musique Contemporaine de Paris conducted by C. Simonovic finally performed Xenakis' challenging piece.

See Xenakis (1963), pp. 161–79. The sophistication of Xenakis' work greatly exceeded that of Balestrini's, both in terms of mathematical logic underpinning the inclusion of aleatory creative methods and computational sophistication. What Balestrini was missing in terms of complexity and logical rigor was however recouped by anticipating larger cultural changes resulting from the use of computers in the arts. The idea of randomized creativity or consumption was not new in literature either. Despite no precedents made any use of computation, in 1962 Marc Saporta completed his *Composition No.1* consisting of 150 loose pages to be read as wished by the reader. This experiment was followed by *The Unfortunates* by B. S. Johnson (1969), which could be purchased as twenty-seven unbound chapters that—with the exception of the first and the last one—could be read in any order. Finally, the use of aleatory methods for composing poems was abundantly employed by historical avant-garde movements, such as Dada and the Beat Generation. Some of these examples can be found in the work of Mallarmé, Arp, Joyce, Queneau, Burroughs, and Corso. What we only find in Balestrini is the convergence of all these previous separate elements.

8. Cassa di Risparmio delle Provincie Lombarde.
9. The exhibition *Arte Programmata* was organized by Italian electronic manufacturer Olivetti in Milan in 1962 and curated by, among others, Umberto Eco. The show opened in Milan to then travel to Dusseldorf, London, and New York.
10. *Tristano*. Webpage. Available at: http://www.versobooks.com/books/1518-tristano (Accessed November 12, 2015).
11. Translation by the author.
12. "L'idea di uno scritto del genere era già più significativa ed importante dello scritto stesso." Eco (1963). *Due ipotesi sulla morte dell'arte*. In *Il Verri*, June 8, 1963, pp. 59–77. Translation by the author.
13. "E' chiaro che, senza voler sovraccaricare di significato un'operazione tranquillamente circoscrivibile, per quanto riguarda i suoi esiti formali, alle modeste dimensioni del suo intento scandalistico, ci troviamo di fronte ad un momento notevolmente alto e riassuntivo dell'ideologia sperimentalistica: definito non più, o non solo, dal campo di progettazione e di innovamento dei contenuti teorico-formali, ma dalla problematica più complessa del modo di produzione di quei contenuti. . . . ciò che il mercato richiede è la definizione di un modello di ripetitività e di un brevetto di riproducibilità di tale costruzione. E' la produzione in serie che subentra alla produzione artigianale, la programmazione che penetra gli argini finora invalicabili del tempio dello spirito." Translated by the author.
14. "L'opera del cervello elettronico, e la sua validitá (se non altro sperimentale e provocatoria) consiste invece proprio nel fatto che le poesie sono tremila e bisogna leggerle tutte insieme. L'opera intera sta nelle sua variazioni, anzi nella sua variabilitá. Il cervello elettronico ha fatto un tentativo di 'opera aperta'" (Eco 1961, p. 176). Translation by the author.
15. Davies (2014).

16. *Tristan Oil* is a video installation (with Giacomo Verde and Vittorio Pellegrineschi) developed for dOCUMENTA 13 (2013) representing the continuous extraction resources at planetary scale. The video is scripted in such a way to be infinite while never repeating itself.
17. http://www.versobooks.com/books/1518-tristano (Accessed November 12, 2015).
18. Lynn (2015).
19. Pritsker, A. A. B. (1979). "Compilation of definitions of simulation." In *Simulation*, August, pp. 61–63. Quoted in Varenne, F. (2001).
20. Specifically, Wolman modelled the deterioration of water conditions in American cities.
21. See *Dictionary of Scientific Biography,* 1972, pp. 476–77; *International Encyclopedia of Statistics*, vol. I, 1978, pp. 409–13.
22. Big Data has been defined as "data sets that are so large or complex that traditional data processing applications are inadequate." These datasets present key characteristics that are often referred to as the three vs: high volume of data which is not reduced but rather analyzed in its entirety, high velocity as data is dynamic, at times recorded in real time, and finally it is highly varied both in terms of types of sources that is conflates (text, images, sound, etc.) and in terms of variables it can record. For a more detailed discussion on this subject, see Mayer-Schönberger and Cukier (2013); and Anderson (2008).
23. Grasshopper3d.com (2016). Available at: http://www.grasshopper3d.com/group/galapagos (Accessed June 15, 2016).
24. In the early 1970s a computer model for land use cost about $500,000. An additional $250,000 had to be spent to include housing data in the model (Douglass Lee 1973).
25. The earth's ecosystem is captured by the following categories: population, capital investment, geographical space, natural resources, pollution, and food production (Forrester 1971, p. 1).
26. Early experiments by MVRDV were *Functionmixer* (2001), *The Region Maker* (2002) and *Climatizer* (2014). See MVRDV (2004, 2005), and (MVRDV, Delft School of Design, Berlage Institute, MIT, cThrough, 2007).
27. *MArch UD RC14* (website). Available at: https://www.ucl.ac.uk/bartlett/architecture/programmes/postgraduate/march-urban-design (accessed on February 20, 2018).

Chapter 7

Scanning

Introduction

An image scanner—often abbreviated to scanner—is a device that optically digitizes images, printed text, handwriting, or objects, and converts it to a digital image.[1] It extracts a set of information from the domain of the real and translates it into a field of binary numbers. As such, it embodies one of the most fundamental steps in the design process: the translation from the empirical to the representational domain; while simultaneously enabling its reversal; that is, the projection of new realities through representation.

There are various types of scanners performing such operations ranging from those we can employ in everyday activities in offices or at home—often referred to as flatbed scanners—to more advanced ones such as hand-held 3D scanners, increasingly utilized by architects and designers to capture 3D objects, buildings, and landscapes. Scanners are input devices rather than computational ones; they work in pairs with algorithms controlling computer graphics to transform real objects into digital ones; strictly speaking they are not part of CAD tools. Though this observation will remain valid throughout this chapter, we will also see how principles informing such technology as well as opportunities engendered by it have impacted design.

To think of digital scanners along the lines of the physiology of sight is a useful metaphor to critically understand how this technology impacts design both in its representational and generative aspects. An incorrect description of the sense of sight would have that what we see is the result of the actions performed by our eyes. The little we know about the human brain has however revealed a rather different picture in which neurological processes play a far greater role than initially thought, adding, recombining, etc. a substantial amount of information to little received through the optical nerves. The brain is even responsible for instructing the eyes the kind of information to seek, reverting what we assumed the flow of information was. Though our description is rather succinct, it nevertheless redirects the discussion toward a much more fruitful and poignant framework to conceptualize digital scanning. This analogy can be taken beyond its metaphorical meaning as digital scanners did develop out of our knowledge of the physiology of sight, as a sort of artificial replica. The brain-eye analogy is also helpful, as it reminds us not to underestimate the crucial role played by algorithms in determining what is scanned and how it is turned into a graphic output. The type of encoding prescribed in the algorithm can either be the consequence of the technology gathering information (lenses will afford a type of information different from photographic camera) or determining how such technology will work.

Historically, scanning therefore conflated a number of technologies: sensing mechanisms—first and foremost, lenses extensively used to observe, magnify, and distort the perception of objects—and then some form of computation—either arithmetical or geometrical—to encode, reconstruct, and alter the optical information initially acquired. This latter element was mostly provided by mathematical perspective, one of the most important elements of modern art and modernity in general, to which a tremendous amount of scholarly research has been dedicated. It suffices to reiterate here that perspective—as rediscovered and developed in the fifteenth century—was understood as a means not only to represent reality, but also to grasp it, to conceptualize it. Filippo Brunelleschi's (1377–1446) famous panels had been first drawn in his studio and then placed in front of the Cathedral of Florence merely for verification purposes. In the centuries following this famous experiment, representation—and consequently scanning—would move from a "passive" technology to acquire measurements and produce visuals to an "active" one to actualize imaginary objects and buildings. Though not central to the topics discussed in this chapter, the history of scanning has always been intertwined with that of fabrication as machines to acquire data from reality could have been turned around to output to make objects. This narrative should not be confined to historical precedents only as it still applied to contemporary design experiments in which digital scanners output data to numerically controlled machines.

The history of scanning technologies would take a radical turn in the mid-nineteenth century with the invention of photography, whereas the introduction of the first digital scanner—approximately one century later—would not only conflate numerical and optical domains but also foreground the relation between neurology and vision as the software encoding images was modeled after on a neurological model accounting for how it was believed images formed in the brain.

The notion of conflation plays a particularly important role to grasp what is at stake when designing with scanners or scanning techniques in CAD. Though drafting software has not changed how orthographic and perspectival views are constructed, it has nevertheless made it infinitely easier as users can effortlessly switch between plans and 3D views. Extracting a plan from a perspective was a laborious process which impacted how buildings were designed: Alberti, for instance, stressed that the plans and elevations were the conventional drawings to design through, as they did not distort distances and angles. By working simultaneously between orthographic and perspectival views has undoubtedly eroded the tight separation between these two modes of representation: in fact, one of the great potentials of CAD modeling is to altogether invert the traditional workflow by designing in three dimensions and then extract plans, sections, and elevations. The recent introduction of photography-based scanners has further reduced the distance between different media, as it has also allowed to merge photography and cinema with architectural representation. As we will see in the conclusion of this chapter, such integration will further extend to the construction site directly connecting digital models to actual building as real areas will be laser-scanned and included in CAD environments in order to reduce tolerances and, literally, physically building the computer model.

The chapter will disentangle this "slow fusion" to trace at which point and under which cultural circumstances new techniques to record physical realities affected the relation between design and construction. At a more technical level, this chapter will also cover different historical technologies to acquire data: from simple direct observation—sometime enhanced by lenses—to the combination of lenticular and chemical technologies—as for photography—to laser. The type of sensing mechanisms employed discriminates between contact and noncontact scanners. Except for direct observation, all the input methods discussed here lend themselves to digitization, that is, the data is translated into a numerical field; this process can result into either a vector-based image or pixel-based one determining in turn the kind of editing operations possible to be performed on the dataset. For instance, while all image-processing software can record basic characteristics such as position (x, y, z) of the point recorded, some can extend these characteristics up to nine—including vector normals (nx, ny, nz) and color (RGB)—by employing the principles derived from photogrammetry.

As mentioned, the quality and type of data acquired already curtails the editing procedures as well as its mode of transmission. Scanning is therefore a technology to translate information, varying the medium storing it, moving from empirical measurement, to abstract computation, finally returning to physical artifact in the form of construction documents or the actual final object. Though apparently a secondary activity in the design process, scanning actually embodies one of the crucial functions of design: the exchange and translation of information. This chapter will analyze some of the more salient technologies performing such translations and their role in the design process; this will of course include the impact that modern computers had on these processes.

Digital scanners employed in design disciplines operate according to two different methods. Laser scanners project a laser beam while spinning at high speed; the time delay between the emission of the ray and its "bounce" off a surface is utilized to establish its position. LIDAR (light imaging, detection, and ranging) scanners automate this process and massively accelerate it—by recording up to a million points per second—to generate high-density scans made up of individual points (referred to as point clouds). LIDAR scanners simply record the positron in the beam bounced back leaving additional information—such as color—to be gathered through complementary technologies. More popular, easy to use, but also far less accurate scans extract information through photogrammetry by pairing up images of the same object taken from different angles. It suffices to take a video with a mobile phone to generate a sufficiently detailed image set for pieces of software such as *Visual SFM* or *Autodesk 123D Catch* to generate decent point clouds even mesh surfaces of the objects scanned. Not only are these scans recording color, but also, by calibrating the quality of the input process, they allow to scan large scenes such as entire buildings or public spaces.

As mentioned, recently developed LIDAR scanners have introduced an unprecedented degree of resolution, precision, and range of action in design, as they can capture about one million points per seconds with a tolerance of 2 millimeters over a length of 150 meters. By moving beyond lenticular technology and gully-integrating digital processing of images, these technologies not only merge almost all representational techniques architects have been using, but also open up the possibility of exploring territories beyond the boundaries of what is visible to humans in terms of both scale and resolution. As we will see toward the end of the chapter, they are likely to affect the organization of the construction site, as they promise a better, almost real-time synchronization between construction and design. Such tendency is surely helped by the prospect of employing robots to assemble architecture also restaging once again century-old questions about the relation between measurement—for example, acquired through a site survey—computation—elaboration of the measurement in the design phase—and construction. Our historical survey will detect the presence of such issues since the development of the very first machines architects conjured up to measure and reproduce large objects or landscapes.

The birth of the digital eye: The perspective machines in the Renaissance

Perspectival distortion was already known by Persian and Greek artists and philosophers who would employ it to correct, for instance, the position of the corner columns in temples. Euclid dedicated some his *Optica* (300 BC) to the basic principles of perspective, whose fundamental laws of proportionality between triangles will constitute the starting point of Alberti's geometrical systematization of perspective. Vitruvius too dedicated part of his treatise on architecture to *scenographia*, a sort of perspectival sketch. However, no scientific understanding of linear perspective existed in ancient Rome and its decisive invention would only happen at the beginning of the fifteenth century, when the laws of optics were coupled with those of geometry to provide a rigorous method to reconstruct what is perceived by the human eye on a piece of paper. This moment precisely occurred in 1435 with the publication of *De Pictura* by Leon Battista Alberti (1404–72) marking the shift from the *Prospectiva naturalis*—empirically constructed—to the *Prospectiva artificialis* underpinned by geometrical construction. Such a revolution also elicited the construction of a series of machines to demonstrate, apply, and popularize the more complex aspects of this new technology. Such contraptions obviously did not involve the use of digital technologies though they did lay out some of the principles that CAD software eventually appropriated and expanded upon.

The foundations of mathematical perspective combined direct observation mediated by elementary contraptions—such as Alberti's *veil*—with geometrical principles; perspective machines consequently conflated advancements from both the domains of optics—considered as "medieval science"—and mathematics of perspective—constituting its "modern" counterpart. This broad division is also consistent with our characterization of scanning as digital vision. In modern computational parlance, we would speak of the human eye—whether enhanced or not—as an input device, whereas the analogue machinery attached to it would store and compute the information gathered. Martin Kemp (1942–) described these perspective machines as the confluence of three main types of devices: instruments for the recording of linear effects according to projective principles; optical devices involving lenses, etc., for the formation of reduced images of the world in a full array of light, shade, and color; and "magic" devices which use optical principles to ambush the spectator's perception (Kemp 1990, p. 167).

Throughout the fifteenth and sixteenth centuries there would be a proliferation of perspective machines built to serve the most disparate professions:

architecture, art, cartography, and the art of war. Whether addressed to architects, artists, cartographers, or artisans, these contraptions promised to turn the more abstract tenets of the new sciences into a series of practical steps that would make perspective part of everyday tools of many professions. There is no direct evidence that most of these devices were actually directly utilized by artists in their work; rather they had a demonstrative quality, almost as "constructed theory." They were analogical computers as they extracted numbers from physical phenomena to further process. We should not entirely overlook the military use of perspective machines which were deployed to survey the outline of the enemy's fortifications to draw first the perspectival view and then extract plans and elevations. Our attention will however go to those contraptions that allow to survey larger objects such as building or landscapes as well as to those presenting similarities with contemporary digital scanning technologies.

In the *Ludi Mathematici* (1450–52) Leon Battista Alberti discussed the use of the "shadow square"—an instrument consisting of astrolabes and quadrants made of straight scales forming right angles when intersecting each other—an ideal device to implement Euclid's law of proportionality between triangles—which he imagined to employ to survey large objects, such as buildings. Alberti himself developed and implemented a similar tool—called *definitor* or *finitorium*—for his survey of Rome (approx. late 1430s to 1940s) to include it in his treatise on sculpture—*De Statua*—bringing together his interest in art and urbanism (Smith 2001, pp. 14–27). The results of Alberti's survey were conflated in a short publication titled *Description Urbis Romae* (Carpo and Furlan 2007) in which, given the technologies of the time, we can witness one of the first examples of digital recording of scanned data. The "shadow square" introduced by Alberti—here utilized horizontally—consisted of a rather simple disk with a rotatory arm, and a plumb-line to guarantee perfect horizontality. The perimeter of the disk was graded into *gradi* and *minuti* so as to read orientation angles. The operator was meant to stand at the center of the Capitol so as to see the outline of Rome and read the various angles. Thanks to this instrument one could pinpoint key points forming the perimeter of Rome. For each point, the instrument would return its polar coordinates consisting of a distance and an angle. In order to preserve the accuracy of the measurements, Alberti decided not to publish an actual map showing the results of the process, but rather he inserted the original polar coordinates arrayed in a chart—an actual spreadsheet by today's standards—that could have been computed to reproduce the map of Rome. By separating the act of measuring from the computation of the data, it was possible to redraw the map in other places and in future times. The scale of the reproduction could also be varied by proportionately altering the original dataset. The media of choice was not visual and therefore based on geometry, but rather digital—based on numbers—to be reinterpreted and potentially elaborated through arithmetic and trigonometry. As Carpo (2008) meticulously pointed out, the full implications of this experiment revealed two important elements in our discussion of the subject. In describing the same method applied to sculpture, Alberti also suggested that once information was recorded "digitally," the manufacturing process could be distributed between different locations. As such Alberti finally implemented Ptolemy's technique for digitizing visual information introduced some thirteen centuries earlier in both the *Geography* and *Cosmography.* Secondly, we have here a clear example of one of the key characteristics not only of scanning technologies, but also of parametric modeling. The sheet of polar coordinates generated by Alberti can be seen as an *invariant* in the process; it is the very fact that physical measurements have been transferred to a different media—that is, numbers—to ensure that they will never vary. The act of reproducing the map at a different scale implied changing these numbers; however, this will not be a random change, but rather one coordinated by the scale factor chosen, that is, parametrically. Each new number will differ from the original set but the rule determining this differentiation will remain the same for all the coordinates.

Not long after Alberti's experiment, Leonardo da Vinci (1452–1519) also turned his attention to the art of mapmaking merging technological and representational advancements. In drafting the plan of Imola—attributed to Leonardo and completed in c.1504—he employed the "*bacolo* of Euclid," a wooden cross he coupled with a wind rose and compass to triangulate the major landmarks and generate a plan of the entire fortified citadel. Whereas Alberti's survey of Rome was particularly important because of the notational system adopted—similar to a spreadsheet, Leonardo's maps stood out for bringing together various technologies which had been employed separately up to that moment. An image of an instrument similar to Leonardo's came to us through the drawings of Vincenzo Scamozzi (1548–1616) and Cosimo Bartoli (1503–72) who mention the use of a special compass—named *bussola* by Leonardo—to measure both the plans and elevations of the existing buildings.[2]

There are at least two important innovations we can infer from Leonardo's plan of Imola: first is the use of devices which have been more specifically crafted to take measurements at the urban scale, thus different from those described to the benefit of artists. Secondly, and perhaps more important, Leonardo managed to produce a visual document, a map—and a very detailed one indeed—of the whole town.

Between 1450 and 1550 numerous machines were developed to apply Albertian principles of mathematical perspective. As mentioned, this phenomenon was largely motivated by practical reasons to allow the everyday use of perspective unencumbered by the complex science behind it. What these devices gained in practicality often lost in terms of rigor. Two devices are particularly important in our survey, as they constituted important developments to respectively the translation of visual observations into numerical data and the range of computational operations to be performed on the dataset. The first experiment to automatically "digitize" the information scanned was conceived by Jacopo Barozzi da Vignola (1507–73) but only illustrated by Ignazio Danti (1536–86) in his *Le Due Regole della prospettiva pratica* (posthumously published in 1583) (Fig. 7.1).

In Danti's etching a rather complex machine is represented operated by two men: one is standing by the contraption using a moveable sight in order to pinpoint specific elements of the subject to measure (in the etching, a statue). The sight was connected to the rest of the apparatus and could be adjusted to determine the point of view from which to survey the statue. A moveable vertical shaft acted as a target allowing the operator to follow the outline of the object scanned. Finally, a system of gradated pulley wheels recorded the position of the target in space: the second operator—crouched below the pulley system—read the values of each point measured and directly plotted it on to the final drawing or canvas. If Alberti's elegant system to construct the plan of Rome was still clearly separating the two phases involved in surveying objects—direct or indirect measurement, and transcription of the data gathered—Vignola's machine merged optical and mathematical elements of perspective into an increasingly seamless, "automatic" process. Though legitimate doubts can be raised as to whether this drawing illustrated a principle rather than a fully functioning machine, we can undoubtedly observe the integration and "automatic" translation of empirical observations into numerical values (Kemp 1990, p. 174). Though the illustration accompanying Vignola's treatise shows the invention applied to sculpture, the machine could have been utilized to measure much larger objects such as landscapes. The use of lenses was a potential source of further distortions, whereas the analogue computing system formed by pulleys provided the numerical, quantifiable, transmittable part of the machine. Similar machines must have nevertheless been utilized by cartographers to survey the enemy's fortifications; here direct observation and geometrical perspective combined in order to extract orthographic drawings

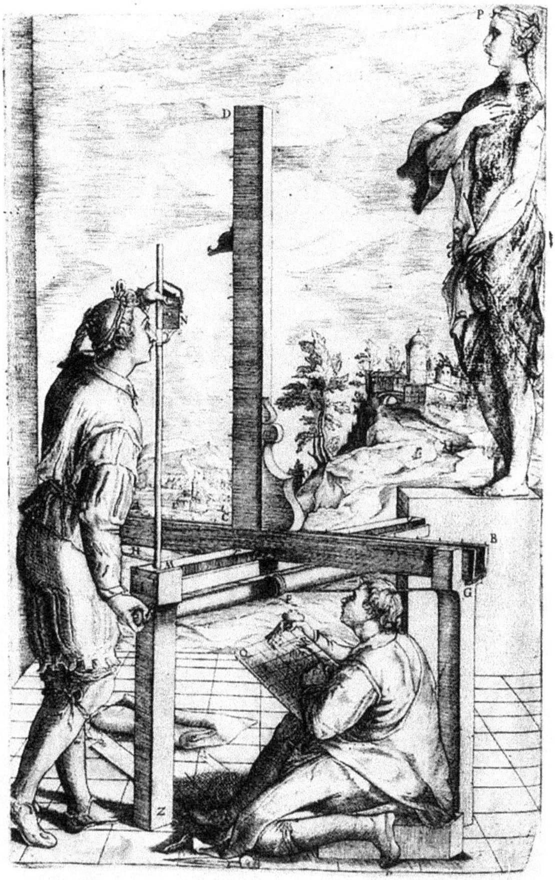

Figure 7.1 Illustration of Vignola's 'analogue' perspective machine. In Jacopo Barozzi da Vignola, *Le Due Regole della Prospettiva*, edited by E. Danti (1583). (image in the public domain, copyright expired). Courtesy of the Internet Archive.

(more useful) from perspectives. It is Danti himself to confirm such use of both these machines and linear perspective:

> [perspective] also offers great advantages in attacking and defending fortresses, since it is possible with the instruments of this Art to draw any site without approaching it, and to have not only the plan, but also the elevation with every detail, and the measurement of its parts in proportion to the distance lying between our eye and the thing we wish to draw. (Danti 1583, quoted in Camarota 2004, p. 182)

This application warranted the invention of numerous other machines which allowed transforming perspectival observations into measurable drawings, such as *distanziometro* by Baldassarre Lanci (1510–71), the *gnomone* by Bernardo

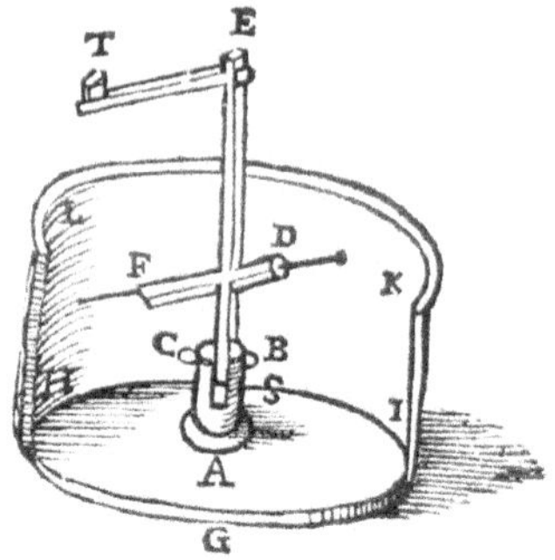

Figure 7.2 Sketch of Baldassare Lanci's *Distanziometro*. In Jacopo Barozzi da Vignola, Le Due Regole della Prospettiva, edited by E. Danti.1583. (image in the public domain, copyright expired). Courtesy of the Internet Archive.

Puccini (1520–1575), and the *proteo militare* by Pietro Accolti (1455–1532) (Camarota 2004, p. 182).

Lanci's *distanziometro* deserves closer examination, as it introduced a series of novelties in the problem of surveying large objects (Fig. 7.2). An exemplar of this device is still on display at the Museum of History of Science in Florence and consisted of a flat circular plate at the center of which a metal shaft was mounted on a pivoting joint. At the top of this vertical element there was a sight to pinpoint specific locations on this object to be measured; whereas at a lower level a metal nail scored points and lines on the actual drawing. The piece of paper to draw on was mounted vertically along the rim of the circular base plate. The user simply needed to follow the outline of the object or landscape to scan while the pointed metal nail would prick the paper leaving behind a scaled copy of the original. Finally, the bottom plate was equipped with a series of moveable intersecting rulers that allowed the operator to directly read the orientation angle of the sight. This last component could have been demounted turning the whole device into a rather light and transportable object. Lanci's ambition to invent a "universal instrument" was well served by the modest weight, size, and complexity of the device whose limits were theoretically only those of the human eye. In commenting this invention Ignazio Danti (1536–86) was unconvinced by the final output: the final image scored on the piece of paper would unavoidably be distorted once the paper was removed from its curved support and unrolled flat. Not only was Lanci well aware of this potential limitation as he provided a series of simple geometrical templates to correct the problem, but he also fitted the bottom plate of two sliding arms to measure the angle of orientation of the pivoting central shaft. By coupling these measurements with the additional diagrams he supplied, the user would have been able to utilize a precise geometrical method to restore visual credibility to the final image. However, perhaps more important than this mendable problem was the fact that Lanci's machine introduced two elements of novelty: first, it did not utilize lenses as in Vignola's and it allowed to draw on a curved surface, thus substituting the prevailing linear projections with cylindrical ones. The relevance of cylindrical projection methods in the history of cartography is beyond the scope of this book but it is still useful to remind the reader that Mercator's famous globe was constructed on this projection technique. Although Lanci did not know who Mercator was or any of his geometrical studies (which he completed in 1569 and published in 1599), this instrument marks an important step in the operations of recording and computing spatial information.

Beyond Lenticular Perception: Piero della Francesca's Other Method

An important step in the evolution of machines to scan real objects and compute them is constituted by Piero della Francesca's *Other Method*. Piero della Francesca introduced it in the third volume of his *De Perspectiva pingendi* (c.1470–80, but only printed in 1899). Not only do we know that Piero was a polymath—a rather common feature among Renaissance painters—but he particularly excelled in mathematics; an area of his activities which only came to the foreground toward the end of his career in the preparation of his *De Perspectiva*. The attention that perspective machines had gained at this point in time was in response to the need of gaining greater control of the space of the painting: Piero's *Other Method* endeavored to conjure up a system through which even irregular objects could be surveyed and accurately reproduced.

Although the tripartite structure of *De Perspectiva* was broadly based on Alberti's, only the second volume maintained the same title as in that of his predecessor (Clark 1969, pp. 70–75). *Commensuratio* was precisely dedicated to the art of measuring objects, an action that in Piero della Francesca acquired a central role in the construction of accurate and aesthetically proportioned perspectival space (Bertelli 1992, p. 164). However, it was only with the third book that Piero discussed his method for representing objects with mathematical precision. The narration moved from simple to complex forms—starting from a square (Proposition 1) while Proposition 7 depicted a Corinthian column—combining concise verbal descriptions of the process with synthetic, stunning diagrams (Field 2005, p. 168). It is these diagrams that have attracted the greatest attention and still fascinate scholars and readers alike.

Proposition 8 portrayed a human head seen from below obtained by connecting with lines a series of points all annotated by numbers. This view was constructed rather than measured from an actual human model as the original dataset resulted from the intersection between the model's head and eight horizontal planes. The profile of the contours obtained was recorded through sixteen points arrayed radially. A total of 128 points were generated to which 2 extra ones were added to survey the "irregular" profile of the nose. The entire set of points was annotated and available to be plotted according to Piero's *Other Method*, whose similarities with Gaspard Monge's (1746–1818) *Projective Geometry* are rather impressive considering that the two examples are some three hundred years apart. Similar to Dürer's methods—which will be analyzed in the next paragraph—Piero's procedure also relied less and less on human intervention or lenses. His process attempted to "automatize" the use of perspective in art practice. We could in fact say that Dürer's and Piero's methods complement each other from the point of view of the use of "automatic" procedures. If Dürer's machine could theoretically survey an object without human intervention, Piero's *Other Method* streamlined the second part of the process as, once the coordinate of each point had been recorded, the original model—in Proposition 8, a human head—was no longer needed to produce all the different drawings of the subject. The method allowed to manually compute, and/or re-compute all the points to portray the head from a different angle or at a different scale by combining linear and auxiliary projections. In this sense, Piero's also differed from Alberti's *Descriptio* as the latter was about a reliable system to "digitize" information—a sort of *ante litteram* spreadsheet—whereas the former focused on a method to compute the data gathered. This was a proper computational operation which is still very much part of the procedures followed by CAD software to visualize and reconstruct three-dimensional geometries. For instance, wherever we rotate the point of view in a digital model, all the key coordinates identifying lines, surfaces, points, etc. are processed through a mathematical matrix that outputs the new, correct positions of each entity. Again we can observe a clear relation between invariant elements—the original coordinates surveyed at the beginning of the process—and the (computing) principle through which they can vary to produce different types of drawings. As Robin Evans (1995, pp. 119–21) succinctly put it; "Piero's achievement was to separate the form of the object from the form of the projection." The British historian went on to also observe a relation between the *Other Method* and Gaspard Monge's *Projective Geometry*—invented toward the end of the eighteenth century. Piero's description was rather superficial compared to the comprehensive system developed by the French engineer and there is also no conclusive evidence that Piero ever employed his own method, whereas Monge saw it as an essential tool to reorganize how buildings were designed and built. The result of the freedom gained through this time-consuming method can still be appreciated in the virtuoso control of the complex geometrical shapes. Testament to this is the fact that Piero's human portrait from below was the first of this kind in the history of art, a feature that some claim had a lasting effect on our image culture (Schott 2008).

The results were not only visually stunning but also showed an early example of wireframe visualization mode as still used in CAD packages.[3] Wireframe is the most basic type of CAD visualization of three-dimensional objects, as it only displays their edges rendering the objects as transparent. In *De pictura*, Alberti described this mode of visualization as aligning it with mathematical representation of object which he described as to "measure with their minds alone forms of things separated from all matter" (Quoted in Braider 1993, p. 22). Piero's method—exactly as for CAD software—rather than describing the whole of the surface, limited its survey to a finite number of points: what was a three-dimensional problem had been reduced to a mono-dimensional one (points as one-degree objects).

The advantages of this method were immediate: once turned into series of points even an irregular shape such as that of the human head could be drawn. The emergence of wireframe representation was also one of the by-products of this method: the amount of data necessary to complete the portrait was drastically reduced, compressed to a series of points eventually connected through lines. Alberti had already suggested artists to think of the body as a faceted surface made up of joined triangles whose main features could be dissimulated by rendering the distribution of light on the curvaceous surfaces of the body.

The complete separation between the technologies for surveying and those for computing would only be enabled by the advancements in field of mathematics. If these two moments conflated in perspective machines, in the work of Girard Desargue (1591–1661), in mathematics they became separate domains. Projections, transformations, etc. could be calculated and plotted on paper eliminating the need to see the actual model to represent. It is therefore not a coincidence that Desargue's treatise in 1639 mostly concentrated on projected, imagined objects. Besides the advantages in terms of precision, this method became a powerful tool to project, investigate, and analyze the formal properties of objects that did not exist yet: a perfect aid to designers.

Finally, the implications of contouring techniques in describing form are the central topic of a different chapter; however, it is worth noticing in passing that both Hans Scharoun and Frank Gehry have been employing these methods to represent their complex architectures. Similarly, we will also see how the introduction of photography to scan a subject would do away with any contact with the object surveyed: if Piero still required a series of points—which he warned the reader to be the complicated and very time-consuming part his method—photography would make computable whatever would fall within the frame of the camera.

Analogous computing: The development of automatic techniques from Albrecht Dürer to the pantograph

The development of perspective machines had both demonstrative and social ambitions: the latter preoccupation was particularly evident in the work of the artists and artisans operating in Nuremberg, particularly for Albrecht Dürer's (1471–1528). Some methods such as Piero's were very time-consuming and unlikely to be ever employed in applied arts. It was within this context that we can appreciate the emergence of "automatic" perspective machines: devices in which some of the mathematical laws governing *Perspectiva artificialis* were physically engrained in the material composition of the machine and in its design. Alberti's "costruzione legittima" was already conceived to provide both precise control over the final image and an "easy" step-by-step procedure that untrained craftsmen could have learned. Famously, the insertion of the veil between object and viewer could "automatically" capture the perspectival image. As Carpo noticed, Alberti lacked the technology but not the conceptual armature to actually record the image impressed by light on the veil, leaving its invention incomplete (Carpo 2008, pp. 47–63).

The systematic theorization of the foundations of perspective was also Dürer's ambition to which he dedicated one volume of his treatise—*Underweysung der Messung mit dem Zirckel un Richtscheyt* (1525)—an art that he had learned intuitively and wished to make accessible to all artists and craftsmen. As Panofsky (1892–1968) pointed out, this was the first time that the mathematical treatment of perspectival problems was the topic of a book, which, by extension, would make Dürer the first theoretician on scanning techniques. However, in the third tome—dwelling on the applications of perspectival methods—we find the most interesting proposition to set up correct perspectival views (1943). The mechanism we are about to describe was first anticipated by Dürer himself in this famous etching *Man Drawing with a Lute* (1525) (Fig. 7.3). However, an even more radical version of this contraption was published by Ignazio Danti in his book on Vignola in 1583. In Danti's woodcut we can actually see Dürer's *sportello* (Italian for "cupboard door") and understand how it was meant to aid the construction of

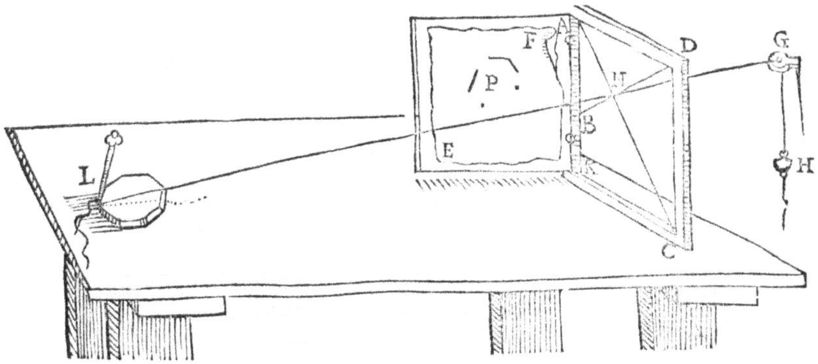

Figure 7.3 "Automatic" perspective machine inspired by Durer's *sportello*. In Jacopo Barozzi da Vignola, *Le Due Regole della Prospettiva*, edited by E. Danti (1583). (image in the public domain, copyright expired). Courtesy of the Internet Archive.

geometrical perspectives. Before we get to discuss how this particular mechanism worked, we should observe that Dürer's machine was completely automatic, able to compute without either human intervention or lenticular technology: humans were only needed to move the pointing nail and read the final measurements (in fact, no human features in Danti's drawing). In fact, the eye of the viewer was replaced by a nail fixed to the wall opposite the figure to represent; a string—a method already suggested by Francesco di Giorgio Martini (1439–1502) which Piero specified to be a horse's hair—connected the nail (G) to a pointing element which was meant to scan the relevant features of the object (L). The string passed through the *sportello* acting as a mechanism recording all the necessary measurements to translate the object observed. Two more strings were stretched between the opposite corners of the *sportello* to both identify the intersection between the line of sight and the picture plane and record the distance between (N) and (B,C,D). The various dimensions were eventually transferred to the piece of paper once the *sportello* was closed. Even if some human presence was still needed to operate the device—as in contemporary contact scanners—we can speak of an automatic contraption as it no longer needed a human to interpret it: the machine "automatically" outputs the various longitudes and latitudes which simply needed to be written down. Dürer's machine outlined a series of operations not too dissimilar from those performed by SOM architects or Frank Gehry some four centuries and a half later.

Another important contact scanning machine conceived was the one illustrated by Johannes Lencker (1523–85) in his *Perspectiva*, published in 1571. Lencker was part of the circle of artists operating in Nuremberg and continuing

Dürer's legacy to develop techniques and contraptions to popularize the use of mathematical perspective in artisanal practices (Fig. 7.4). In describing his work we should talk of scanning rather than perspective machines, as the unique feature of Lencker's device was to record projected measurements, therefore allowing to directly draw plans and elevations. His machine consisted of a dry-pin (pencil led) that could move in space along the *x*, *y*, and *z* axes in order to follow the profile of the object to scan—in the most famous illustration, a sphere wrapped by a square section ring. A pivoting table could be aligned with the scanning pointer to transfer the measurements onto the paper and immediately trace the top view of the sphere. Again, we have not only a device

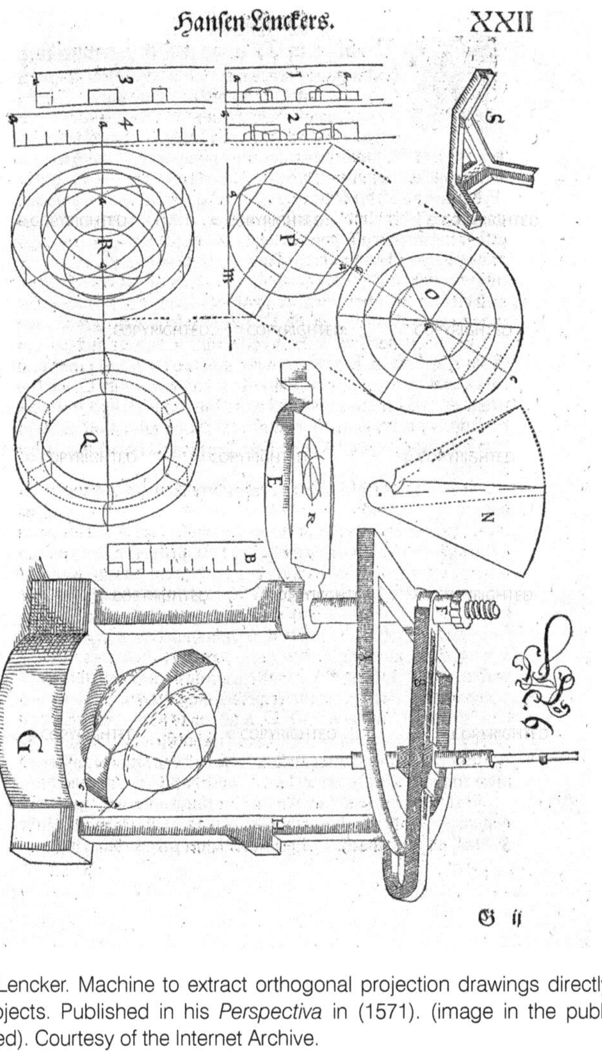

Figure 7.4 J. Lencker. Machine to extract orthogonal projection drawings directly fro three-dimensional objects. Published in his *Perspectiva* in (1571). (image in the public domain, copyright expired). Courtesy of the Internet Archive.

performing analogue computation, but also a new type of calculations that no longer adhered to the laws of *Prospectiva artificialis* that Alberti had introduced at the beginning of the fifteenth century.

More precise devices to record data scanned would only emerge in the seventeenth century. Lodovico Cigoli (1559–1613)—artist and Galileo's friend—in fact set out to construct a machine that would do away with veils or chords to pinpoint precise features of the subject to portray. His *perspectograph* roughly consisted of a system of pulleys and sights to be manually operated by sliding them across the picture plane. These were simultaneously coordinated by the operator to draw the outline of the scene identified—not unlike tracing over a shape with a mouse or a digital pad. Cigoli also showed—and partially demonstrated—two rather important additional features that his *perspectograph* supplied: by tilting the horizontal plane of work, the instrument could compute distortions such as anamorphic projections and, perhaps more important in this discussion, it allowed for the whole workflow to be reversed to go from the drawing to physical reality by plotting points (one of the illustrations shows its applications to a vaulted ceiling). Despite the technical difficulties of simultaneously operating the pulleys with both hands, this machine took advantage of the properties of both optics and mathematics to make directly possible—for the first time—to automatically generate images, a feature that was only latent in Dürer's *Man Drawing a Lute* (Kemp 1990, p. 179). Moreover, as we have seen for other devices, the innovation introduced by the device was not just technical: it well served the cultural desire to explore more complex, deceiving forms such as optical illusions for which it could be used.

These instruments should also be seen as the progenitors of the pantograph, a drafting device that formalized most of the notions we have discussed thus far. Invented by Christoph Scheiner (1573–1650), who introduced it in his *Pantographice seu ars delineandi* published in 1631, the pantograph would enjoy an outstanding longevity which would only begin to fade with the introduction of photography in the nineteenth century. The operation of copying and scaling drawings or images would become extremely simple and precise so much so that this instrument was still rather popular in the twentieth century. The basic operations it engendered such as copying and scaling also bore close resemblance to those enabled by digital scanners. Most importantly, the pantograph was easily shifting from an input device—to survey—to an output one—to design. As such it could be seen as a primitive robotic arm able to augment human gestures, replicate prescribed shapes, and maintain some level of precision due to its mechanical constraints. These technologies would find renewed interest in the nineteenth century when the introduction of photography would change the process to acquire and plot data.

Photosculpture: The rise of photography

Though machines for scanning objects in the nineteenth century were much faster, more precise and efficient than the ones we have analyzed, their principles had remained unchanged. For instance, the *Physionotrace*, invented by Gilles-Louis Chrétien (1754–1811) in 1786, basically consisted of a large pantograph whose size allowed to directly replicate and scale portraits, a burgeoning artistic genre at the time. Portraiture would play an important role in the development of the modern scanning technologies; as a popular subject for inventions and experiments that would employ a range of technologies—optics, drawings, and sculpture—posing the problem of both accurately measuring real objects and manufacturing exact copies of them. In Britain Charles Gavard (1794–1871) would develop a particular type of pantograph to draw panoramas, another fashionable genre at the time.

The invention of photography radically changed all that. Photography conflated the optical developments of the camera obscura with chemical properties to produce images. Photographic cameras were combined with perspective machines to improve the quality and speed of reproduction. Perhaps the most convincing and successful of these experiments was *Photosculpture* invented by François Willème (1830–1905) in 1859. The introduction of photography would change not only the process of data acquisition but also that of manufacturing anticipating the technologies currently employed in CAM such as 3D printing and robotics (Hoskins 2013).

His subjects would sit at the center of a special circular room on whose walls 24 cameras—one every 15 degrees—were mounted. Willème's team would simultaneously trigger all twenty-four cameras obtaining different views of the same subject. The set of photographs was then developed and used as templates to carve out the head's profile from wooden tablets. The final setup vaguely reminds of the special cinematic devices utilized to shoot the combat sequences in *The Matrix* movies (*The Matrix*, 1999). In doing so, Willème created a powerful noncontact, completely automatic scanner. Recording information on photographs not only removed, for the first time, the use of geometry to compute information, but also obviated to the common problem arising from capturing landscapes with camera obscura. The literature on the subject would in fact invariably warn the reader about the importance of fixing the point of view from which to survey the scene: a step that not only would determine all the subsequent ones, but also would not be possible to adjust later on in the process. Monge's *Projective Geometry*—and its early antecedent, Piero's *Other Method*—allowed manipulating the acquired data with agility and precision; however, all these operations were only manipulating a given dataset which could have not been altered. The obvious rule of thumb was to only record the minimum quantity of information in order to avoid redundancies and, consequently, complications and mistakes. Recording data through photography relaxed such constraints, as it was no longer necessary to predetermine which points were important to survey, the reductivist approach was superseded: anything captured by the photographic plate could have been turned into data. The resulting dataset—the invariant element of scanning—not only was much greater than previous methods, but it also allowed to defer any decision to curtail data to a more manageable size. Similar problems have also recently resurfaced in treating very large databases—often referred to as "Big Data"—in which the same promise to indefinitely defer reduction also featured as one of its innovative methods (Mayer-Schönberger and Cukier 2013). Though Willème was not interested in theorizing his discoveries, his *Photosculpture* nevertheless had an indirect impact on artistic production as it inspired, among others, artists such as Auguste Rodin (1840–1917) who used it to examine his subjects from numerous angles to create a mental "profils comparés" (Quoted in Sobieszek 1980).

However, the digitization of the data recorded was not available yet and Willème had to fall back onto an older technology, the pantograph. Each photographic plate would be translated into cut-out wooden profiles and organized radially to reconstruct the final three-dimensional portrait. The organization of his atelier was also interesting as it signaled an increasing level of industrialization of the creative process with consequent significant economic advantages. The team of assistants would take care of large parts of the process: from photographing the subject, to producing rough three-dimensional models of the head that Willème would finish by adding his "creative" touch. The atelier resembled more a shop than an artist studio. Spread over two levels, all the machinery was on the upper, private floor, whereas the ground floor provided the more public area for clients. This layout was also suggested by the speed at which the atelier was able to churn off sculptures: *Photosculpture* allowed Willème to go through the entire process delivering a statuette approximately 40–45 centimeters tall in about 48 hours. Clients were given a choice of materials for the finishing: plaster of Paris—by far the most popular choice—terra-cotta, biscuit, bronze, alabaster, and they could even be metal-plated by galvanoplasty. The nascent scanning process underpinning *Photosculpture* also enabled the production of multiple copies of the same sculpture whose scale could have been changed into very large sculptures, theoretically at least. For this reason, the atelier had to also be equipped with adequate storage space to preserve all the photographic records (Sobieszek 1980). The range of plausible subjects to portray through *Photosculpture* also widened. This technology grew in parallel with the nascent mercantile class of the nineteenth century whose preferred subjects went beyond those of traditional paintings and sculptures to embrace family portraits, etc.

It is useful to treat separately the developments of technologies dealing with the two separate problems the *Physionotrace* had conflated. On the one hand, the problem of coordinating the digitization of images with a manufacturing process that would ensure precision; on the other, the technologies for the accurate transmission of data. The former marked the beginning of a strand of innovations we currently still enjoy through rapid-prototyping and CNC machines, whereas the latter—which we will concentrate on—will take us to the invention of the computer scanner and, consequently, its application in architectural design processes.

The digital scanner

Prior to the invention of the digital scanner, several others anticipated its arrival. Among the many attempts, two stood out. First was Frederick Bakewell's (1800–1869) invention in 1848 which finally allowed to materialize Alberti's vision of distributing information independently of its place of creation. His scanner could transmit simple documents to remote locations: the message—written on a metal foil with a special non-conducting ink—was put through a mechanical drum and scanned by a metal stylus moving back and forward. The principles behind the combined action of the drum rotating and the pendulum-like movement of the stylus are still part of modern flatbed scanners. Each time the stylus interjected a mark made with insulating ink, the flow of electrical current suspended. A similar instrument at the other end reversed the sequence of operations to copy the message down on a metal foil. Later on, Giovanni Caselli (1815–91) patented his *Pantèlègraphe* (1861), which improved the synchronization of the two clocks at each end and, therefore, the quality of the data transmitted. The nature of data transmission had definitely abandoned photographic reproduction and fully relied on electric signals.

The year 1957 marked the last radical twist in the development of this technology as the first digital image was scanned. This breakthrough occurred at the US National Bureau of Standards where the team led by Russell A. Kirsch (1929–)—also responsible for major advancements in early numerical analysis, memory mechanisms, graphic display, pattern recognition, etc.—was confronted with numerous tasks that could have been efficiently automated through the introduction of computational methods. One of these involved developing working processes able to acquire large quantities of documents. By evolving some of the technologies just surveyed, the team was able to develop an early version of an image recognition software that could detect an alphabetical character from its shape. The result was the Standards Eastern Automatic Computer (SEAC) scanner which combined a "rotating drum and a photomultiplier to sense reflections from a small image mounted on the drum. A mask interposed between the picture and the photomultiplier tessellated the image into discrete pixels" (*Earlier Image Processing* no date). The final image was 176 × 176 pixels (approximately 5 centimeters wide) portrait of Kirsch's newly born son.

In this crucial innovation we also see the reemergence of the metaphor of the digital eye. The algorithm written to process images was built on the best neurological and neuroanatomical knowledge of the time. "The emphasis on binary representations of neural functions led us to believe that binary representations of images would be suitable for computer input" (ibid.). The algorithm would operate according to a 0/1 logic, thus coloring each pixel either white or black. Though this was a pioneering machine, inaugurating a series of inventions in the field of computational image analysis and shape recognition, the team immediately understood that the problem did not rely in the technology but rather in the neurological paradigm accounting for the physiology of vision. By overlaying different scans of the same image with different threshold parameters, they were able to improve the quality of the results producing a more subtle gradation of colors.

Scanners in architecture

Digital scanners—often also referred to as three-dimensional input devices or optical scanning devices—had already been developing for about two decades when they landed in an architecture office. Other complementary technologies helped such technological transfer. The RAND Tablet—developed at the RAND Corporation in September 1963—consisted of a pen-like device to use on a tablet of 10 inches × 10 inches (effectively a printed-circuit screen) able to record 10^6 positions on the tablet. The pen was only partially utilizing scanning technologies but it could be made to work as a scanner by, for instance, tracing over existing maps, etc. The information received from the pen was "strobed, converted from grey to binary code" (Quoted in Davis and Ellis 1964). By expanding on Laposky's experiments, the tablet could also retain "historical information," that is, adding new pen positions without deleting the previous ones and therefore tracing continuous lines.

The *Lincoln WAND* was developed at MIT's Lincoln Laboratories in 1966 under the guidance of Lawrence G. Roberts.[4] The WAND allowed moving from 2D to 3D scanning by positioning four ultrasonic position-sensing microphones that would receive sound information from a fifth emitting device. The range of coverage of the WAND was a true novelty, as it allowed to operate at the scale of a room and therefore could be used to scan architectural spaces or models. The working space was 4 × 4 × 6 feet with an absolute tolerance of 0.2 inches. As mentioned, the output were sets of *x*, *y*, *z* values for each potion recorded through a hand-held device (Roberts 1966). Around the same period at the University of Utah, a mechanical input device was also developed. The contraption could be seen as a digital version of the device Vignola designed some four centuries ago. By substituting lenses with a mechanical pointer—a needle—the team at the University of Utah had turned Vignola's vision into a contact digital scanner. The pointer could be run along the edges of an object while its position in space would be electronically recorded and transferred to a workstation. The shift from optics to mechanics made these devices significantly more precise than Vignola's as lens distortion had been completely removed: however, by turning it into a contact scanner greatly limited the range of action of the instrument.

The first use of digital scanners by an architectural practice occurred in 1981 when SOM took on the commission to build a large sculpture by Joan Miró (1893–1983) to be placed adjacent to their Brunswick complex in Chicago. Confronted with the complex and irregular shapes proposed by Miró, SOM proceeded by digitally scanning a small model (36 inches tall) to eventually scale up the dataset to erect the thirty-foot tall sculpture made of concrete, bronze, and ceramic. The process followed was reminiscent of *Photosculpture*, as SOM employed a CAT body-scan which produced 120 horizontal slices of the model in the form of images. These were eventually traced over in CAD and stacked up for visual verification. The dataset was triangulated into a mesh by using SOM's very own software and then engineered to design a structural solution to support it.

Perhaps the most famous use of digital scanners in architecture coincided with the adoption of this technology by Frank Gehry's office in the 1990s. The production of the Canadian architect has always been associated with the constant pursuit of ever-freer, dynamic forms in his architecture. The anecdote that led Gehry's office to adopt digital tools is well documented in the documentary *Sketches of Frank Gehry* (2006) and it also summarizes all the issues at stake with the use of scanning technologies in architectural design: measurements, computation, data transmission, and fabrication. Upon completing the *Vitra Museum* in Weil am Rhein in 1989, Gehry expressed his dissatisfaction with the translation of some of the most daring sculptural parts of the design: particularly, the dramatic twisting cantilever containing the spiral staircase was forming a kink when joining the main volume of museum instead of the seamless connection the office had designed. The search for more adequate tools liaising design to construction started under James Glymph's supervision. The office eventually ended up acquiring *CATIA* (CAD interactive application), manufactured by the French company Dassault Systèmes, which had already been employed in the aviation industry to design, among others, the Mirage fighter jet.

The combination of digital scanners and CAD software specifically geared toward manufacturing would not only change the organization and the formal language of Gehry's office, but also impact on the entire profession. The first project completed by the office with *CATIA* was the *Vila Olimpica* (1989–92), a biomorphic roof structure in steel, part of the development for the Olympic Games in Barcelona. However, it was only with the *Lewis House* (1989–95) that the office developed a more holistic workflow that also included digital scanners. The design of the house spanned over a particularly long period of time, with various changes to the brief—often increased in size and ambition—which allowed Gehry to experiment with different formal configuration and design methodologies that would inform several of the following commissions. Gehry has himself often described the project as "a research fellowship or the ultimate study grant" (Quoted in Rappold and Violette 2004, p. 102). The design process for this house started like any other Gehry's commission: that is, by constructing large-scale physical models directly sculpted and manipulated by Gehry himself and his team. Once a satisfactory configuration was attained, the models were digitized by scanning the position of specific markers placed on the model. The markers corresponded to the key points to capture in order to be able to replicate the physical model inside the computer. *CATIA* tools would allow digitally reconstructing all ruling geometries and output the key document to both communicate and eventually build the house. Again, elements of the physiology of vision informed these developments: to scan an object meant using *both* the digitizers and computational tool able to handle the information set. On closer examination, it was perhaps the latter to constitute the element of greater novelty and importance in Gehry's work: the ability to reconstruct and manipulate geometries freed the office from previous constraints and injected new energy in their designs. Gehry's office was also a paradigmatic example of how deeply perspective machines influenced the design process: both prior and subsequent to the introduction of computers, the office still relied on techniques first introduced in the Renaissance. Before adopting digital scanners, Richard Smith—a *CATIA* expert that had joined the office at the time the software had been acquired—recalled how elevations were drawn up in the office:

> The architects built a box that had a frosted glass window, and they set up an elevation. They'd shine a light behind the box, which would cast a shadow on the frosted glass. They'd take tracing paper, trace the shadow, and they'd say, "Well, that's our elevation." I came in and asked, "How do you know that the dimensions are right?" And they told me, "Hey, Michelangelo did this. This is the way it's been done for centuries. Don't buck it." (Quoted in Friedman and Sorkin 2003, p. 17)

The method is also rather close to Alberti's "costruzione legittima" in which the insertion of a *veil* between object and viewer would act as a screen to capture the desired image. The shift to digitally assisted design enhanced rather than changed the practices the office had been working on: less interested in computer-generated images, CAD software was more opportunistically adopted to align design and construction.[5] In this context it is more fruitful to see the introduction of the digital scanners against Piero della Francesca's *Other Method*, as physical models had to be first reduced to a series of key points to be digitized, transferring all the necessary information in the language of Cartesian coordinates—an invariant media engendering further manipulations. The first experiments carried out on scanning opted for a more traditional approach as information gathered was rationalized by applying algebra-based geometries: curves were turned into arcs, centers and radii became the guiding principles to represent but also simplify the fluid surfaces of the physical models.

This approach too presented similarities with those enabled by the mathematics of the Renaissance based on analogue computing measurements extracted through chord and compass. These were obviously not adequate to compute the geometrical intricacy Gehry was after: each step in the process was effectively reducing the quantity of data to handle, eventually generating a coarse description of curves and surfaces. Digital tools provided a powerful and systematic way of handling and modifying data according to a consistent logic. The relation between invariant and variable data required the introduction of differential calculus in the treatment of surfaces, which *CATIA* could aptly provide. By moving from the overarching principles of algebra to localized descriptions based on calculus, the need to discard information at every step of the process became redundant and so did the idea of having unifying geometrical principles guiding the overall forms. This facilitated the workflow both upstream and downstream. The latter allowed to describe surfaces much more accurately despite their irregular profiles with a potentially radical impact on the economy of the building—which would become an essential factor in the construction of the *Guggenheim Bilbao Museum* (1991–97). The latter allowed Gehry to experiment much more freely with shapes: digital scanners established a more "direct" relation between real objects—often derived from a take on vernacular traditions—and their virtual translation. Operating through a sort of "ready-made" approach—one of the signatures of Gehry's work—was enhanced by the introduction of digital scanners, allowing the office to continue experimenting with methods often inspired by artistic practices.[6] While working on the *Lewis House*, the office also had to change the range of materials to use for the construction of working models; felt was introduced to better encapsulate the more experimental and fluid forms such as the so-called Horse Head which Gehry initially developed for this project and eventually built in a slightly different iteration for the headquarters of the *DZ Bank* in Frankfurt (1998–2000).[7] Despite Gehry's notorious lack of interest in digital media, these examples show not only the extent of the impact of CAD systems on the aesthetics and methods embraced by the office, but also an original approach to digital tools characterized by the issue of communication in the design and construction processes, the widening of the palette of vernacular forms and materials to be appropriated and developed in the design process, and an interest in construction—in the Master Builder—rather than image processing, also confirmed by the persistent lack of interest in computer-generated imagery, such as renderings.

The success of the integration of digital tools in the office has been limited not only to production of evermore daring buildings, but also to the very workflow developed which eventually—first among architects—led Gehry in 2002 to start a sub-company dedicated to the development of digital tools for the construction of complex projects: Gehry Technologies. The whole ecology of tools developed by Gehry finally demonstrates how much these technologies have penetrated into the culture and workflow of commercial practices far beyond the role of mere practical tools impacting the aspects of the design process.

Contemporary landscape

In conclusion, it is perhaps surprising to observe how little the technologies for architectural surveying and representation have changed since Brunelleshi's experiment in Florence at the beginning of the fifteenth century. This chapter, perhaps better than others, highlights a typical pattern of innovation in digital design; one in which novelties result from layering or conflating technologies and ideas that had previously been employed separately. CAD packages have not changed the way in which perspective views are constructed; they simply absorbed methods that had been around for centuries. However, the ease with which perspective views can be constructed and manipulated as well as how CAD users can rapidly switch or even simultaneously work between orthographic and three-dimensional views has enabled them, for instance, to conceptually change the way a building is designed by modeling objects in three dimensions first to then extract plans and sections.

Digital scanners promise to add to the representational repertoire all the qualities of photographic images, charging digital modeling with perceptual qualities. The stunning images produced by combining LIDAR scanning and photographic recordings suffice to demonstrate their potential. However, the representational tools may afford new, more generative capabilities for further research.

One potential element of novelty involves exploiting further the artificial nature of the digital eye. Laser or other types of scanners see reality in a way that only partially resembles those of humans. The powerful coupling of sensing technologies and image processing can give access to aspects of reality falling outside human perception in the same way in which the introduction of the microscope in the seventeenth century afforded a foray into scales of material composition inaccessible to human eyes. As early as the 1980s, software analysis of satellite imagery made visible the long lost city of Ubar by revealing the traces of some old caravan routes (Quoted in Mitchell 1992, p. 12). A similar exercise was recently commissioned by the BBC to *ScanLAB* (2016) to analyze the ruins of Rome's Forum: a team of architects and archaeologists ventured into Rome's underground tunnels and catacombs to produce detailed scans of these underground spaces. A more contentious, but spatially very original project was developed in collaboration with the Forensic Architecture group combining "terrestrial scanning with ground penetrating radar to dissect the layers of life at two concentration camps sites in former Yugoslavia" (Scanlab 2014) (Fig. 7.5).

A second area of research one has perhaps deeper roots in the history of surveying and computation as it employs scanners to close the gap between representation and construction. Pioneered by *Autodesk*, among others, digital scanners are employed to regularly survey construction sites in order not only to check the accuracy of the construction process, but also to coordinate digital model and actual physical reality. The transformations promised by both technologies has prompted architects such as Bob Sheil (2014, pp. 8–19) to hypothesize the emergence of a high-definition design in which not only tolerance between parts is removed, but also, more importantly, representation and reality collapse into one another. The conflation of these two technologies

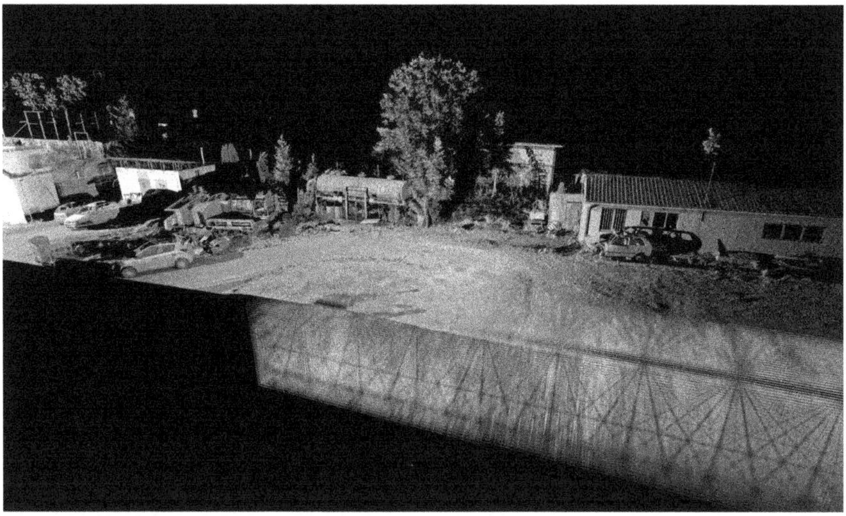

Figure 7.5 Terrestrial LIDAR and Ground Penetrating Radar, The Roundabout at The German Pavilion, Staro Sajmiste, Belgrade. © ScanLAB Projects and Forensic Architecture.

allows us to imagine a scenario in which CAD environments are in constant dialogue with building sites adjusting to varying conditions. The vast amount of data to manage such processes to successfully work questions again the relation between information and architecture. As for other areas of design—for instance, the so-called Smart Cities—techniques for gathering, mining, and acting on large datasets should also involve the relation between the construction site—surveyed by laser scanners—and designer's office. The processing power required to fluidly manage such relations has not been available to standard computers yet, but design and cultural implications of such shift can be already sensed.

Notes

1. *Image Scanner*. In *Wikipedia*. online. Available from: http://en.wikipedia.org/wiki/Image_scanner (Accessed June 2, 2015).
2. Bartoli (1559, p. 170).
3. "A wire-frame model is a visual presentation of a three-dimensional (3D) or physical object used in 3D computer graphics. It is created by specifying each edge of the physical object where two mathematically continuous smooth surfaces meet, or by connecting an object's constituent vertices using straight lines or curves. Its name derives from the use of metal wires to give form to three-dimensional objects." See *Wire-frame Model* (2001). *Wikipedia*. Available from: http://en.wikipedia.org/wiki/Wire-frame_model (Accessed June 9, 2015).

4. Roberts' work will also be discussed in the chapter "Pixels."
5. "When I'm looking at a computer image of my buildings, when I'm working with it, I have to keep an 'ideal' dream in my head. I have an idea for a building and it's visually clear in my head, but I have to hold on to this image while looking at some terrible image on a screen. That requires too much energy and concentration for me, and I can only do it for a few minutes at a time. Then I have to run out of the room screaming" (Quoted in Rappolt and Violette 2004, p. 92).
6. Perhaps the best and most famous example of such design aesthetic is exemplified by Gehry's own house (*Gehry Residence*, 1989–92).
7. For a comprehensive visual description of this process see Greg Lynn's exhibition and catalogues (2016).

Chapter 8

Voxels and Maxels

Introduction

Voxels are representational tools arranging a series of numerical values on a regular three-dimensional grid (scalar field). Voxels are often referred to as three-dimensional pixels, as stacks of cubes, enabling to abstract spatial representation, a capacity key to understand the relation between digital tools and design. Just as pixels and other digital concepts voxels too are scaleless tools for visualization. At a basic level, voxels thus provide a model for representing three-dimensional space with computers. For those familiar with the world of videogames, Minecraft—in which every element be it a human figure or a natural feature are modeled out of cubes—is a good reference to imagine how such space may look like. As we will see in this chapter, the translation of voxels into cubes only captures one of the many ways in which the scalar field can be visualized. In fact the scalar field can encapsulate more values than the mere geometrical description and position of cubical elements. According to the type of numerical information stored in each point in the grid we can respectively have Resels (recording the varying resolution of a voxel or even pixel space), Texels (texture elements), Maxels (embodying material properties such as density, etc.), etc. For designers, one important difference between voxels and polygons to take notice of is the ability of the latter to efficiently represent simple 3D structures with lots of empty or homogeneously filled space—as they can do so by simply establishing the coordinates of their vertexes—while the former are inherently volumetric and therefore can better describe "regularly sampled spaces that are non-homogeneously filled."[1] This is a very important distinction that will be reflected in the organization of this chapter: to think of space in terms of voxels we have to move beyond descriptive geometrical models based on singular points (e.g., the edge coordinates of a polygon) to explore more continuous, volumetric descriptions of space which better exploit the capacities engendered by voxels. We should also point out that the kind of continuity implied through voxels is still an approximation of analogue, truly continuous phenomena occurring in reality as digital computation, and voxels are a perfect example of this, ultimately rests on the discrete logic of binary numbers.

Despite having a marginal role in the discussions on digital design, voxels have been playing an important part in expanding the range of spatial manipulations available to designers. For instance, they are extensively employed in videogame design to compute real-time renderings of large, complex scenes, such as landscapes. The lack of deep design research in this specific area of digital design partially comes from the limitation of the computational architecture of CAD software. CAD packages model and visualize geometries according to "Boundary Representation" (B-Rep) models. In order to make files lighter and interaction more agile, only the outer surfaces of objects are modeled and displayed; in other words, every object modeled in CAD is hollow.[2] As a result the digital models we interact with in CAD are highly abstract: surfaces do not have thicknesses and we can conceive of zero volume entities such as points which could not exist outside the conventions of the software employed. The representational language adopted by CAD is geometry, which acts as a filter between the reality of an object and its digital representation, with a consequent loss of information attached to the object modeled. If, on the one hand, the resulting workflow is highly efficient, on the other, the resulting digital model has no materiality whatsoever; only texture images can be applied to surfaces to give the visual impression of weight and material grain. If we also add that modeling takes place in a space bereft of all forces acting on real objects and spaces—starting, obviously, from gravity—we realize that materials are the great missing element of current digital-design tools. At the moment, this lacuna is circumvented by integrating design software packages with other ones explicitly dedicated to the analysis of structural properties in which the user can assign specific material and mechanical properties to objects. Though these software packages are efficient and often easy to use, materials are not yet integral to the design process and only considered after modeling has been completed. These possibilities are on the contrary at the core of animation software mainly utilized in the movie industry. Complex simulations or explosions cannot be solely defined by geometry; material properties must be taken into account to compute collisions, etc. Pieces of software such as *Autodesk Maya*, *Cinema 4D*, *Houdini*, or *Blender* are among those allowing designers—including architects—to exploit the possibilities engendered by voxel space. Besides the immediate promise of integrating material considerations in the design process, voxel-based modeling could impact digital design more profoundly by moving it beyond the strict tenets of geometry. Tracing of this "expanded" notion of voxel will involve reflecting on different, "volumetric" spatial sensibilities to conceptualize matter as they first emerged in a number of disciplines, such as medical imaging, meteorology, and photography toward the end of the nineteenth century.

The geometrical definition of voxels as small cubical elements and that of a more continuous material distribution seem to be partially at odds with each other; while the former seeking immediate identification with geometrical form, the latter constantly postponing it. Undoubtedly the history of architecture has favored the first of these two interpretations, perhaps because less abstract and therefore directly applicable to design. This chapter aims at retracing their history to better grasp their design potential. Before we proceed in our survey, it is important to acknowledge the importance that algorithms have to interpret the "raw" numerical fields of voxel space. Algorithms in fact set the numerical values above which the original numbers of voxel space into forms. In other words, they determine an actual "threshold of visibility" above which the continuous space of voxels can be discretized. Voxel space can in fact be visualized directly through volume rendering or by extracting polygons from isosurfaces.[3] In the latter case the marching cubes algorithm (Lorensen and Cline 1987)—to only name the most popular of these methods—has been utilized since the late 1980s: such kind of algorithm scans the scalar field by subdividing it into small virtual cubes—consisting of eight points each—and eventually places a geometrical marker (a polygonal mesh variously placed within the cube analyzed) every time one or more numbers among those analyzed exceed a predetermined value. This process is not an obvious one, and several studies have been dedicated to the resolution of special cases (which normally occur at the corners of the isosurfaces). Eventually the individual meshes are merged into a single surface joining all points sharing certain values, forming an image we have become familiar with due to its widespread use in the field of medical imaging (in the case of Magnetic Resonance Imaging [MRI] scans, such meshes identify the shape of the brain or parts of it). This last example implies that the numbers processed by the marching cube algorithm can stand for a variety of properties: from pure algebraic entities to physical ones such as temperature or pressure. To reiterate the spatial shift introduced by modeling with voxels, numerical scalar fields are coordinate-independent values whose relation with a final form or surface directly results from the analysis carried out by an algorithm which arbitrarily singles out values out of an otherwise continuous space.

The data-gathering process to construct the scalar field in medical imaging is also indicative of the different sensibility toward space and matter instigated by voxel modeling. MRI scans send out magnetic beams resonating with the neutrons and protons in each nucleus which once hit immediately reorient along a single direction. As the beam moves on, they return to their original position and the scanner measures their relaxation time (how long it takes for each proton to return to its initial position), which is stored to form the actual scalar field. It is not coincidental that upon its invention MRI scans attracted more attention from chemists than medical students, as the numerical field recorded by the machine does not describe geometrical properties but rather purely material ones. In fact, we owe to chemist Paul Lauterbur (1929–2007) the invention of the first working computer algorithm to reconvert the single points of data output by the machine into a spatial image (Kevles 1997).

Cubelets

The idea that space is not an inert element but rather a filling substance within which things exist and move is not a novel idea. Both Aristotle and Newton theorized the presence of what in the nineteenth century increasingly became referred to as ether. Vitruvius also alludes to it in his illustration of the physiology of sight, where he justified optical corrections by claiming that light was not traveling through a void but through layers of air of different densities (Corso 1986). Toward the end of the eighteenth century Augustin-Jean Fresnel (1788–1827) spoke of "luminous ether" to theorize the movement of light from one media to another. Though his studies still implied matter to be homogeneous, allowing him to massively simplify his mathematics, they also announced the emergence of a sensibility no longer constrained by the domain of the visible and, by extension, by the laws of linear perspective. The "imperfections" of matter could therefore be explored and the art of the early twentieth century decisively moved in that direction. The idea that bodies—be that of humans or planets—were not moving in a void was a powerful realization brought about by the discoveries of Herztian waves, X-rays, etc. Artists such as Umberto Boccioni (1882–1916), Wassily Kandinsky (1866–1944), and Kazimir Malevich (1878–1935) all referred in their writings—albeit in very different ways—to an "electric theory of matter" as proposed by Sir Oliver Lodge (1851–1940) and Joseph Larmor (1857–1942) (Quoted in Henderson 2013, p. 19).[4] These thoughts were only the first signals of a different understanding of matter that was rapidly accelerated by the discovery of radioactivity—which revealed that matter was constantly changing its chemical status and emitting energy—and eventually by the general theory of relativity by Einstein.

All these examples, however, greatly preceded the official introduction of voxels in the architectural debate which would only happen in 1990 when William J. Mitchell in his *The Logic of Architecture* (1990) by actually crediting Lionel March (1934–) and Philip Steadman (1942–) to first introduce this concept in their *The Geometry of the Environment* (1974). March and Steadman however did not refer to it as voxel but rather as cubelets, a cubic unit utilized to subdivide architectural shapes. Confirming the importance of materials in thinking of space in such terms, they located the origin of the cubelet in a field directly concerned with studying matter: crystallography. The *Essai d'une Théorie sur la Structure des Crystaux, Appliquée à Plusieurs Genres de Substances Cristallisées* published by Abbe Hauy (1743–1822) in 1784 suggested the introduction of a *molécule intégrante* as the smallest geometrical unit to dissect and reconstruct the morphology of crystals. Compellingly, the study of minerals is far less concerned with spatial categories concerning architects such as interior/exterior, up/down, as space is conceived volumetrically, as a continuous entity, from the outset. Though not presenting all the characteristics of voxels yet, cubelets did exhibit some similarities as they also allowed to both construct and reconstruct any given shape with varying degrees of resolution; they were rational systems allowing to reduce and conform any geometrical anomaly to a simpler, more regular set of cubes. March and Steadman linked J. N. L. Durand's (1760–1834) *Leçons d'Architecture* (1819) to Abbe Hauy's investigations on form, as Durand also employed a classificatory method for building typologies based on cubical subdivision and its combinatorial possibilities (Durand 1819). This connection appears to us to be too broad as Durand's focused on formal composition rather than materiality and as such would better pertain to conversations on composition.

The notion of the *molecule integrante* migrated from crystallography to architecture to provide formal analysis with robust methods. It was no longer just a purely geometrical device to slice crystals with; cubelets had also acquired a less visible, but more organizational quality affording a new categorization of shapes regardless of their morphology and irregularities. An example of this transformation is the writings of Eugène Viollet-Le-Duc (1814–79)—who was trained both as an architect and geologist—in which architectural form can be seen as an instantiation of *a priori* principle constantly governing the emergence of form and its growth (Viollet-Le-Duc 1866). Such principles could not be detected and described without a rational, geometrical language to reveal the deeper logic of apparently formless shapes. It is possible to trace in the growing importance of structural categorization the early signs of structural thinking which would find a decisive contribution in Sir D'Arcy-Thompson's (1860–1948) morphogenetic ideas published in *On Growth and Form* (1917) which, in turn, would have a deep and long-standing influence on contemporary digital architects.

March and Steadman finally pinpointed the most decisive contribution to integrate cubelets and design methods in the work of Albert Farwell Bemis

(1870–1936). His hefty *The Evolving House* (1934–36)—written with structural engineer John Burchard—consisted of three volumes aligning the formal logic of the cubelets with the possibilities offered by industrialization and its rational paradigms. The convergence of these two trends "naturally" produced a design manual for prefabricated housing units to which Bemis' third and last volume was entirely dedicated. The formal mechanism conflating these two domains was a three-dimensional lattice both providing a modular system to manage complexity during the design process—a sort of data compression mechanism—and to streamline the translation from conception design to construction. The third installment of *The Evolving House*—compellingly subtitled "The Rational House"—reinforced the focus on the notion of voxel as a reductive and "visible" mechanism to rationalize forms. Bemis was explicit in his intentions when he stated that "I have approached [it] with the distinct preconceived idea that the chief factor of modern housing is physical structure. A new conception of structure of our modern houses is needed, better adapted not only to the social conditions of our day but also to modern means of production: factories, machinery, technology, and research" (Bemis and Burchard 1936, p. viii). This particular aspect would be only be strengthened in March and Steadman's discussion consolidating the understanding of voxels as directly geometrical elements. One of the most interesting, and in many ways, visionary elements of Bemis' plan was to focus not on physical qualities of the design—for example, materials, etc.—but rather on the design process itself. It was this very element that in Bemis' mind needed urgent renewal; as such the "theory of cubical design" (p. 92) was not intended to turn houses into stacks of small cubes, but rather to provide an abstract three-dimensional grid coordinating successive design stages and manufacturing processes. In other words, it was the design media—what in the context of this study we refer to as CAD—that must have been reconceptualized to supply an effective, pragmatic link to the transformations going on in other societal sectors (i.e., industrialization). The formal result was a form of proto-associative design in which any variation of the dimensions of the smallest modular elements has a rippling effect on the whole building.

Despite the strong emphasis on rationalization and industrial production (the chapter on design is relegated to Chapter 7 in the second part of the book), Bemis' design approach did resonate with the notion of voxel, as it was conducive to a more continuous and volumetric mode to conceptualize and represent space.

To illustrate his design principles Bemis provided three successive diagrams (Fig. 8.1). The first simply consisted of a box made up of many individual little cubes (i.e., cubelets). This was the virtual volume of the house into which the

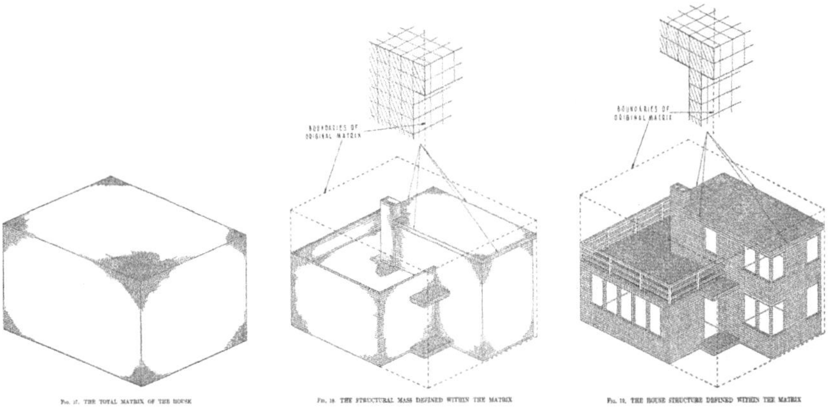

Figure 8.1 Albert Farwell Bemis, The Evolving House, Vol.3 (1936). Successive diagrams showing how the design of a house can be imagined to take place "within a total matrix of cubes" to be delineate by the designer through a process of removal of "unnecessary" cubes.

designer would carve—as the second and third diagrams exemplify—to obtain the desired design. Besides ensuring to be perfectly modular and therefore mass-producible, these diagrams also evidenced a volumetric approach to design. The whole of the house was given from the outset, as virtual volume to manipulate and give attributes to. The designer only needed to subtract the unnecessary parts for openings and specify the desired finishing. Rather than designing by aggregating individual parts to one another, cubelet—or proto-voxels—allowed Bemis to conceive of space volumetrically.

Despite the pragmatic bias, Bemis' work showed consistency between tools and ambitions. If the architects of the modern movement had suggested dynamism and fluidity through lines—translated into columns—and planes—be it those of the floor slabs, internal partitions, or façades; volumetric design called for a representational device able to carry the design intentions and coherently relate individual parts of the house to the whole. The cubelet did that.

The architectural merits of these experiments were never fully exploited, perhaps leaving a rather wide gap between the techniques developed and the resulting design. To find an architectural exploration of volumetric design through components we would have to look at some of the production of F. L. Wright (1867–1959) in the 1920s. These projects take some of the ideas proposed by Bemis to resolve them with far greater elegance and intricacy. Besides his colossal unbuilt *Imperial Hotel* in Tokyo (1919–23), in two occasions Wright managed to actually build projects developed around the articulation of a single volumetric element: *Millard House* (La Miniatura) in Pasadena (1923) and *Westhope* (1929) for Richard Lloyd Jones (Wright's cousin). These designs shared the use of the so-called textile block as generative geometry (respectively

4 and 20 inches in size). The block could be compared to the cubelet, which was here conceived not only as a proportioning system for the overall design but also as an ornamental and technological one (yet, not structural ones as both houses employ concrete frames). The addition of ornamental patterns to the block was important not only for their aesthetic effect, but also because they began to reveal the spatial potentials unleashed by conceiving space and structure through a discretized language, a preoccupation still shared by contemporary digital designers.

Leonardo and Laura Mosso: *Architettura programmata*

If Bemis can be credited as the first architect to introduce a proto-voxel tool in architecture, it will only be in the second part of the twentieth century that these ideas begin to deeply and systematically impact on architecture both in terms of forms afforded and design processes. Starting from the 1960s the notion of voxels as a discrete architectural component would provide the opportunity to link up with other emerging fields of research, such as linguistic studies, prefabrication, and, of course, digital computation. The first of the two examples we will discuss takes us to Italy whose architectural production at the time has been rarely considered in relation to computation. The landscape of the 1960s was in fact dominated, on the one hand, by La Tendenza, with its neo-rationalist take on the typological studies and structuralism—which found in Aldo Rossi (1931–97) its most distinctive designer and in Manfredo Tafuri (1935–94) its polemicist—or, on the other, by the experimental approach of the radical architects such as Archizoom, Superstudio, and Gianni Pettena (1940–) who aimed at questioning the very basis of the architectural production and its role in society. Between these two factions Leonardo Mosso (1926–) stood out for his original take on language and design. Born in the Italian Northwest, in 1955 Mosso won a scholarship to study in Finland and work in Alvar Aalto's studio until 1958. Upon returning to Italy and becoming Aalto's Italian associate working with Finnish Maestro on both commissions and exhibitions, Mosso began to develop his distinctive approach to design through both commissioned projects and academic research. Since his initial projects such as *Benedetto Croce Library* in Pollone (1960) and the *Chapel for the Mass of the Artist* in Turin (1961–63) it was evident his interest in "discretized" architecture composed of small, finite elements of simple morphology which could join in a variety of configurations giving rise to complex spatial organizations (Chiorino 2010). Structure was here understood both in operational terms as physical elements able to withstand loads and form enclosures and in regulating linguistic principles providing hierarchy and syntax between elements. The design for the small chapel—a subterranean religious space consisting of only one congregational hall which is no longer extant—was of rare elegance and designed through the modulation of a single morphology: a 5 × 5 centimeters wooden section. The individual elements were then layered onto each other at 90-degree angle thickening toward the opposite corners of the chapel to add further drama to the overall spatial experience. Gio Ponti unreservedly praised the spatial qualities of this design without dedicating equal attention to the logic of the process followed, which has never been adequately analyzed (Ponti 1964). Rather than thinking of it as a composition of heterogeneous elements, the chapel was designed in a more continuous fashion by generating spatial differentiation through varying the distribution of a single piece of wood. Mosso (1989) asked the viewer to imagine it made up of a single wood beam of the length of 8 kilometers cut into small pieces and eventually joined with exposed nails. This process extended to every component, including furniture resulting in a space whose complexity and elegance—somehow reminiscent of Japanese architecture—was enhanced by the artificial light filtering through the wooden members (Tentori 1963). In the words of its author this was the "first example of 'programmed architecture' organised serially, three-dimensionally, and, potentially, self-manageable by the users" (Mosso 1989, ibid.).

The use of proto-voxel, discretized components deliberately echoed the process followed in the construction of language as emerging from determining the basic symbols first—letters—and then the rules governing their aggregation—grammar. This analogy was extremely productive for Leonardo and Laura Mosso (now working together) who, since the very beginning of the 1960s, had been dedicating his academic research to the development of a "theory of structural design" weaving relations between phonology, structuralism, and architecture. This research resulted in the development of elementary structures, held together by universal joints able to be appropriated by end users who could add to, make alterations, or even remove them. It was their organizational logic based on elemental geometrical forms to give a new, expanded meaning to Bemis' cubelets. The search for a volumetric, programmable language for architecture was here seen as part of larger social and cultural project no longer simply related to industrialization and efficiency, but rather aimed at transferring power from the hands of the architect to those of the users. Key to developing such "open" alphabet was the resolution of the node aggregating the individual elements. Mosso dedicated a large part of his research to this issue designing first mobile and then elastic, universal (omnidirectional) joints tested with students through 1:1 prototypes. The social ambition of the work, however, demanded of structural joints to provide far more than simple structural integrity; they should have been able to encourage and absorb change over time. Mosso could no longer interpret the joint as the rigid, static element of the construction, the point in which dynamism stopped. In his architecture the node must have rather acted as an "enabler" of all its future transformations. The individual members were organized so as to rotate outward from the center of the node in 90-degree steps. This method—which also reminds of the work of Konrad Wachsmann (1901–80)—opened the joint up to multiple configurations without ever mixing different materials or structural logics. The effects of this approach to space were evident in both experimental designs, namely, the entry for the competition the Plateau Beauburg (1971)—emblematically titled *Commune for Culture*—and the completed *Villa Broglia* in Cossila Biellese (1967–72), whose overall massing and articulation through cubical modules reminds of F. L. Wright's experiments in the 1920s (Baccaglioni, Del Canto, and Mosso 1981).

However, the couple's research introduced new, profoundly different elements to the notion of cubelet. First, the formal language developed was a product of the very cultural context in which their ideas formed. Structuralism, whose impact on Italian culture had been steadily growing throughout the 1950s and 1960s, brought a deeper understanding of linguistic analysis. Mosso's structures were basic, rational elements deliberately designed so as to have no *a priori* meaning; their lack of expressivity was one of the features guaranteeing of their combinatorial isomorphism. Their neutrality determined Mosso's preference not only for simple geometries but also for conceiving the joint as a direct and universal device engendering almost infinite numbers of permutations. Mosso—who at this point in his career shared all his activities his wife Laura—compared the role of the architect to that of the linguist whose work was to foreground the mechanisms of a language rather than describing all the ways in which it could be used. Both architects and linguists worked in "service of" a language that the final users would develop by using it and taking it in yet unforeseen directions; the architect only provided the individual signs and grammar but not a preconceived, overall form (Mosso 1970). The strict logic on which this discretized architectural language rested on naturally drew them to computers to study the delicate balance between control and indeterminacy.

Mosso, like Bemis, saw industrial production as the key ingredient to implement his ideas which he conceives as cultural and political instruments for change. The idea of an architecture developing from basic elements was conceived as a vehicle for self-determination, for emancipation in which the construction of communities was not mediated by the architect but directly controlled by its inhabitants. The Mosso's called it "a general theory of non-authoritarian design" alluding to the necessity for architecture to provide the structure for mankind's interior and exterior realization (Baccaglioni, Del Canto, and Mosso 1981, p. 83). In developing his research, Mosso started with his wife Laura, Sandro De Alexandris (fine arts), Enore Zaffiri (electronic music), and Arrigo Lora Totino (concrete poetry) the "Centre for the Studies of Informational Aesthetic" in 1964 as well as began contributing to *Nuova Ecologia* (New Ecology), a magazine in which structuralism, politics, and environmental awareness conflated.

Finally, in the 1960s the computer was introduced to manage the complex range of options involved in the design, construction, and management of "structures with universal joints." Working with Piero Sergio Rossato and Arcangelo Compostella on a Univac 1108 provided by Politecnico of Milan the team—in a manner that was perhaps already implicit in Bemis' work—both scripted computer programs to control the coordination between design and prefabrication[5] and simulated possible pattern of use of the future community that will inhabit his architectures. From 1968, Mosso worked on a theoretical model for a "programmed and self-managed city-territory": the physical model illustrating the idea is composed of 10,000 blocks of either wood or Plexiglas extruded at different lengths (Fig. 8.2). The size of each of these slim columns

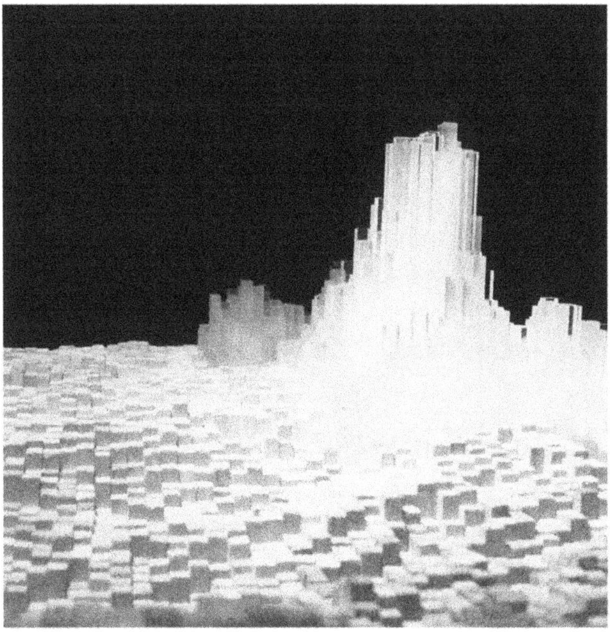

Figure 8.2 Leonardo Mosso and Laura Castagno-Mosso. Model of the La Cittá Programmata (Programmed City) (1968-9). © Leonardo Mosso and Laura Castagno-Mosso.

changed over time depending on the needs and desires of its inhabitants. Each element was imagined to be made up of stacks of voxels, individual cubes of varying size and density. As for cybernetic systems, the computer's role was to manage the relation between the different streams of information such as the user's feedback and the structural and material grammar of the architecture in order to strike a balance between stability and change. The result was an "automatic, global design model for self-determination of the community" represented through a series of computational simulations in which the growth and distribution of voxels occurred according to statistical and random rules (Mosso 1971).[6] The strong link between politics and computation should not be confined to historical studies, but rather act as a powerful reminder that these two disciplines are not mutually exclusive and that the use of computation in the design process can be tasked with radical social and political ideas.

By designing through voxels, that is, through elastic modules whose density, organization, and rhythm could greatly vary, the architectures promoted by Mosso abandoned definitive spatial classifications, to embrace a more open, porous, distributed model of inhabitation. In presenting his work to the 1978 Venice Architecture Biennale, Mosso did not hesitate to describe his research as pursuing a "non-object-based architecture" (Mosso 1978). The constant reference to "Programmed" architecture alluded to both the possibility to script computer programs to manage the structural growth of his architectures and the vast range of experiments—including Nanni Balestrini's poems discussed in the chapter on randomness—that were eventually collated by Umberto Eco in 1962 in the *Arte Programmata* exhibition promoted by Italian computer manufacturer Olivetti. In anticipating the creative process of *Arte Programmata*, Eco 1961 had already pointed out how the combination of precise initial rules subjected to aleatory processes would have challenged the notion of product by favoring that of process: Mosso's work had individuated in the use of voxel-based, discretized architectural language the spatial element able to translate these cultural concerns into architecture.

SEEK: Voxels and randomness

Cubical elements also made an appearance in the work of *The Architecture Machine* group led by Nicholas Negroponte (1943–) at the MIT in Boston. Ten-foot cubes were first use in the 1967 as modular elements in an experimental piece of software called *URBAN 5*. The software was part of a long-term project by the group to apply cybernetics ideas about human/machine dialogue to computer-aided tools. Developed in the late 1960s, *URBAN 5* was specifically intended to assist urban designers by not only eliminating any language barrier between computers and users, but also feeding the user back with important information about the steps taken or about to be taken (Negroponte 1970, pp. 70–93). Negroponte was quick to point out that the large cubes used to sculpt buildings were only rough abstractions and in no way could be understood as a sufficiently articulate palette of forms to match designers' ambitions. Perhaps as a result of the technical limitations presented by 1960s' computers, Negroponte's team also affirmed that one of the principles of their project was that "urban design is on based on physical form" (1970, p. 71), a statement whose implications exceeded that of the technology of the time. Cubical forms also feature in a successive project by the group in which they stood in for generic building blocks. *SEEK*—presented at the exhibition *Software* held at The Jewish Museum in New York in 1970—sought to draw a potential parallel between computational systems and social ones.[7] The installation consisted of a series of cubical structures arranged inside a large glass container in which gerbils moved freely. Any disruption caused by the erratic actions of the animals was regularly scanned by a digital eye which in turn triggered the intervention of a robotic arm. If the block had been dragged by the gerbils within a given distance from their original location, the robotic arm would place it back; otherwise it would simply realign it with the grid, de facto "accepting" the alterations caused by the gerbils. Though being based on cubic geometries, *SEEK* was an exercise in meta-design, as it avoided issues of scale and material to display the potential of infinitely reconfigurable environment. This short excursion in application of cubical elements to design systems ends with the realization of the *Universal Constructor* by Unit 11 students at the Architectural Association in London in 1990 under the guidance of John and Julia Frazer. This project should be seen as the culmination of a line of research that the Frazers had been pursuing since the 1970s. In this outstanding project cubes are augmented by integrated circuits turning this "voxelised" architecture into a sentient, dynamic configuration.[8]

Maxels: Or the geometrical deferral

Lewis Fry Richardson: Climatic continuity

An unexpected transition point between the two notions of voxels posited at the beginning of this chapter came from the germinal field of climatic studies. By examining the work of Lewis Fry Richardson (1881–1953) we begin to trace the development of voxels no longer as mere formal devices—represented by small cubes—but rather as representational tools to approximate and conceptualize material continuity. The geometrical deferral alluded to in the title of this section encapsulates a series of experiments in which geometry was not used to directly give rise to form but rather it was employed as a means to survey forms which had been generated according to different principles. It is therefore not coincidental that these transformations could be first observed in the field of climatic studies at the beginning of the twentieth century. Not only is climate a complex system resulting from multiple variables unfolding over long periods of time, but it is also an abstraction, more precisely the result of statistical calculations averaging empirical data. As such it lends itself well to computational studies, as they too are abstractions borne out of logical (algebraic/semantic) constructs. The protagonist of this development was the English mathematician Lewis Fry Richardson who completed the first numerical—based on data—weather prediction in 1922. Strictly speaking Richardson's was not an actual weather prediction, though. Due to the scarcity and imprecision of respectively empirical data and instrumentation available, the idea of accurate weather forecasting was simply impossible. However, this remained a key piece in the history of weather prediction because of the methods it employed and its volumetric approach.

In order to have a sound set of criteria to test its experiment, Richardson decided to work with a historical weather dataset. He based his calculations on "International Balloon Day," which had taken place in the skies over Germany and Austria in 1910. On the day an exceptionally high quantity (for the time) and range of data had been recorded: the presence of balloons in the atmosphere provided "three-dimensional" recordings of climatic data in the atmosphere—a very rare occurrence at the time. Although the readings were still quite sparse, Richardson proceeded with his idea to "voxelise" the entire area considered: a rhomboid shape covering Germany and parts of Austria was divided into regular cells by overlaying a grid coinciding with latitude and longitude lines. Each of the resulting skewed rectangles measured about 200 kilometers in size spanning between meridians and parallels. The grid was then multiplied vertically four times—to an overall height of approximately 12 kilometers—to obtain 90 rectangular volumes, de facto subdividing a continuous phenomenon such as the weather into discrete cells (Fig. 8.3). The mathematics of this system directly evolved from Vilhelm Bjerknes (1862–1951) whose seven equations had been used to describe the behavior of the basic variables of weather: pressure, density, temperature, water vapor, and velocity in three dimensions. In order to reduce complexity, Richardson abandoned differential equations able to account for temporal transformations based on derivatives, in favor of finite-difference methods in which changes in the variables are represented by finite numbers. If this decision might have caused a massive reduction of the complexity of the phenomenon

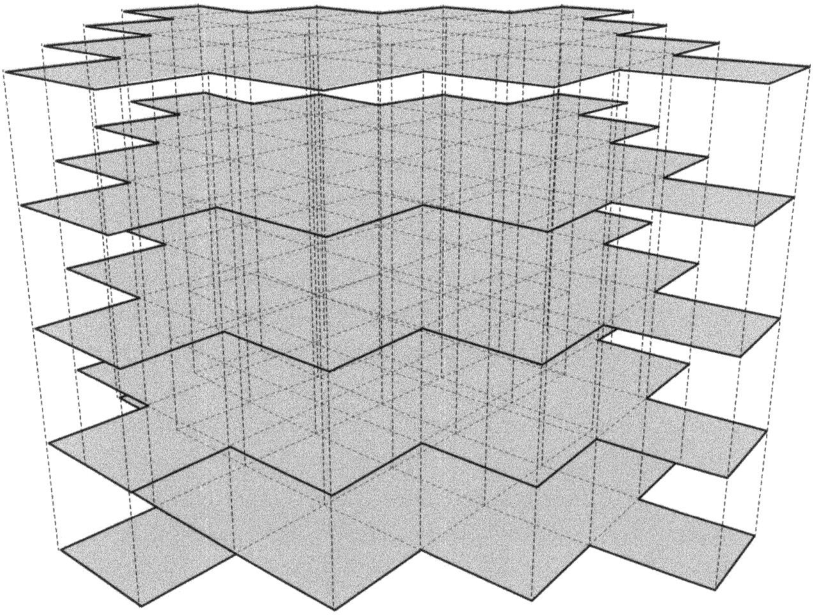

Figure 8.3 Diagram describing Richardson's conceptual model to "voxelise" of the skyes over Europe to complete his numerical weather prediction. Illustration by the author.

observed and consequent mistakes, Richardson compensated it by increasing the number of variables to compute as many elements as possible, such as the curvature of the earth, etc. This way of operating struck the best possible balance between constructing a precise model and what was conceivably computable by humans. Richardson singlehandedly took up the task to re-calculate the weather over a period of six hours for two locations within the voxel space laid out. What the system gained in simplicity it lost in precision: by fixing the actual fluctuation of the variables meant to proceed by averaging out values with the consequent risk of overlooking important changes in the dataset. However, weather systems are inherently nonlinear, and sudden, unpredictable changes of their behaviors can be induced by small variations in the initial conditions governing them. To further simplify the calculations, Richardson assumed the seven variables to be constant and data was extracted by interpolation from empirical readings in order to obtain a more evenly distributed grid of values to start from. Each cell was calculated independently by using Bjerknes' equations and the results were then carried over to the neighboring cell in which the same procedure was reapplied. It took Richardson about two weeks to complete his weather prediction, which, not surprisingly, turned out to be completely wrong. However, the deficiencies of this method were not in the process followed but rather in poor quality of the input empirical data and in the approximations of the mathematical model. Unfortunately, the apparent failure of this experiment convinced researchers to overlook numerical methods to move their attention to different mathematical models to study climate; the development of modern computers made complex calculations faster and more precise, which in turn allowed to rediscover Richardson's methods (Nebeker 1995).

Despite the disappointing results, Richardson made two further contributions of relevance in our discussion. The first one referred to his idea of a Forecast-Factory, a sort of human computer whose importance links it up with the development of simulation models discussed in "Random" chapter. While singlehandedly completing his calculations, Richardson had the idea of building a large space in which people could have been arrayed to replicate the spatial organization of his numerical method. He calculated that about 64,000 people could have sat in a large spherical hall representing the planet, each representing—so to speak—one voxel. Each person would have been given a form with twenty-three step-by-step equations to compute—practically a computer program formed by sequential instructions—through which to calculate the basic climatic variables in each cell and then pass them on to the adjacent one.

> Imagine a large hall like a theater, except that the circles and galleries go right round through the space usually occupied by the stage. The walls of this chamber are painted to form a map of the globe. The ceiling represents the North Polar regions, England is in the gallery, the tropics in the upper circle, Australia on the dress circle, and the Antarctic in the pit. A myriad of computers are at work upon the weather of the part of the map where each sits, but each region is coordinated by an official of higher rank. Numerous little "night signs" display the instantaneous values so that neighboring computers can read them. Each number is thus displayed in three adjacent zones so as to maintain communication to the North and South on the map. From the floor of the pit a tall pillar rises to half the height of the hall. It carries a large pulpit on its top. In this sits the man in charge of the whole theater; he is surrounded by several assistants and messengers. One of the duties is to maintain a uniform speed of progress in all parts of the globe. In this respect he is like the conductor of an orchestra in which the instruments are slide-rules and calculating machines. But instead of waving a baton he turns a beam of rosy light upon any region that is running ahead of the rest, and a beam of light upon those who are behindhand.
>
> Four senior clerks in the central pulpit are collecting the future weather as fast as it is being computed, and dispatching it by pneumatic carrier to a quiet room. There it will be coded and telephoned to the radio transmitting station. Messengers carry piles of used computing forms down to a storehouse in the cellar.

> In a neighboring building there is a research department, where they invent improvements. But there is much experimenting on a small scale before any change is made in the complex routine of the computing theater. In a basement an enthusiast is observing the eddies in the liquid lining of a huge spinning bowl, but so far the arithmetic proves the better way. In another building are all the usual financial, correspondence, and administrative offices. Outside are playing fields, houses, mountains, and lakes, for it was thought that those who compute the weather should breathe of it freely (Richardson 1922, quoted in Edwards 2010, pp. 94–95).

In his detailed description, Richardson is once again affirming the role of architecture as a computational device as extensively explored in the "Database" chapter, but he is also describing what is today known as finite-element method (FEM) for analysis. This method—which could be understood as his second major contribution to computational culture—is largely employed in design and particularly in structural analysis where it provides numerical techniques approximating the behavior of a system within a boundary—be it identified by values or geometrical constraints. The process usually involves the division of the whole domains into a series of smaller subdomains which are analyzed through a set of given equations; finally, they are recombined into a final matric resulting into the final, global forecast. FEM would only become an established model for design with the introduction of modern computers. It is once again the "inhuman" quality of computation Leibniz had already spoke of some three centuries earlier to resurface here. Richardson's was not conceptually incorrect, but simply lacked empirically measured data and the tools to compute very large numbers of equations. Despite its imprecise results, Richardson's model already proposed a subdivision pattern based on a three-dimensional geometry which presented some definite advantages, such as an accurate representation of complex geometries, the inclusion of dissimilar material properties, and the ability to capture of local effects bridging the gap between the two genealogies of the voxel.

X-rays: Apprehending the invisible

The examples we have analyzed so far fundamentally understood voxels as small, often cubical geometrical elements. However, the mathematical, and consequently digital, definition of voxels far exceeds that of mere geometrical entities to incorporate additional properties, including material ones. These additional properties are in many ways the most original contribution of voxels to the definition and representation of space which digital designers and architects have somehow often adopted without fully grasping its theoretical implications. The tradition we have been tracing utilized geometry to define, to structure matter both in literal and abstract terms; geometry operated as a sifting mechanism to reduce any anomaly or formal complexity. A voxel-based mapping of space, however, inverts this procedure: material qualities are recorded first with varying degrees of precision and resolution to be successively processed by some formal system in the form of an algorithm. In other words, geometrical attribution is deferred for as long as possible. This approach to matter particularly suits complex, "formless" situations such as those constantly encountered by geologists and meteorologists in whose fields in fact proto-voxel thinking first emerged.

The development and potential nested in representing space through voxels cannot be fully appreciated if discussed in isolation from the very machines that allowed its emergence as Lorraine Daston and Peter Galison (2010) so convincingly demonstrated how we see is also what we see. The fundamental technological shift to propel this "non-geometrical" thinking coincided with the discovery of X-rays' properties and wireless communication. X-rays in particular gave an unprecedented impetus to research and experimentation within the realm of the invisible. Since its discovery by Wilhelm Conrad Röntgen (1845–1923) in December 1895, X-rays were an immediate success both as a medical discovery and as a social phenomenon. It is this latter aspect that we would like to dwell on, as not only scientists but also artists were attracted and employed it for all the more diverse usages. This new way of seeing impacted on societal costumes such as individual privacy as it promised a direct access to the naked body. In London special X-ray-proof underwear was advertised, whereas French police was first to apply X-rays—more precisely the popular and portable fluoroscope—in public spaces by screening passengers at the Gare du Nord in Paris inaugurating what is now part of the common experience of going through major transportation hubs (Kevles 1997, pp. 27–44).

In 1920 Louis Lumière—who with his brother Auguste had already projected the first modern movie, coincidentally also in 1895—finally brought his experiments on new technologies for cinematography to a conclusion by completing his *Photo-stereo-synthesis*. Moved by the desire to eliminate lenticular distortion—and consequently perspectival alterations—on moving images, Lumière's device was a rather simple photographic camera in which both the distance between and the angle formed by the lens and photographic plate were kept constant. The lens was set so as to have a very limited depth of field so that only a limited region of the subject photographed was in focus while all remaining areas were blurred. Because of the particular settings, the area in focus happened to be at approximately at the same distance from the lens, therefore virtually cutting a slice through the object photographed. The fixed relation between lens and plate finally allowed the operator to move the camera around the target object to bring other areas of the subject into focus, or, in other words, keep slicing it. By methodically moving the contraption by regular intervals an object—regardless of its geometry—could be sliced with acceptable precision. Once developed, the individual images were laminated onto plastic blocks whose thickness matched that the length of each stepped movement of the *Photo-stereo-synthesis*, thus returning a three-dimensional sculpture out of 2D-images. Although Lumière quickly realized that such a process was too complicated to be able to shoot a whole movie with it, the potential provided by this technology would have a lasting impact, albeit in a different field. Despite using lenses, the *Photo-stereo-synthesis* was not recoding pictorial images—the look of the object—rather it was recording the object itself; the shallow depth of field produces minimal perspectival distortion turning the final photographs into orthographic drawings rather than traditional images (Cartwright and Goldfarb 1992). The outcome of the process was a precise, volumetric representation of a subject constructed out of flat images without any use of geometrical constructions. The similarities with *Photosculpture* are inevitable to draw: both technologies attempted to eliminate lenticular deformations to turn photography into a more objective, almost scientific instrument. However, Lumière's machine went much further as it operated outside the realm of perspectival space to enter a different kind of spatial representation, one that was no longer attempting to emulate human sight. Such an image was no longer interesting for its visual appeal, rather for its ability to foreclose new material dimensions. It was a machinic image as its emergence was inextricably linked to the very technology generating it. Throughout the twentieth century we would witness an increase in the construction of machines which will improve their ability to record even more abstract images of reality, consequently increasing the role of additional machines to decode the initial, abstract dataset into visual artifacts. In time such machines would coincide with computers, whose algorithms would actively shape how data is encoded implicitly contributing to the design of the final image.

All the ingredients for the development of a comprehensive, working technology to map space through voxels were already present in the two inventions discussed, so much so that the merits of the successive contributions were to improve *Photo-stereo-synthesis* by adding complementary technologies. It is still unclear who should be credited for the idea of combining Lumière's and Röntgen's apparatuses, as a number of very similar claims were made both in

Europe and in the United States around the same time (Kevles 1997, pp. 108–10). Nevertheless, each inventor did manage to patent various technologies, but did not manage to construct any working prototype. In 1930 Alessandro Vallebona (1899–1987) finally completed this long project by building a machine that could take X-ray photographs—so to speak—through the human body. He called his invention stratigraphy and compared the images of the body produced by his instrument to that of a stack of paper sheets each corresponding to one photographic section taken through a body.

If Lumière had opened the doors to the possibility of reproducing volumetric figures, Vallebona's machine gave access to the interior of the body, to its invisible organs which could now be seen in action. The space of the human body was not represented through geometry as in Dürer's drawings, for instance: no proportions, or elemental figures to reduce it to, rather the body was expressed through its materiality by simply recording its varying densities organized through gradients or sharp changes in consistency. These early experiments would constitute the fundamental steps toward tomography first, in the 1950s, and then computer tomography (CT) in which algorithms would translate the data field produced by machines into images. The introduction of MRI would eventually remove the last visual element of the process; photography would in fact be replaced by magnets able to trigger protons to realign. MRI scanners entirely bypassed geometrical description as they directly targeted material properties, whose abstracted material qualities were inaccessible to human senses and could only be made visible through algorithmic translation. Computation therefore not only was essential to completing this process, but also became one of the key variables affecting what is visible in the final visual outcome, a proper design tool affecting what could be seen. The definition of voxels as introduced at the beginning of the chapter finds in these experiments a renewed meaning allowing to move away from strict geometries to venture into the complex nature of matter. At this point our journey moves back to the creative disciplines to examine how it impacted on artistic and architectural practices.

Form without geometry

Artists too were deeply influenced by the idea that matter could have been understood as a continuum composed by both visible and invisible substances, prompting Lord Balfour to imagine the universe as a completely saturated with ether. (Balfour 1904, p. 7). Consequently the supremacy of retinal perception was questioned and with it the notion of object as finite element with clear boundaries. New types of mathematics began to appear from Henri Poincaré's (1854–1912) non-Euclidian topologies—which hypothesized that objects deformed when subjected to transformations—to the general theory of relativity which Albert Einstein (1879–1955) published in 1915.

Marcel Duchamp, Pablo Picasso, and Kazimir Malevich—to name a few—all showed varying degrees of interest in scientific discoveries, which—with the exception of Duchamp—were explored through bi-dimensional paintings. Umberto Boccioni's (1882–1916) works particularly resonate with the discussion on matter and technology we have analyzed so far. His iconic *Unique Forms of Continuity in Space* (1913) was anticipated by the *Technical Manifesto of Futurist Painting* (1910) in which he rhetorically asked "Who can still believe in the opacity of bodies . . . when our sharpened and multiplied sensibility allows us to perceive the obscure disclosures of mediumistic phenomena? Why should we continue to create without taking into account our perceptive powers which can give results analogous to those of X-rays?" (Boccioni, quoted in Henderson 2013, pp. 53–54). Boccioni's interest in continuity prompted him to dissolve any distinction between the description of the figure represented and the "exterior" space in which this was moving. As stated in his manifesto and embodied in his sculptures, such relation was invisible but apprehensible through mathematics, as the movement of a body in space should be understood as the intersection between two different types of matter—that of the body and that of the ether in which it moves. Boccioni called his vision "physical transcendentalism" in which form indexically carried the traces of its own movement and deformation in space (not unlike the principles of non-Euclidean geometry developed around the same time in mathematics). The result was a plastic fluidity with distinct volumetric qualities unknown to the cubists. Besides the lasting impact that Henry Bergson's (1859–1941) ideas had on the Italian artist upon his arrival in Paris in 1911, more central in this narrative was his renewed relation between form and matter which impacted on representational and creative methods. Grounded on relatively accurate readings of the mathematical discoveries of the late eighteenth century, Boccioni's sculptures began to suggest a spatiality akin to the one promised by voxels: liberated from geometrical reduction, form was conceived as an interaction between matter and forces. Where cubism proposed fragmented, angular shapes by concentrating on perception, Boccioni morphed fluent forms under material tension. In a letter to Severini, Ugo Giannattasio (1888–1958) even managed to summarize such a relation into a mathematical formula: Object | 3 dimensions + weight + expansion > resistance | absolute value = fourth dimension (Giannatassio quoted in Henderson (1913, i)). No reference to geometry is made.

Finally, a brief mention to the parallel developments in the field of theater helps us to better contextualize the emergence of a different spatial sensibility. Theater is an artistic discipline that naturally conflates different artistic fields, including architecture which forms its environment. Particularly we refer to the experiment carried out by Oskar Schlemmer (1888–1943) at the Bauhaus in which actors' costumes were equipped with all sorts of prosthetics, including long metal sticks that allowed them to magnify their actions and extend the effects of body's movements onto the space of the scene. It is not a coincidence that theater will play a central role in the architectural production of the architect who more than anybody else began to grasp and translate the potential of material continuity in design: Frederick Kiesler.

Kiesler: Maxels and architecture

It is rather arduous to find architectural examples in which the influence of proto-voxel spatiality can be detected. The notion of continuity that so radically changed fine arts proved difficult to scale up to inhabitable volumes. Boccioni spoke of his sculptures as spiral architectures but it would only be with Frederick John Kiesler (1890–1965) that we will encounter a comprehensive attempt to translate these ideas into spatial design. The appreciation of Kiesler's work can only be fully grasped if we move beyond mere formal analysis of his oeuvre to embrace the full ecology of ideas, technologies, and techniques he conjured, developed, and seldom completed to develop a continuous, volumetric spatial experience resonating with the broader ideas elicited by voxels. The fascination for Kiesler's work is a recurrent feature in the history of architecture since its first international successes in the 1920s. The nature of his architectural production—Philip Johnson famously described him as "the greatest non-building architect of our times"—is often quickly labeled as belonging to the realm of conceptual design consisting of a series of ideas on space and architecture rather than a traditional series of blueprints that could be built. This approach to design is traceable in many of Kiesler's projects culminating in his best-known project: *The Endless House*, a lifelong endeavor constantly redrawn and developed, which never materialized beyond a series of physical models. It is in this context that we can re-engage with his work and scrutinize it from the vantage point of voxel modeling.

Kiesler's career started in Vienna but quickly acquired an international status. After a short period in Paris—in which he got to know De Stijl ideas thorough his close relationship with Theo van Doesburg—he moved to New York where he spent the rest of his life. Here too, the exchange with the artistic community was intense: besides forming a close friendship with Marcel Duchamp—with whom he also shared an apartment—it was Peggy Guggenheim who eventually commissioned him for his crucial design for *The Art of Century* (1942), a gallery space to house her recently acquired works of art. Since the Viennese years, Kiesler had been attracted by theater design, a building type that he would constantly revisit throughout his career. As in the research carried out by Schlemmer at the Bauhaus, Kiesler too saw in stage design the possibility, if not the necessity, to merge space, actors, and spectators as well as to provide highly dynamic settings able to adapt to the movement of actors and the temporal dimension of the performance.

In projects such as the *Endless Theatre* (Paris, 1925), the *Film Guild Cinema* (New York, 1929), or *The Space House* (New York, 1933) Kiesler never hesitated to deploy the most advanced building technology of his time to make his architectures as dynamic as possible. Each design exhibited a range of components—rubber curtains, dynamic lighting, adjustable components, etc.—engendering constant manipulations of spatial qualities by the users. Kiesler never made use of computers in his work (he died in 1965), probably not for lack of interest or openness to experimentation but simply because computation at the time was an extremely complex business which still largely belonged to military and scientific milieus where it had first emerged. We can nevertheless speculate that the contemporary world of embedded sensors and ubiquitous computing would have suited his ideas allowing him to explore further notions of continuity. Though his interest in technology was one of the consistent features of his work, it would be unfair to simply consider his projects as examples of techno-fetishism, as attempts to parade the wonders of modernity; they were, and still are, radical exercises to create a continuous spatial experience in which space, bodies, and architecture endlessly interacted. Space was indeed the protagonist of Kiesler's work; no longer considered as an "inert" substance, but rather as an active medium, a "saturated" volume modulating the inner psychological complexity of individuals and the architectural elements choreographing their existence. His interest in space—the invisible matter that architectural elements frame and alter—was well documented since his European years. Early experiments on *Vision Machines*—small devices aimed at altering spatial perception—later on influenced his designs for exhibitions, a decisive exercise in the development of his spatial language. *The Art of Century* provided an opportunity to reconceive space to enhance rather than limit the interaction between object displayed and visitors. The final layout consisted of thematically different galleries housing Miss Guggenheim's recently acquired collection of European art. All walls were removed in favor of a continuous, volumetric experience; spatial fluidity was achieved by proposing curvaceous geometries and smoothing any junction between floors, external walls, and ceiling. Most elements proposed had a dynamic quality: they could be moved, altered, or removed over time. With Miss Guggenheim's permission, all frames were removed from the paintings which "floated" in the gallery space hanging from ropes. The orientation of the paintings could be adjusted to suit the viewer; the Daylight Gallery—one of the four spaces proposed—was conceived as a picture library in which "the spectator has a chance of sitting in front of mobile stands, and to adjust any painting to angles best suited for his own studying, also to exchange some of them from a built-in storage" (Kiesler 1942, p. 67). Paintings were individually lit in order to best enhance their qualities, and, in the original plan, an automatic system would randomly turn lights on and off. One of the proposals made involved modifying a Theremin to control the lighting system of the gallery. The Theremin—invented in 1920s in the Soviet Union[9]—is one of the few noncontact musical instruments in which the performer seems to be magically playing with an invisible substance—the electromagnetic fields generated by two metallic antennae. It is the material density of the human body—more precisely, the hands of the performer—to produce sound by shielding and deflecting the waves, an interaction which occurs in three dimensions. In Kiesler's hands this idea turned architecture into a dynamic, materially based affair. The three-dimensional space of the gallery was itself the generator of spatial experiences: the bodies moving in it were not a post facto occurrence but rather the triggers of this system signaling the presence of different material densities—today we could speak of maxels—aiming at constructing constantly changing atmospheres. Theremin defined a system of relationship in which space, perception, body, and architecture blended materializing the logic of the *Vision Machine* Kiesler had been working on since 1924. In the light of these experiments, it also becomes clearer why Kiesler rejected so drastically primitive geometries in favor of continuous forms in a state of tension. Organic, continuous surfaces coherently supported his idea to conflate multiple scales; that of the paintings, the viewers, and the very environment in which this encounter was taking pace. All these elements were now appearing as fluctuating, interacting dust, reverberating one another regardless of their size and materiality. Despite the idea had to be eventually abandoned, it presented remarkable similarities with the nascent spatial sensibility we have seen developing in the field of medical imaging in which scientists, and later artists, were also interested in volumetric, invisible phenomena (spatial and bodily arrangements) that allowed them to consider space in all its material and dynamic complexity.

If Kiesler delineated his ideas in the famous article "On Correalism and Biotechnique" (Kiesler 1939), it was his lifelong project—*The Endless House*—to provide the ideal testing ground for design experimentation. The aim to exceed received notions of space and interaction was clear from the outset as Kiesler pursued them with all media available: from sketches, to drawings, photography, and physical models were all employed at some point. The house can be succinctly described as a series of interpenetrating concrete shells supported by stilts. Central to our discussion is not so much the final formal outcome of a project as this was anyway meant to be endless, but rather the procedures and techniques followed or invented during the design process in which we can detect the emergence of a design sensibility responding to a different—proto-voxel—spatial sensibility. The house was often sketched in section—a mode of representation particularly akin to emphasizing relations between spaces rather than discrete formal qualities. Tellingly, these studies did not describe architectural elements through a continuous, perimeter—be it a wall or a roof—differentiating between interior and exterior but rather exploded the single line into a myriad of shorter traits creating an overall blurred effect in which the physical envelop expanded and contracted in a constant state of flux. Different from the sketches of German expressionist architects such as Hermann Finsterlin (1887–1973) and Hans Scharoun, Kiesler's do not emphasize the plastic, sculptural nature of the forms conceived. The line marking Finsterlin's architectures was sharp, precise, "snapping," and, ultimately, plastic. Kiesler's sketches were rather nebulous, layered, the dynamism of the architecture was not suggested as potential movement—as in the case of German expressionism—but rather as series of superimposed configurations, almost a primitive form of digital morphing. The architectural elements reverberated with the space they enclosed, a choice that sectional representation strengthened. The trembling lines of Kiesler's sketches were suggestive of the continuous nature of space, of the interplay between natural and artificial light in the house and its effects on the bodies inhabiting it and on their psychological well-being. The treatment of the skin of the house revealed how space was here not understood as an "empty" vessel, but rather as an active volume which could only be modulated by a type of architecture which also shared the same volumetric and dynamic characteristics. Geometry gave way to more elastic, impure, geometrically irreducible forms which would be better described as topologies subjected to forces, tensions, and transformations; the result was a total space—understood both as material and immaterial effects—a Gesamtkunstwerk based on time-space continuity (Kiesler 1934). Rather than using geometrical terms, it was the language of thermodynamics, chemistry, and energy to supply a better characterization of

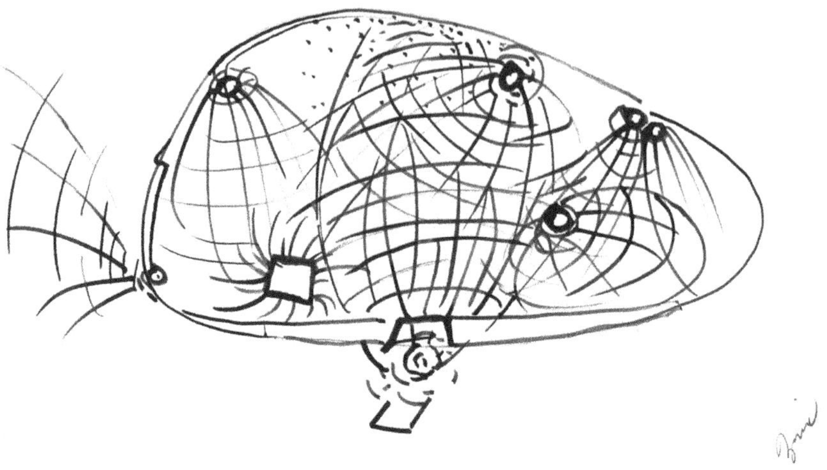

Figure 8.4 Frederic Kiesler, Endless House. Study for lighting part of the (1951). © The Museum of Modern Art, New York/Scala, Florence.

Kiesler's ideas: he spoke of "anabolic and catabolic" processes, of "nuclear-multiple forces," of "physico-chemical reactions" (Kiesler 1942, p. 60). The balance between environment and its inhabitants was mediated by an elastic architecture whose ultimate promise was to pulverize itself into continuously reacting particles (Fig. 8.4).

A second key moment in which the interaction with Kiesler's spatial sensibility gave rise to innovative design methods occurred in 1959 when he was invited by the Museum of Modern Art in New York to build a prototype of his house. After long vicissitudes, a scale model rather than a 1:1 prototype was constructed. Kiesler meticulously documented the preparation of the model through a series of carefully staged photographs which often portrayed him directly sculpting the continuous shapes of *The Endless House*. The final configuration resulted from tensioning metal meshes on which cement was eventually applied to both give structural rigidity and its iconically ragged, unfinished look. Though the images of the final model are normally circulated, the photographs showing the construction in progress, in an incomplete state before the final cement coat is laid onto the mesh are perhaps the most compelling to grasp the novelty of this experiment. At that stage *The Endless House* was incredibly suggestive not only because the effects of light on the meshes enhanced the sense of spatial continuity, but also because multiple scales—from the body to architecture—could be read simultaneously. The craft with which these photographs were taken was indicative of their importance, making photography the most successful media in capturing the dynamic spatial complexity of this project: the images produced registered light, shadows, all the invisible volumetric effects toward which Kiesler had been devoting so much of his time and design efforts. As a result, space expanded from the inside-out, geometrical determination was deferred or altogether substituted by the interaction between forces and material consistencies. They offered a layered, volumetric, "voxelized" image of the house which still acts as a useful precedent for multi-material architecture.

Contemporary landscape

The developments in robotic fabrication and modeling software have been generating the conditions to literally designing and building within a voxel space. Voxel-based modeling tools particularly allow to represent, simulate, and mix materials within a voxel space. This has reignited the discussion on many of the themes touched in this chapter, as it is possible to imagine that standard CAD software will soon absorb some of the features today only available in advanced modelers. The possibilities provided by rapid-prototyping machines to combine different types of materials can only be exploited through the development of software interfaces that can directly work with material densities. Although this area of research is still at an embryonic stage, examples such as *Monolith*—a piece of software designed by Andrew Payne and Panagiotis Michalatos—begin to reveal such potentials as this modeling tool allows designers to work in a voxel space and therefore include material densities—albeit represented through color channels—from the outset.[10] A multi-material approach to design represents a very interesting area of research largely debated among architects and designers, which is also likely to grow in importance in the near future. In this area the research designers such as Kostas Grigoriadis (Grigoriadis, 2016) (Fig. 8.5), Neri Oxman, Rachel Armstrong, Benjamin Dillenburger and Biothing (Alisa Andrasek) stand out for both their rigor and formal expressivity. A different, albeit very original take on the relation between voxels is represented by the *AlloBrain@AlloSphere* (2007) developed at the University of California by Markos Novak in which the architect's brain is scanned in real time as he models at the computer (Thompson, J., Kuchera-Morin, J., Novak, M., Overholt, D., Putnam, L., Wakefield, G., and Smith, W. 2009).

In general, this kind of work promises to impact architecture on a variety of levels. First, by making the designer's workflow more integrated: from conception, to representation, to material realization as data manipulated within the software environment will be directly employed in the design stage—for example, through rapid manufacturing. On a disciplinary level the implications of moving from the frictionless and material-less space of current software

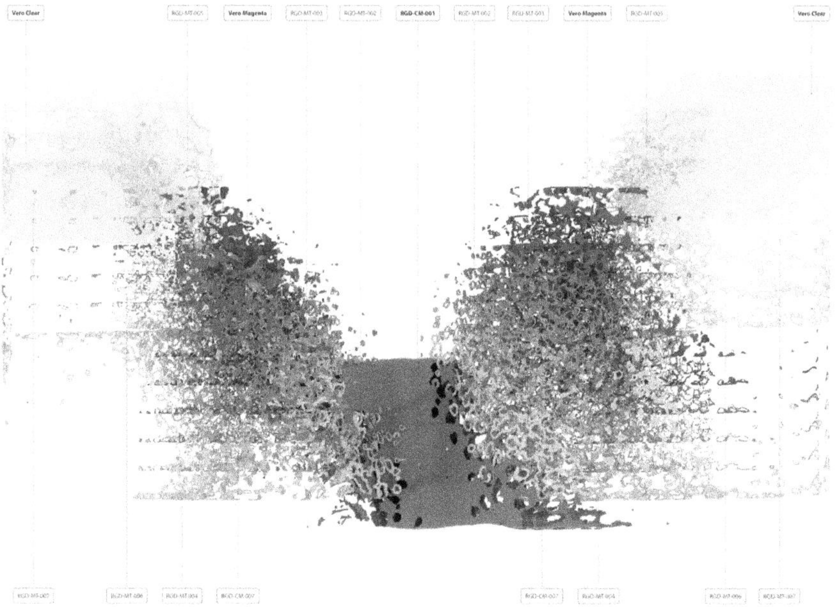

Figure 8.5 K. Grigoriadis: Multi-Material architecture. Detail of a window mullion (2017). © K. Grogoriadis.

to a voxel-based one are profound and could mark a radical departure from boundary-defined architecture firmly relying on geometrical reductivism toward more continuous, processual notion of space. Finally, the social and political organization of labor in the building industry may also be challenged perhaps finally finding an adequate response to Kiesler's lament in 1930: "a building wall today is a structure of concrete, steel, brick, plaster, paint, wooden moldings. Seven contractors for one wall!" (Kiesler 1930, p. 98).

Notes

1. *Voxel. Wikipedia* entry. [online]. Available from: https://en.wikipedia.org/wiki/Voxel (Accessed October 12, 2015).
2. In some software packages such as *Grasshopper* it is possible to visualize, deconstruct, and modify B-Rep envelops of a single or group of geometries to extract information or compute them more efficiently.
3. An isosurface is a surface—either flat or curved—grouping points sharing the same values in regard to a predetermined characteristics: for example, same air pressure in meteorological maps.
4. Incidentally, Fresnel calculations on light reflection and reflation still play an important role in computer graphics as they are employed to render liquid substances.

5. Mosso's key texts were included in one of the first Italian publications on the relation between prefabrication and computer (Mosso 1967).
6. The same computational model was also proposed for the entry to the competition for the Plateau Beauburg in 1971. The physical model submitted for the competition was particularly telling in this conversation. What was shown was not the actual building, but rather its *spatium*, that is the maximum virtual voxel space which was technologically possible to build. Users' needs would eventually determine which parts and how such voxel space would be occupied.
7. *Software* was an important show in the development of computer-generated aesthetics which was curated by another important figure of the 1960s, American art and technology critic Jack Burnham (See Burnham 1970).
8. All the major experiments developed by Unit 11 at the Architectural Association are gathered in Frazer (1995).
9. The Theremin was invented by Russian physicist Leon Theremin in the 1920s (but only patented in 1928) as part of his experiments with electromagnetism. His use as a musical instrument will only occur after its discovery and will be popularized in 1950s by the likes of Robert Moog. Famously featuring in Beach Boys' *Good Vibrations* (1966), it consists of two antennae emitting an electromagnetic field which can be "disturbed" by the hands of the player. The distance from the one antenna determines frequency (pitch), whereas the distance from the other controls amplitude (volume). Glinsky (2000).
10. http://www.monolith.zone/#introduction (Accessed on February 8, 2017).

Afterword

Frédéric Migayrou

How to elaborate the forms of a critical history of digital architecture where the limits have not yet been established or well defined; a short history in which a chronological account is difficult to establish? Moreover, within this frame, it is difficult to distinguish between digital culture within aeronautic and car manufacturing industries and the digital within computational architecture.

We might first be tempted to link the emergence of digital architecture to the proliferation and general accessibility of software. The 3D software which has been developed since the early 90s—surface modelling programs for the most part (Form Z, CATIA, and Solidworks), or parametric modelers (Top Solid, Rhino, etc.)—offered radically new morphogenetic explorations of forms which prompted an entire generation of experimental architects to participate in numerous publications and group exhibitions. However great the temptation to 'make a history' by uncovering an 'archaeology of the digital' might be, it would consequently refute an approach that links the origins of computational architecture to the accessibility of first generation computers in large universities. This project would correspond to a larger vision of the historical spectrum which also paralleled other disciplines such as art, music or literature. While Cambridge University's *Center for Land Use and Built Form Studies* (LUBFS, 1967) and M.I.T's *Architecture Machine Group* (1969), among others, have recently regained scholarly attention, it seems essential to reconsider these architectural computer labs and their relationship with universities and industries as they began speculating on the possibility of a programmed art and creativity.

If we are to assume that digital architecture development is to be found at the heart of the history of computation and complexity theories, this must also be located within an expanded field of computational history including computers and programming languages. Returning to the seminal figures of Kurt Gödel, Alan Turing or John von Neumann, a third level stands out offering the full measure of the epistemological domain that must be taken into account, weaving links between the foundation of computation and the mathematical sources of logic. *Digital Architecture Beyond Computers* opens up a broader history of logic, numbers, and calculus to a more complex reading across a wide range of historical periods (from the representational models of the Renaissance to the origins of differential calculation, from topology to group theory across exemplary mutations and consequences of these evolutions within multiple fields of application).

Within the eight chapters, Bottazzi explores fields of knowledge from the history of science and technology, to logic and mathematics, to philosophy and artistic practices, which are all key to the shared understanding of the digital realm. *Digital Architecture Beyond Computers* is considered within a wider epistemological field where the history of science and technology feeds into various conceptual analyses, highlighting both the ruptures and positive outcomes of these formalizing strategies. His transversal approach is not dogmatic or linear but rather forms connections between various references. The eight notions explored within these chapters constitute within themselves mini-archaeologies forming a sort of map, or rather a constellation of references, and studies, both historical and contemporary. Each section concludes with a small appendix, "Contemporary Landscape", which leaves the field open to an analysis of current innovative projects exemplifying each of the notions. This historically and critically situates research on computational architecture giving it legitimacy, and ensuring critical cohesion to better analyze and judge the contemporary architectural scene.

The intelligence of Roberto Bottazzi's book is to avoid a monolithic singular reading structure in favor of a more discursive reasoning, setting up an "economy" of the reading tailored to our own management of the different parts. This reminds us of the contemporary cognitive universe distributed along sites, islands of knowledge where interpretation and comprehension are segmented and determined by relational games. The chapters function as binding agents to organize texts regarding different meanings and definitions of concepts (data and information, geometrical or digital paradigms, physical computation and parametric, random numbers in history ...). They articulate key moments of a calculated archaeology consisting of renaissance philosophers, architects, authors as well as the engineers and theoreticians of the first computational investigations (Ramon Llull, Giulio Camillo, Gottfried Leibniz, Luigi Moretti, Leonardo Mosso, Michael Noll, Jay Forrester ...). It is thus necessary to analyze the book by crossing these multiple platforms through which such an archeology of computation is constructed; these multiple entries thus mark the analogies, the correspondences as well as the breaks animating this "infra-history" of the computational. From this semantic field, originating first in the theories proposed by Quillian and Collins (1969) in which concepts are defined as units of meaning hierarchically related to one another in order to form either layered assemblages or intersected combinations, ultimately the possibility of a new set of meanings arises. Framed around two distinct readings, Bottazzi's book attempts straddle between objective and intuitive intentions. It is driven on the one hand by a rigorous comprehension of the vast literature of computation and, on the other hand, by an ambitious reorganization of the categories linking back to the scientific and cultural fields. Down to the chapters, it becomes evident that this book constitutes a thesaurus of sorts, a set of indexical relationships that build up into this porous-like cloud, ever-expanding over the cultural field of digital architecture.

The sequence of the chapters could well be moved around or rearranged depending on the reading. However, Database and Networks remains the first entry point by proposing that the process of discretization and binary code are at the source of ruptures requiring a new order of calculus. Even if the alphabet can also be considered a discrete system, it is important to stress that they belong to two fields of syntax each with their perfectly distinguished symbolic economies. One is founded on the word, and not directly on the alphabet, while the other on a reduced number. In other words, binary code constitutes a conversion that tilts domains of expression into a logical system, therefore bringing together existing agencies into unity. As mentioned by George Boole (quoted here by Bottazzi) "Binary numeration was finally introduced as the symbol 0 represents nothing whereas the symbol 1 represent the Universe". Going beyond the military research into coding, encoding remains a founding disciplinary principle to formalize information predicted by Claude Shannon using Boole's (0–1) to describe the various links between machines. In his seminal piece *A Mathematical Theory of Communication* (1948), Shannon sketches the notion of a byte, describing it as the smallest unit of measure in a numbering system. The definition of units of digital information such as the bit, constitutes a conversion of information into digital forms which infers a notion of data. Beyond the existing diversity of encoding principles and the process of transcoding data, the question emerging is that of the status of idealization of the number as an ideal construct. These forms of logic constitute the intellectual pillars of mathematics, algebra and geometry, relating to the issue arising from the specialization of numbers and space. Principles of computability, as defined by Alonzo Church (Lambda Calculus), Kurt Gödel (Recursive Functions), and Alan Turing (Computable Functions—Turing Machine) constitute a domain of formal simulation raising issues of transcription, and translatability pertaining to all the systems of notation. The problems of the ontology of the number and the principles of its formal ontology present themselves whilst marking a distance with the phenomenological concept initiated by Edmund Husserl, Roman Ingarden and then later reconstituted by Barry Smith's analytical lens through the oeuvre of Franz Brentano as well as his own work *Parts & Moments, Studies in Logic and Formal Philosophy* (1982). Formal ontology, Smith claims, presents itself as the counterpoint of formal logics constituted by elements of a regional ontological, axiomatization and modelization.

Founded on a theory of dependencies and relations, formal ontology directly contraposes to Set theory which, on the other hand, is founded on abstract entities, on the relations between a set and its parts to privilege a modelization of specific ontologies that define the categories of objects organized by their formal between their concepts. Introducing new ideas to explain the relationship between parts and wholes will constitute mereology as an alternative to Set Theory, giving rise to Mererotopology as a 'Dot Free Geometry'; a geometry whose most basic assumption considers not the point but the region. This is also a proposition by Karl Menger (*Dimensions Theory*, 1928), when he claims that mereotopology turns into a concrete formalization of space also developed by Casati or Achille Varzi (*Parts, Whole and Part-Whole Relations: The Prospects of Mereotopology*, 1996). While there remain problems with the principle of identification, indexation and,classification, formal ontology establishes new systems of interpretation. Before any reconfiguration by the Speculative Realism philosophical approach, which following Alain Badiou, comes back to formal principals of Set Theory, a semantic turn towards fields of application such as object oriented ontologies were largely developed within industries and its computational applications. In some respect, Bottazzi employs a similar argument to Barry Smith's semantic ontology in his analysis of spatial operativity of databases when he elaborates on the recursive function of data and its use, but also its intrinsic formal limitation of such 'object oriented modelling'. His study, focusing on Aby Warburg' *Atlas*, fully corresponds to a proposed mereotopology which analyses the relations between images as "an ever-expanding landscape dynamically changing according to the multiple relations by the objects in the database". Databases cannot simply be considered as models exportable in physical space according to a vision of networks underpinned by the morphology of territories. Bottazzi's analysis demonstrates that interrelated datasets can also be recomposing the geography of influence and sovereignty zones. From the first territorial coding—the first postcodes network—to the emergence of a power that, according to Michel Foucault, recomposed morphological territories using algorithms, instead of an exercised control over territory. The apparition of data mapping established correspondences between databases, changing the paradigm where a globalized and universal system would lead to an erasure to profit the economical and political business of Big Data. Richard Buckminster Fuller's *World Game* (1961), Constanrin Doxiadis' *Electronicmaps* and *Cartographatron* (1959–1963), and Stafford Beer's *Cybersin* (1971–1973) all preempted a universalization of data at a territorial scale by Map Overlay Statistical System (MOSS) in 1978, followed by Geographical Information System (GIS) and Global Positioning System (GPS). These exploitative geodata technologies provide a saturated web accessible from our mobile telephones. Bottazzi's reading of the specific digital architectural field stems from a generic architecture, one that responds to a mereotopological condition and escapes the current dominant discourse. On the one hand, it is propagated as an understanding of morphogenetics issued by a neo-structuralist syntax model such as the diagram, on the other, by generic simulation defined by complex systems of emergence and self-organization. In fact, the large part of his experimental research on materials respond to morphologenic strategies by their traditional formation and production of geometries. Space remains an extended domain and real algebraic mathematical principles still depend on a particular doxa where CAD software define a new formal grammar. Morphing techniques enable a dynamic control over a large organic vocabulary of NURBS (Non-Uniform Rational B-Spline) by generalizing the use of these curves and Bezier surfaces which have allowed a polynomial interpolation enabling the construction of points with a discreet ensemble. As a consequence, the diffuse use of software employing cellular automata algorithms has changed the approach to geometry and reintroduced the problematic of an ontology of numbers whose sources are found within the logic of cellular automata proposed by Stanislav Ulam, John von Neumann or more recently by Marvin Minsky. Bottazzi's analysis allows for a continuous reading through the voxel-based modeling definition where he determines references from by Leonardo Mosso in *Architettura Programmata* (1968), but also by Lionel March's or Philip Steadman's definition of cubelets (LUBFS). This method can be applied to architecture history to further reinterpret the visual constructions of Leon Battista Alberti (*Ludi Mathematici*, 1450–1452), Piero della Francesca (*De Prospectiva Pigendi*, 1460–1480), and Albrecht Dürer (*Man drawing with a Lute,* 1525) as well as other descriptive geometries such as Girard Desargues (*Brouillon projet d'une atteinte aux évènements des rencontres d'un cône avec un plan*, 1639).

By doing so, the book avoids an analogical reading of geometry which seeks to find continuity and constants through different sources that ever since Euclid established would preserve a certain status of spatiality and by extension preserve a certain identity of architecture. Looking for structural constants through history allows us to reaffirm links between a history of computing and that of a critical aesthetic of architecture. Here, Bottazzi invents an integrative archeology in the manner of Alfred Korzybski, a general semantics to update meta-models establishing a hermeneutics to better understand the most contemporary research of digital architecture. The issues of chance, stochastics then emerges through the theories of complexity imposing new types of modeling and returning to the sources of cryptography (Ramon Llull, Gustavus Selenus, Alan Turing, etc.). Such type of modelization will eventually be accomplished by the invention of the Monte-Carlo method (Ulam-von Neumann, 1946) which will employ a class of algorithms that will approach the final result through iteration. Understanding this new order of rationality, at odds with a certain orthodoxy of post-modern architecture, means to accept the notion of computability, to grasp how it has permeated through all human practices as well as given back to architecture its function of organizing heterogeneous domains. It is in terms that Roberto Bottazzi's work becomes a guide, a manual establishing on the one hand a *quid juris* historical foundation for digital architecture, and, on the other, offering a critical instrument for future research.

Frédéric Migayrou, October 2017

Bibliography

Agamben, G. 2009. *The Signature of All Things: On Method*. Translated by L. D'Isanto and K. Attell. New York: Zone Books.

Anderson, C. 2008. The End of Theory: The Data Deluge Makes the Scientific Method Obsolete [online]. Available at: http://www.wired.com/2008/06/pb-theory/ [Accessed on May 20, 2016].

Arup Group and RIBA. 2013. *Designing with Data: Shaping our Future Cities*. Available at: https://www.architecture.com/Files/RIBAHoldings/PolicyAndInternationalRelations/Policy/Designing withdata/Designingwithdatashapingourfuturecities.pdf [Accessed on September 3, 2016].

Baccaglioni, L., Del Canto, E., & Mosso, L. 1981. *Leonardo Mosso, architettura e pensiero logico*. Catalogue to the exhibition held at Casa del Mantegna, Mantua.

Balestrini, N. 1961. Tape Mark I. In *Almanacco Letterario Bompiani 1962: Le Applicazioni dei Calcolatori Elettronici alle Scienze Morali e alla Letteratura*, edited by S. Morando. Milan: Bompiani, pp. 145–51.

Balestrini, N. 1963. Come Si Agisce. Milan: Feltrinelli.

Balestrini, N. 1966. *Tristano. Un Romanzo*. Milan: Feltrinelli.

Balestrini, N. 1969. Tape Mark I. In *Cybernetic Serendipity: The Computer and The Arts*, edited by J. Reichardt. New York: Praeger, p. 55.

Balfour, A. J. 1904. *Address by The Right Hon. A. J. Balfour. Report of the Seventy-Fourth Meeting of the British Association for the Advancement of Science*. London: John Murray, p. 7.

Bartoli, C. [1559] 1990. *Del modo di misurare*. In Kemp M. *The Science of Art: Optical Themes in Western Art from Brunelleschi to Seurat*. New Have and London: Yale University Press, p. 170.

Baxandall, M. 1985. *Patterns of Intention: On the Historical Explanation of Pictures*. New Haven and London: Yale University Press.

BCS Academy Glossary Working Party. 2013. *BCS Glossary of Computing and ICT*. 13th edition. Swindon: The Chartered Institute for IT.

Beaman, J. J., Barlow, J. W., Bourell, D. L., Crawford, R. H., Marcus, H. L., McAlea, K. P. 1997. *Solid Freeform Fabrication: A New Direction in Manufacturing: With Research and Applications in Thermal Laser Processing*. Dordrecht and London: Kluwer Academic Publisher.

Beer, S. 1967. *Cybernentics and Management*. London : English University Press.

Beer, S. 1972. *The Brain of the Firm*. London: Allen Lane.

Beer, S. (April 27, 1973). On Decybernation: A Contribution to Current Debates. Box 64, The Stafford Beer Collection, Liverpool John Moores University.

Beer, S. 1975 [1973]. Fanfare for Effective Freedom: Cybernetic Praxis in Government. In *Platform for Change: A Message from Stafford Beer*, edited by S. Beer. New York: John Wiley, pp. 421–52.

Bellini, F. 2004. *Le Cupole del Borromini*. Milan: Electa.

Bemis A. F. and Burchard, J. 1936. *The Evolving House, vol. 3: Rational Design*. Cambridge, MA: MIT Press.

Bendazzi, G. 1994. *Cartoons: One Hundred Years of Cinema Animation*. London: Libbey.

Berardi, F. 2011. *After the Future*. Edited by G. Genosko and N. Thoburn. Translated by A. Bove. Oakland, CA and Edinburgh: AK Press.

Bertelli, C. 1992. *Piero della Francesca*. Translated by E. Farrelly. New Haven, CT and London: Yale University Press.

Blanther J. E. 1892. *Manufacture of Contour Relief-map*. Patent. US 473901 A.

Boccioni, U. 1910. *Technical Manifesto of Futurist Painting*.

Bolzoni, L. 2012. *Il Lettore Creativo: Percorsi cinquecenteschi fra memoria, gioco, scrittura*. Naples: Guida.

Bolzoni, L. 2015. *L'Idea del Theatro: con "L'Idea dell'Eloquenza," il "De Trasmutatione" e altri testi inediti*. Milan: Adelphi.

Booker, P. J. 1963. *A History of Engineering Drawing*. London: Chatto & Windus.

Boole. G. 1852. *An Investigation of the Laws of Thought on Which Are Founded the Mathematical Theories of Logic and Probabilities*. London : Walton & Maberly.

Borromini, F. 1725. *Opus Architectonicum*. Rome.

Bottazzi, R. 2015. The Urbanism of the G8 Summit [1999–2010]. In *Critical Cities, vol. 4: Ideas, Knowledge and Agitation from Emerging Urbanists*, edited by N. Deepa and O. Trenton. London: Myrdle Court Press, pp. 252–70.

Bouman, O. 1996. *Realspaces in QuickTimes: Architecture and Digitization*. Rotterdam: NAI Publishers.

Bowlt, J. E. 1987. The Presence of Absence: The Aesthetic of Transparency in Russian Modernism. *The Structurist*, vol. 27, no. 8 (1987–88), pp. 15–22.

Braider, C. 1993. *Reconfiguring the Real: Picture and Modernity in Word and Image, 1400–1700*. Princeton, NJ: Princeton University Press.

Bratton, B. 2016. *The Stack: On Software and Sovereignty*. Cambridge, MA and London: The MIT Press.

Burnham, J. 1970. *Software – Information Technology: Its New Meaning for Art*, New York: The Jewish Museum, September 16–November 8, 1970.

Camarota, F. 2004. Renaissance Descriptive Geometry. In *Picturing Machines 1400–1700*, edited by W. Lefêvre. Cambridge, MA: The MIT Press, p. 178–208.

Camillo, G. 1552. *Discorso in materia del suo theatro*. Venice: apresso Gabriel Giolito de Ferrari.

Camillo, G. 1544. *Trattato dell'Imitazione*. Venice: Domenico Farri.

Camillo, G. 1587. *Pro suo de eloquentia theatro ad Gallos oratio*.

Cantrell, B. and Holzman, J., ed. (2015). *Responsive Landscapes: Strategies for Responsive Technologies in Landscape Architecture*. London: Routledge.

Cardodo Llarch, D. 2012. *Builders of the Vision: Technology and Imagination of Design*. PhD Thesis. Massachusetts Institute of Technology, Department of Electrical Engineering.

Cardodo Llarch, D. 2015. *Builders of the Vision: Software and the Imagination of Design*. New York and London: Routledge.

Carpo, M. 2001. *Architecture in the Age of Printing: Orality, Writing, Typography, and Printed Images in the History of Architectural Theory*. Translated by S. Benson. Cambridge, MA and London: The MIT Press.

Carpo, M. 2008. Alberti's Media Lab. In *Perspective, Projections and Design: Technologies of Architectural Representation*, edited by M. Carpo and F. Lemerle. London and New York: Routledge, pp. 47–63.

Carpo, M. 2013a. *Notations and Nature: From Artisan Mannerism to Computational Making*. Lecture delivered at *9th Archilab: Naturalizing Architecture* (October 25, 2013). Available at: https://vimeo.com/86102570 [Accessed on July 2, 2016].

Carpo, M. 2013b. Digital Indeterminism: The New Digital Commons and the Dissolution of Architectural Authorship. In *Architecture in Formation: On the Nature of Information in Digital Architecture*, edited by P. Lorenzo-Eiroa and A. Sprecher. New York: Routledge and Taylor and Francis, pp. 47–52.

Carpo, M. and Furlan, F., eds. 2007. *Leon Battista Alberti's Delineation of the City of Rome (Description Urbis Romae)*. Translated by P. Hicks. Tempe, Ariz: Arizona Center for Medieval and Renaissance Studies.

Cartwright, L. and Goldfarb, B. 1992. Radiography, Cinematography and the Decline of the Lens. In *Zone 6: Incorporations*, edited J. Crary and S. Kwinter. New York: Zone Books, pp. 190–201.

Caspary, U. (2009). *Digital Media as Ornament in Contemporary Architecture Facades: Its Historical Dimension.* In *Urban Screens Reader*, edited by S. Mcquire, M. Martin, and S. Niederer. Amsterdam: Institute of Network Cultures.

Ceruzzi, P. E. 1998. *A History of Modern Computing*. Cambridge, MA and London: The MIT Press.

Ceruzzi, P. E. 2012. *Computing: A Concise History*. Cambridge, MA and London: The MIT Press.

Chaitin, G. J. 1987. *Algorithmic Information Theory*. Cambridge: Cambridge University Press.

Chaitin, G. J. March, 2006. The Limits of Reason. *Scientific American*, vol. 294, no. 3, pp. 74–81.

Chiorino, F. 2010. Né periferia, né provincia. L'incontro tra un grande scienziato e un giovane architetto a pochi passi dall'eremo biellese di Benedetto Croce. In *Leonardo Mosso, Gustavo Colonnetti, Biblioteca Benedetto Croce, Pollone, 1960*, in *Casabella* n. 794, October, pp. 84–97.

Chu, H.-Y. 2009. Paper Mausoleum: The Archive of R. Buckminster Fuller. In *New Views on R. Buckminster Fuller*, edited by H.-Y. Chu and R. G. Trujillo. Stanford, CA: Stanford University Press.

Cingolani, G. 2004. Il Mondo in quarantanove caselle. Una lettura de l'"Idea del Teatro" di Giulio Camillo. In *Microcosmo-Macrocosmo. Scrivere e pensare il mondo del Cinquecento tra Italia e Francia*, edited by G. Gorris Camos. Fasano: Schena, pp. 57–66.

Clark K. 1969. *Piero della Francesca: Complete Edition*. London: Phaidon Press.

Colletti, M. 2013. *Digital Poetics: An Open Theory of Design-Research in Architecture*. Farnham, Surrey, and England: Ashgate Publishing.

Comai, A. 1985. *Poesie Elettroniche. L'esempio di Nanni Balestrini*. Master Thesis in Italian literature from the University of Turin – Faculty of Literature and Philosophy. Available at: http://www.adcorsi.com/analisidisegno/a_comai/TESI.html [Accessed on May 3, 2016].

Computer Technique Group. 1968. Computer Technique Group from Japan. In *Cybernetic Serendipity: The Computer and the Arts*, edited by J. Reichardt. New York: Frederick A. Praeger, p. 75.

Coop Himmelb(l)au. 1983. *Open House*. [Unbuilt project]. Available at: http://www.coop-himmelblau.at/architecture/projects/open-house/ [Accessed on May 16, 2016].

Corso, A. 1986. *Monumenti periclei: Saggio critico sulla attività edilizia di Pericle*. Venice: Istituto Veneto di Scienze, Lettere ed Arti.

Crossley, J. N. 1995. Llull's Contributions to Computer Science. In *Ramon Llull: From the Ars Magna to Artificial Intelligence*, edited by A. Fidora and C. Sierra. Barcelona: Artificial Intelligence Research Institute, IIIA, Consejo Superior de Investigationes Cientifícas. pp. 41–43.

Crossley, J. N. 2005. *Raymond Llull's Contributions to Computer Science*. Clayton School of Information Technology, Monash University, Melbourne, technical report 2005/182.

Dalston, L. and Galison, P. 2010. *Objectivity*. New York: Zone Books.

Danti, E. edited and expanded. 1583. *Le Due Regole della Prospettiva Pratica del Vignola*.

Davies, L. 2014. Tristano: The Love Story that's Unique to Each Reader. *The Guardian*, published on February 13, 2014. Available at: http://www.theguardian.com/books/2014/feb/13/nanni-balestrini-tristano-novel-technology [Accessed on March 15, 2015].

Davis, D. 2013. *Modelled in Software Engineering: Flexible Parametric Models in the Practice of Architecture*. PhD. RMIT University.

Davis, M. 2001. *The Universal Computer: The Road from Leibniz to Turing*. New York and London: W. W. Norton.

Davis, M. R. and Ellis, T. O. 1964. *The RAND Tablet: A Man-Machine Graphical Communication Device*. Memorandum RM-4122-ARPA, August 1964, p. 6. Available at: http://www.rand.org/content/dam/rand/pubs/research_memoranda/2005/RM4122.pdf [Accessed on August 25, 2015].

Deleuze, G. 1992. *The Fold: Leibniz and the Baroque*. Minneapolis, MN: University of Minnesota Press.

Deleuze, G. 1976. *Rhizome: Introduction*. Paris: Les Éditions de Minuit.

Depero, F. 1931. Il Futurismo e l'Arte Publicitaria. In *Depero Futurista and New York: il Futurismo e L'Arte Publicitaria: Futurism and the Art of Advertising*. 1987. Edited by M. Scudiero. Rovereto: Longo.

Dictionary of Scientific Biography. New York: Scribner's, 1972.

Dilke, O. A. W. 1971. *The Roman Land Surveyors: An Introduction to the Agrimensores*. Newton Abbot: David & Charles.

Douglass Lee, B. Jr. 1973. Requiem for Large-Scale Models. *Journal of the American Institute of Planners*, vol. 39, no. 3, pp. 163–78.

Durand, J. N. L. 1819. *Leçons d'Architecture*. Paris.

Earlier Image Processing. No date. The SEAC and the Start of Image Processing at the National Bureau of Standards. Available at: http://museum.nist.gov/panels/seac/EARLIEST.HTM [Accessed on July 15, 2015].

Eckhardt, R. 1987. Stanislav Ulam, John von Neumann, and the Monte Carlo Method. *Los Alamos Science*, vol. 15, Special Issue, pp. 131–41.

Eco, U. 1961. La Forma del Disordine. In *Almanacco Letterario Bompiani 1962: Le Applicazioni dei Calcolatori Elettronici alle Scienze Morali e alla Letteratura*, edited by S. Morando. Milan: Bompiani, pp. 175–88.

Eco, U. June 1963. Due ipotesi sulla morte dell'arte. *Il Verri*, no. 8, pp. 59–77.

Eco, U. 1989. *Open Work*. Translated by A. Cancogni. Cambridge, MA: Harvard University Press.

Eco, U. 2009. *The Infinity of Lists: From Homer to Joyce*. Translated by A. McEven. London: MacLehose.

Eco, U. 2014. *From the Tree to the Labyrinth: Historical Studies on the Sign and Interpretation*. Translated by A. Oldcorn. Cambridge, MA: Harvard University Press.

Edgar, R. 1985. *Memory Theatres*. Online. Available at: http://www.robertedgar.com/memory-theatres/ [Accessed on April 14, 2015].

Edwards, P. N. 2010. *A Vast Machine: Computer Models, Climate Data, and the Politics of Global Warming*. Cambridge, MA and London: MIT Press.

Esposito, R. 1976. *Le Ideologie della Neoavanguardia*. Naples: Liguori.

Evans, R. 1995. *The Projective Cast: Architecture and Its Three Geometries*. Cambridge, MA and London: The MIT Press.

Fano, D. (2008). *Explicit History is now Grasshopper*. http://designreform.net/2008/06/explicit-history-is-now-grasshopper. Blog (Accessed July 8, 2016).

Farin, G. E. 2002. *Curves and Surfaces for CAGD: A Practical Guide*. 5th edition. San Francisco, CA and London: Morgan Kaufmann; Academic Press.

Field J. V. 2005. *Piero della Francesca: A Mathematician's Art*. New Haven, CT and London: Yale University Press.

Forrester, J. W. 1961. *Industrial Dynamics*. Cambridge, MA: The MIT Press; New York; London: John Wiley & Sons.

Forrester, J. W. 1969. *Urban Dynamics*. Cambridge, MA: The MIT Press.

Forrester, J. W. 1973. *World Dynamics*. Cambridge, MA: Wright-Allen Press.

Forrester, J. W. 2009. *Some Basic Concepts in System Dynamics*. Available at: http://www.cc.gatech.edu/classes/AY2013/cs7601_spring/papers/Forrester-SystemDynamics.pdf [Accessed on June 12, 2016].

Foucault, M. 2003. *The Abnormals: Lectures at the Collège de France*. London: Verso.

Frazer, J. 1995. *An Evolutionary Architecture*. London: Architectural Association Press.

Frazer, J. 2016. Parametric Computation: History and Future. In *Architectural Design: Parametricism 2.0: Rethinking Architecture's Agenda for the 21st Century*, edited by P. Schumacher, vol. 86, March/April. Chichester: John Wiley & Sons, pp. 18–23.

Frazer, J. and Graham, P. 1990. Evolving a Tuscan column using the parametric rules of James Gibbs (1732). In *Architectural Design: Parametricism 2.0: Rethinking Architecture's Agenda for the 21st Century*, edited by P. Schumacher, Vol. 86, March/April. Chichester: John Wiley & Sons, p. 22.

Friedman, Y. 1975. *Towards a Scientific Architecture*. Translated by C. Lang. Cambridge, MA and London: The MIT Press.

Friedman, M. S. and Sorkin, M., eds. 2003. *Gehry Talks: Architecture + Process*. London: Thames & Hudson.

Fuller, R. B. and McHale, J. 1963. *World Design Science Decade 1965 – 1975: Phase 1 - Document 1: Inventory of World Resources Human Trends and Needs*. Carbondale: Southern Illinois University, World Resources Inventory.

Fuller, R. B. and McHale, J. 1965. *World Design Science Decade 1965 – 1975: Phase 1 - Document 4: The Ten Year Program*. Carbondale: Southern Illinois University, World Resources Inventory.

Fuller, R. B. 1965. "Vision '65," Keynote Lecture, Carbondale: Southern Illinois University, October 1965. In *Database Aesthetic: Art in the Age of Information Overflow*, edited by V. Vesna. Minneapolis, MN: University of Minnesota Press.

Fuller, R. B. 1981. *Critical Path*. New York: St. Martin's Press.

Gardner, M. 1958. *Logic Machines and Diagrams*. New York, Toronto, and London: McGraw-Hill Company.

Geach, P. and Black, M., eds. 1952. *Translations from the Philosophical Writings of Gottlob Friege*. Oxford: Blackwell.

Giannattasio, U. November 19, 1913. Letter to Severini. In *Archivi del Futurismo*, edited by Gambillo and Fiori.

Glinsky, A. 2000. *Theremin: Ether Music and Espionage*. Urbana: University of Illinois Press.

Goldstine, H. H. 1972. *The Computer – From Pascal to von Neumann*. Princeton, NJ and Chichester: Princeton University Press.

Goodman, C. 1987. *Digital Visions: Computers and Art*. New York: Harry N. Abrahams.

Gouraud, H. 1971. *Computer Display of Curved Surfaces*. PhD. University of Utah.

Grigoriadis, K., ed. 2016. *Mixed Matters: A Multi-Material Design Compendium*. Berlin: Jovis Verlag.

Grima, J. 2008. Content-Managing the Urban Landscape. *Volume – Content Management*, no.17, pp. 64–65.

Gropius, W. and Wesinger, A. S., eds. 1961. *The Theatre of the Bauhaus*. Translated by A. S. Wensinger. Middletown, CT: Wensleyan University Press.

Gruska, J. 1999. *Quantum Computing*. London and New York: McGraw-Hill.

Guarnone, A. 2008. Architettura e Scultura. In *Lo scultore e l'Architetto. Pietro de Laurentiis e Luigi Moretti. Testimonianze di un sodalizio trentennale."* Conference Proceedings. Rome: Archivio di Stato.

Hegedüs, A. 1997. Memory Theatre VR. Available at: https://www.digitalartarchive.at/database/general/work/memory-theatre-vr.html [Accessed on April 15, 2016].

Henderson, L. D. 2013. *The Fourth Dimension and Non-Euclidean Geometry in Modern Art*. 1st edition 1983. London, England and Cambridge, MA: MIT Press.

Hersey, G. L. 2000. *Architecture and Geometry in the Age of the Baroque*. Chicago, IL and London: The University of Chicago Press.

Herzog, K. 2015. How James Cameron and His Team made *Terminator 2: Judgment Day*'s Liquid-Metal Effect. Online blog. Available at: http://www.vulture.com/2015/06/oral-history-of-emt2ems-liquid-metal-effect.html [Accessed on September 12, 2016].

Hoskins, S. 2013. *3D Printing for Artists, Designers and Makers*. London: Bloomsbury Press.

Huhtamo, E. 2009. Messages on the Wall: An Archaeology of Public Media Display. In *Urban Screens Reader*, edited by S. McQuire, M. Martin, and S. Niederer. Amsterdam: Institute of Network Cultures.

Jenkins, H. 2006. *Convergence Culture: Where Old and New Media Collide*. New York and London: New York University Press.

Kamnitzer, P. September, 1969. Computer Aid to Design. *Architectural Design*, vol. 39, pp. 507–08.

Kay, A. C. 1993. *The Early History of Smalltalk*. Online. Available at: http://gagne.homedns.org/~tgagne/contrib/EarlyHistoryST.html [Accessed on May 22, 2016].

Kemp, M. 1990. *The Science of Art: Optical Themes in Western Art from Brunelleschi to Seurat*. New Haven and London: Yale University Press.

Kendall, D. G. 1971. Construction of Maps from "Odd Bits of Information." *Nature*, no. 231, pp. 158–59.

Kenner, H. 1973. *Bucky: A Guided Tour of Buckminster Fuller*. New York: William Morrow & Company Inc.

Kepes, G. 1944. *The Language of Vision*. Chicago, IL: Theobold.

Kevles, B. H. 1997. *Naked to the Bone: Medical Imaging in the Twentieth Century*. New Brunswick, NJ: Rutgers University Press.

Kiesler, F. J. 1930. *Contemporary Art Applied to the Store and its Display*. New York: Brentano.

Kiesler, F. J. January–March, 1934. Notes on Architecture: The Space-House. *Hound & Horn*, p. 293.

Kiesler, F. J. 1939. On Correalism and Biotechnique: A Definition and Test of a New Approach to Building Design. *Architectural Record*, no. 86, pp. 60–75.

Kiesler, F. J. 1942. Notes on Designing the Gallery (extended version). Unpublished typescript. In *Frederick Kiesler: Function Follows Vision, Vision Follows Reality,* edited by L. Lo Pinto, V. J. Müller and the Austrian Frederick and Lillian Kiesler Private Foundation. Berlin: Sternberg Press, 2016.

Kilpatrick, J. J. 1984. *The Writer's Art*. Kansas City: Andrews, McMeel, and Parker.

Kline, M. 1972. *Mathematical Thought from the Ancient to Modern Times*. New York: Oxford Press.

Kruskal, W. H. 1978. *International Encyclopedia of Statistics*, vol. 1. New York: Free Press.

Laposky, B. 1969. Oscillons Electronic Abstractions. *Leonardo*, vol. 2, pp. 345–54.

Laugier, M.-A. 1775. *Essai sur l'Architecture*.

Le Corbusier. 1987. The Decorative Art of Today, Boston, MA: MIT Press. Quoted in M. Wigley, The Architectural Brain. In *Network Practices: New Strategies in Architecture and Design*, edited by A. Burke and T. Tierney. New York: Princeton Architectural Press, 2007, pp. 30–53.

Lee, A. 2013. Cost-Optimized Warehouse Storage Type Allocations. Thesis (PhD), Massachusetts Institute of Technology. Available at: https://dspace.mit.edu/bitstream/handle/1721.1/81004/857789705-MIT.pdf?sequence=2 [Accessed on May 4, 2015].

Lee Douglas, B. Jr. May, 1973. Requiem for Large-Scale Models. *Journal of American Institute of Planning*, vol. 39, no. 3, pp. 163–78.

Leibniz, G. W. 1666. *Dissertatio de art combinatoria*.

Leibniz, G. W. 1667. *Nova Methodus Discendae Docendaeque Iurisprudentiae*.

Lipetz, B.-A. 1966. Information Storage and Data Retrieval. In *Information: A Comprehensive Review of the Extraordinary New Technology of Information*. San Francisco: W. H. Freeman and Company, pp. 175–92.

Llull, R. 1512. *Liber de ascensus et descensu intellectus*, Ed. of Valencia.

Longo, G. 2009. Critique of Computational Reason in the Natural Sciences. In *Fundamental Concepts in Computer Science*, edited by E. Gelenbe and J.-P. Kahane. London: Imperial College Press, pp. 43–70. Available at: http://www.di.ens.fr/users/longo/files/PhilosophyAndCognition/CritiqCompReason-engl.pdf [Accessed on August 15, 2016].

Longo, G. 2013. *Guiseppe Longo Lecture* [sic]. Available at: https://vimeo.com/71491465 [Accessed on April 8, 2016].

Lo Pinto, L. and Miller, V. J. 2016. The Exhibition as Medium. In *Frederick Kiesler: Function Follows Vision, Vision Follows Reality*, edited by L. Lo Pinto and V. J. Miller. Berlin: Sternberg Press, 2016, p. 13.

Lorensen, W. E. and Cline, H. E. 1987. Marching Cubes: A High Resolution 3d Surface Construction Algorithm. *ACM Computer Graphics*, vol. 21, no. 4, pp. 163–69.

Lunenfeld, P. 2011. *The Secret War Bzetween Downloading and Uploading*. 1st edition. Cambridge, MA: MIT Press.

Lynn, G. 1998. *Folds, Bodies and Blobs: Collected Essays*. Bruxelles: La Letree Volée.

Lynn, G. 1999. *Animate Form*. New York: Princeton Architectural Press.

Lynn, G., ed. 2013. *The Archaeology of the Digital: Peter Einsenman, Frank Gehry, Chuck Hoberman, Shoei Yoh*. Berlin: Sternberg.

Lynn, G. 2015. *Canadian Centre for Architecture – Karl Chu and Greg Lynn Discuss X Phylum and Catastrophe Machine*. [E-Book] Montreal: Canadian Centre for Architecture. Available at: https://itunes.apple.com/gb/book/karl-chu-x-phylum-catastrophe/id1002168906?mt=11.

Lyotard, J. F. 1988. *The Inhuman: Reflections on Time*. Cambridge: Polity Press.

Malthus, T. R. 1817. *Additions to the Fourth and Former Editions of an Essay on the Principle of Population*. London, 1st edition published anonymously in 1798.

Manovich, L. 2007. *Database as Symbolic Form*. In *Database Aesthetics: Art in the Age of Information Overflow*, edited by V. Vesna. Minneapolis, MN and Bristol: University of Minnesota Press; University Presses Marketing, pp. 39–60.

Manovich, L. 2013. *Software Takes Command*. New York, NY and London: Bloomsbury Academic.

March L. and Steadman P. 1974. *The Geometry of the Environment: An Introduction to Spatial Organisation in Design*. London: Methuen.

Martin, G. 2001. *The Universal Computer: The Road from Leibniz to Turing*. New York and London: W. W. Norton.

Martin, M. W. 1968. *Futurist Art and Theory*, 1909–1915. Oxford: Clarendon Press.

Marx, K. 1964. *Economic and Philosophical Manuscripts of 1844*. 1st edition, 1932. Edited with an introduction by Dirk J. Struik. New York: International Publisher.

Mayer-Schönberger, V. and Cukier, K. 2013. *Big Data: A Revolution That Will Transform How We Live, Work and Think*. London: John Murray.

Meadows, D. H., Meadows, D. L., Randers, J., Behrens III, W. W., eds. 1972. *The Limits of Growth: A Report for the Club of Rome's Project*. New York: Universe Books.

Medina, E. 2006. Designing Freedom, Regulating a Nation: Socialist Cybernetics in Allende's Chile. *Journal of Latin American Studies*, no. 38, pp. 571–606.

Medina, E. 2011. *Cybernetic revolutionaries: Technology and Politics in Allende's Chile*. Cambridge, MA and London: MIT Press.

Menges, A., ed. 2012. *Material Computation: Higher Integration in Morphogenetic Design. Architectural Design*, 2016, March/April. Hoboken, NY: John Wiley & Sons.

Miralles, E. and Prats, E. 1991. How to Lay out a Croissant. *El Croquis* 49/50: Enric Miralles/Carme Pinos 1988–1991, no. 49–50, pp. 192–93.

Mitchell, W. J. 1990. *The Logic of Architecture: Design, Computation, and Cognition*. Cambridge, MA and London: The MIT Press.

Mitchell, W. J. 1992. *The Reconfigured Eye: Visual Truth in the Post-Photographic Era*. Cambridge, MA and London: The MIT Press.

Mole, A. 1971. Art and Cybernetics in the Supermarket. In *Cybernetics, Art, and Ideas*, edited by J. Reichardt. London: Studio Vista.

Morando, S., ed. 1961. *Almanacco Letterario Bompiani 1962: Le Applicazioni dei Calcolatori Elettronici alle Scienze Morali e alla Letteratura*, Milan: Bompiani.

Moretti, L. 1951. Struttura come Forma. In *Spazio* no. 6 (December 1951 – April 1952), pp. 21–30. In *Luigi Moretti: Works and Writings*, edited by F. Bucci and M. Mulazzani, 2002. New York: Princeton Architectural Press. pp. 175–77.

Moretti, L. 1971. Ricerca matematica in architettura e urbanistica. *Moebius*, vol. 4, no. 1, pp. 30–53.

Morton, T. 2013. *Hyperobjects: Philosophy and Ecology After the End of the World*. Cambridge: Cambridge University Press.

Mosso, L. 1967. Architettura programmata e linguaggio. In *La Sfida Elettronica, Realtà e Prospettive dell'Uso del Computer in Architettura*, edited by M. Foti and M. Zaffagnini. Bologna: Ente Autonomo per le Fiere di Bologna, pp. 130–37.

Mosso, L. 1970. L'architecture programmée et langage and Conception fundamental de la cité- territoire programée. *L'Architecture d'Aujourd'hui*, no. 148, pp. 18–21.

Mosso, L. 1971. Rapporto su di un modello di progettazione automatica globale per l'autoprogrammazione della communità. Centro Vocational del I.M.S.S., Mexico, "Memoria de la Conferencia Internacional Mexico 1971 IEEE sobre sistemas, redes, y computadoras," vol. 2, pp. 765–69.

Mosso, L. 1978. La progettazione strutturale, per una architettura della non oggettualità. In *Topologia e Morfogenesi, utopia e crisi dell'antinatura, momentidelle intenzioni architettoniche in Italia*, edited by L. V. Masini. Venice: Venice Biennale, pp. 160–63.

Mosso, L. 1989. 1961–1963. Cappella per la Messa dell'Artista, sotterranei di via Barbaroux 2, Torino. Available at: http://www.leonardomosso.it/home3/pagina.php?p=11&img=35 [Accessed on October 15, 2015].

Mumford, E. 2000. *The CIAM Discourse on Urbanism*, 1928–1960. Cambridge, MA; London: The MIT Press.

MVRDV. 2004. *The Region Maker: Rhein Ruhr City*. Berlin: Hatje Cantz Publishers.

MVRDV. 2005. *KM3: Excursions on Capacity*. Barcelona: Actar.

MVRDV, Delft School of Design, Berlage Institute, MIT, cThrough. 2007. *The Space Fighter: The Evolutionary Game*. Barcelona: Actar.

Nebeker, F. 1995. *Calculating the Weather: Meteorology in the 20th Century*. New Brunswick, NJ: Rutgers University Press.

Negroponte, N. 1970. *The Architecture Machine: Toward a More Human Environment*. Cambridge, MA, London: The MIT Press.

Noll, M. A. 1969. A Subjective Comparison of Piet Mondrian's "Composition with Lines" 1917. In *Cybernetic Serendipity: The Computer and The Arts*, edited by J. Reichardt. New York: Praeger, p. 74.

Olivato, L. 1971. Per Serlio a Venezia: documenti nuovi e documenti rivisitati. *Arte Veneta*, vol. 25, pp. 284–91.

Ören, T. 2011a. The many facets of simulation through a collection of about 100 definitions. *SCS Modeling and Simulation Magazine*, Vol. 2, 82–92. Available at: http://www.scs.org/magazines/2011-04/index_file/Files/Oren(2).pdf [Accessed on August 11, 2015].

Ören, T. 2011b. A Critical Review of Definitions and About 400 Types of Modeling and Simulation. http://www.scs.org/magazines/2011-07/index_file/Files/Oren-July-11(2).pdf [Accessed on August 12, 2015].

Pane, R. 1953. *Bernini Architetto*. Venice: Neri Pozza Editore.

Panofsky, E. 1943. *The Life and Art of Albrecht Dürer*. Princeton: Princeton University Press.

Poletto, M. and Pasquero, C. 2012. *Systemic Architecture: Operating Manual for the Self-Organising City*. London: Routledge.

Parisi, L. 2013. *Contagious Architecture: Computation, Aesthetics, and Space*. Cambridge, MA: The MIT Press.

Pascal, B. 1654. Pascal to Fermat. In *Fermat and Pascal on Probability*. Available at: https://www.york.ac.uk/depts/maths/histstat/pascal.pdf [Accessed on November 12, 2015].

Paul, C. 2007. *The Database as System and Cultural Form*. In *Database Aesthetic: Art in the Age of Information Overflow*, edited by V. Vesna. Minneapolis, MN: University of Minnesota Press.

Perrault, C. 1676. *Cours d'Architecture*.

Pine, B. 1993. *Mass-Customization: The New Frontier in Business Competition*. Boston, MA: Harvard Business School Press.

Plimpton, G. 1984. *Fireworks*. New York: Garden City.

Ponti, G. 1964. Una "Cappella Simbolica" nel Centro di Torino. *Domus*, no. 419, pp. 28–29.

Poole, M. and Shvartzberg, M., eds. 2015. *The Politics of Parametricism: Digital Technologies in Architecture*. London and New York: Bloomsbury Academic.

Portoghesi, P. 1964. *Borromini nella Cultura Europea*. Rome: Officina Edizioni.

Portoghesi, P. 1974. *Le Inibizioni dell'Architettura Moderna*. Bari: Laterza.

Postcodes. Available at: http://www.postalheritage.org.uk/explore/history/postcode [Accessed on May 11, 2016].

Pugh, A. L. 1970. *DYNAMO User's Manual*. 3rd edition. Cambridge, MA: The MIT Press.

Quatremère de Quincy. 1825. Type. In *Encyclopédie Méthodique*, vol. 3. Translated by Samir Younés, reprinted in *The Historical Dictionary of Architecture of Quatremère de Quincy*. London: Papadakis Publisher, 2000.

Raper, J. F., Rhind, D. W., and Sheperd, J. W., eds. 1992. *Postcodes: The New Geography*. Harlow and New York: Longman; John Wiley & Sons.

Rappold, M. and Violette, R., eds. 2004. *Gehry Draws*. Cambridge, MA and London: The MIT Press in association with Violette Editions.

Ratti, C. and Claudel, M. 2015. *Open Source Architecture*. London: Thames & Hudson.

Reed, C. *Short History of MOSS GIS*. Available at: https://sites.google.com/site/reedsgishistory/Home/short-history-of-the-moss-gis [Accessed on March 3, 2015].

Reichardt, J., ed. 1969a. *Cybernetic Serendipity: The Computer and The Arts*. New York: Praeger.

Reichardt, J., ed. 1971. *Cybernetics, Art, and Ideas*. London: Studio Vista.

Richardson, L. F. 1922. *Weather Prediction by Numerical Process*. Cambridge: Cambridge University Press.

Riegl, A. 1912. *Filippo Baldinuccis Vita des Gio. Lorenzo Bernini*. Translation and commentary by A. Riegl, A. Burda, and O. Pollak, eds. Vienna: Verlag Von Anton Schroll & Co.

Roberts, L. G. 1963. *Machine Perception of Three-dimensional Solids*. PhD Thesis. Massachusetts Institute of Technology.

Roberts, L. G. 1966. The Lincoln WAND. In: *AFIPS '66*, Proceedings of the November 7–10, 1966, fall joint computer conference, pp. 223–27.

Rosenstiel, P. 1979. Labirinto. In *Enciclopedia VIII: Labirinto-Memoria*, edited by R. Romano. Turin: Einaudi, pp. 620–53.

Ross, D. T. 1968. *Investigations in Computer-Aided Design for Numerically Controlled Production*, Report ESL-FR 351. Cambridge, MA: Electronic Systems Laboratory, Electrical Engineering Dept., Massachusetts Institute of Technology. Available at: http://dspace.mit.edu/bitstream/handle/1721.1/755/FR-0351-19563962.PDF. txtjsessionid=3469E7BE3780EDAF65F833757A0 12AF4?sequence=2 [Accessed on November 12, 2015].

Rossi, P. 1960. *Clavis Universalis: Arti Mnemoniche e Logica Combinatoria da Lullo a Leibniz*. Milan; Naples: Riccardo Ricciardi Editore.

Rowe, C. and Slutzky, R. 1963. Transparency: Literal and Phenomenal. *Perspecta*, vol. 8, pp. 45–54.

Santuccio, S., ed. 1986. *Luigi Moretti*. Bologna: Zanichelli.

Saunders, A. 2013. Baroque Parameters. In *Architecture in Formation: On the Nature of Information in Digital Architecture*, edited by P. Lorenzo-Eiroa, and A. Sprecher, New York: Routledge, pp. 224–31.

Scanlab. 2014. *Living Death Camps*. Available at: http://scanlabprojects.co.uk/projects/forensicarchitecture [Accessed on September 3, 2015].

Scanlab. 2016. *Rome's Invisible City*. Available at: http://scanlabprojects.co.uk/projects/bbcrome [Accessed on September 3, 2015].

Schott, G. D. October 2008. The Art of Medicine: Piero della Francesca's projections and neuroimaging today. *The Lancet*, vol. 372, pp. 1378–79. Available at: http://www.thelancet.com/journals/lancet/article/PIIS0140673608615767/fulltext [Accessed on June 8, 2015].

Schumacher, P. 2008. *Parametricism as Style – Parametricist Manifesto*. Available at: http://www.patrikschumacher.com/Texts/Parametricism%20as%20Style.htm [Accessed on June 8, 2015].

Schumacher, P. 2010. *The Autopoiesis of Architecture, vol. 1: A New Framework for Architecture*. Chichester: John Wiley & Son.

Schumacher, P. 2012. *The Autopoiesis of Architecture, vol. 2: A New Agenda for Architecture*. Chichester: John Wiley & Son.

Schumacher, P., ed. 2016. *Parametricism 2.0: Rethinking Architecture's Agenda for the 21st Century, Architectural Design*, 2, vol. 86. Chichester: Wiley and Son.

Scoates, C. 2013. *Brian Eno: Visual Music*. San Francisco: Chronicle Books.

Selenus, G. 1624. *Cryptomenytices et cryptographiae libri ix*. Lunaeburgi: Excriptum typis Johannis Henrici Fratrum.

Shannon, C. July, October, 1948. A Mathematical Theory of Information. *The Bell System Technical Journal*, vol. 27, pp. 379–423, 623–56.

Sheil, B., ed. 2014. High Definition: negotiating zero tolerance. *In High-Definition: Zero Tolerance in Design and Production. Architectural Design,* no. 227. Chichester: John Wiley & Sons, pp. 8–19.

Shop, ed. 2002. *Versioning: Evolutionary Techniques in Architecture. Architectural Design*, no. 159. Chichester: John Wiley & Sons.

Smith, B. 2001. True Grid. In *Spatial Information Theory: Foundations of Geographic Information Science: International Conference*, edited by D. R. Montello, COSIT 2001, Morro Bay, CA, USA, September 19–23, 2011: Proceedings. Berlin and London: Springer, pp. 14–27.

Smith, B. 2003. Ontology. In *The Blackwell Guide to Philosophy of Computing information*, edited by L. Floridi. Malden: Blackwell, pp. 155–66.

Sobieszek R. A. December, 1980. Sculpture as the Sum of Its Profiles: François Willème and Photosculpture in France, 1859–1868. *The Art Bulletin*, vol. 62, no. 4, pp. 617–30.

Souchon, C. and Antoine, M. E. 2003. La formation des départements, Histoire par l'image. [online]. Available at: http://www.histoire-image.org/etudes/formation-departements [Accessed on May 13, 2016].

Spieker, S. 2008. *The Big Archive: Art from Bureaucracy*. Cambridge, MA; London: The MIT Press.

Sterling, B. 2005. *Shaping Things*. Cambridge, MA and London: The MIT Press.

Strachey, C. S. 1954. The Thinking Machine. *Encounter*, vol. 3, pp. 25–31.

Sutherland, I. E. 1963. *Sketchpad: A Man-machine Graphical Communication System*. PhD. Massachusetts Institute of Technology. Available at: https://dspace.mit.edu/handle/1721.1/14979 [Accessed on April 28, 2016].

Sutherland, I. E. 1968. A Head-Mounted Three-Dimensional Display. Proceedings of the *Fall Joint Computer Conference*, pp. 757–64.

Sutherland, I. E 2003. Sketchpad: A Man-machine Graphical Communication System. *Technical Report*, no. 574. Available at: https://www.cl.cam.ac.uk/techreports/UCAM-CL-TR-574.pdf [Accessed on December 12, 2015].

Taton, R., ed. 1958. *A General History of the Sciences: The Beginnings of Modern Science from 1450 to 1800*. Translated by A. J. Pomerans, 1964. London: Thames and Hudson.

Tentori, F. 1963. L. Mosso, una cappella a Torino. *Casabella*, no. 277, pp. 54–55.

Teresko, J. December 20, 1993. *Industry Week*. 1993. Quoted in Weisberg, D. E. (2008). *The Engineering Design Revolution: The People, Companies and Computer Systems That Changed Forever the Practice of Engineering*. [online]. Available at: http://www.cadhistory.net./16%20Parametric%20Technology.pdf [Accessed on June 10, 2016].

Thom, R. 1989. *Semio Physics: A Sketch*. Translated by V. Meyer. Redwood City, CA: Addison-Wesley Publishing Company, The Advanced Book Program.

Thompson, D. W. 2014. *On Growth and Form*. 1st edition 1917. Cambridge: Cambridge University Press.

Thompson, J., Kuchera-Morin, J., Novak, M., Overholt, D., Putnam, L., Wakefield, G., and Smith, W. 2009.The Allobrain: An Interactive, Stereographic, 3D Audio, Immersive Virtual World. *International Journal of Human-Computer Studies* Vol. 67, no. 11, pp. 934–46.

Tschumi B. 1981. *Manhattan Transcripts*. London: Academy Editions.

Tsimourdagkas, C. 2012. *Typotecture: Histories, Theories, and Digital Futures of Typographic Elements in Architectural Design*. PhD Thesis. Royal College of Art, School of Architecture.

Turing, A. M. 1936. On Computable Numbers, with an Application to the Entscheidunsproblem. In *Proceedings of the London Mathematical Society,* November 30–December 23, pp. 230–65.

UN Studio. 2002. *UN Studio: UN Fold*. Rotterdam: NAi Publisher.

Vallianatos, M. 2015. Uncovering the Early History of "Big Data" and the "Smart City" in Los Angeles. *Boom: A Journal of California* [on-line magazine]. Available at: http://boomcalifornia.com/2015/06/uncovering-the-early-hisory-of-big-data-and-the-smart-city-in-la.html [Accessed on February 15, 2016].

van Berkel, B. 2006. *Design Models: Architecture Urbanism Infrastructure*. London: Thames & Hudson.

van Eesteren, C. 1997. *The idea of the functional city: A lecture with slides 1928 – C. van Eesteren*. With an introduction of V. van Rossem. Rotterdam: NAi publishers.

Van Rossen, V. ed. (1997). *The idea of the functional city: A lecture with slides 1928 – C. van Eesteren*. Rotterdam: NAi publishers, p.19–23.

Varenne, F. 2001. What does a computer simulation prove? The case of plant modelling at CIRAD (France). Published in *Simulation in Industry*, proceedings of the 13th European Simulation Symposium, Marseille, France, October 18th–20th, 2001, edited by N. Giambiasi and C. Frydamn, Ghent: SCS Europe Byba, pp. 549–54.

Varenne, F. 2013. The Nature of Computational Things: Models and Simulations in Design and Architecture. In *Naturalizing Architecture*, edited by F. Migayrou and M.-A. Brayer. Orleans: HYX, pp. 96–105.

Venturi, R. and Scott-Brown, D. 2004. *Architecture as Sign and System: For a Mannerist Time*. Cambridge, MA: Belknap Press.

Venturi, R., Scott-Brown, D., and Izenour, S. 1972. *Learning from Las Vegas*. Cambridge, MA: The MIT Press.

Vesna, V. 2007. *Database Aesthetics: Art in the Age of Information Overflow*. Minneapolis, MN and Bristol: University of Minnesota Press; University Presses Marketing.

Viollet-Le-Duc, E. 1866. *Dictionnarie Raisonné de l'Architecture Francaise*. Paris: A. Morel & C. Editeurs.

von Neumann, J. 1945. *First Draft of a Report on the EDVAC*. Available at: http://www.wiley.com/legacy/wileychi/wang_archi/supp/appendix_a.pdf [Accessed on August 15, 2016].

von Ranke, L. 1870. *Englische Geschichte vornehmlich im siebzehnten Jahrhundert*, Ranke, Sämmtliche Werke, vol. 14. Leipzig: Duncker and Humbold.

Wardrip-Fruin, N. 2003. Introduction to "Sketchpad: A Man-Machine Graphical Communication System". In *New Media Reader*, edited by N. Wardrip-Fruin and N. Montfort. Cambridge, MA and London: The MIT Press, pp. 109–26.

Washington Post, 1965. Computers Help Lay Plan at Watergate. *The Washington Post*, February 19, 1965.

Weisberg, D. E. 2008. Parametric Technology Corporation. In *The Engineering Design Revolution: The People, Companies and Computer Systems That Changed Forever the Practice of Engineering*. [online]. Available at: http://www.cadhistory.net./16%20 Parametric%20Technology.pdf. [Accessed June 10, 2016].

Weisstein, E. 1988. *Concise Encyclopaedia of Mathematics*. Boca Raton, London and New York, Washington DC: CRC Press.

Wigley, M. 2007. The Architectural Brain. In *Network Practices: New Strategies in Architecture and Design*, edited by A. Burke and T. Tierney. New York: Princeton Architectural Press, pp. 30–53.

Williams, M. R. 1997. *A History of Computing Technology*. Los Alamitos, CA: IEEE Computer Society Press.

Winsberg, E. 2010. *Science in the Age of Computer Simulation*. Chicago: The University Chicago Press.

Wolfram, S. 2002. *A New Kind of Science*. Champaing, IL and London: Wolfram Media; Turnaround.

Wolfram, S. 2012. *The Personal Analytics of my Life*. Stephen Wolfram Blog. Available at: http://blog.stephenwolfram.com/2012/03/the-personal-analytics-of-my-life [Accessed on September 15, 2015].

Wolman, A. (1965). *The Metabolism of Cities. In Scientific American*, Vol. 213, pp.179–190.

Woodward, S. 2007. Russell Kirsch: The Man who taught computers to see. In *Oregon Live*. Available at: http://www.oregonlive.com/living/index.ssf/2007/05/russell_kirsch_the_man_who_tau.html [Accessed on September 24, 2015].

Xenakis, I. 1963. *Musique Formelle*. Paris: Richard-Masse.

Yates, F. 1966. *The Art of Memory*. London: The Bodley Head.

Young, M. 2013. Digital Remediation. *Cornell Journal of Architecture 9: Mathematics*, no. 9, pp. 119–34.

Movies

The Abyss. 1989. Movie. Directed by James Cameron. USA: Lightstorm Entertainment.

Inland Empire. 2006. Directed by David Lynch [Film]. USA/France: Absurda and Canal Plus.

The Matrix. 1999. Movie. Directed by The Wachowski Brothers. USA: Warner Bros.

Sketches of Frank Gehry. 2006. Movie. Directed by Sydney Pollack. USA: Sony Pictures Classics.

Terminator 2. 1991. Movie. Directed by James Cameron. USA: Carolco Pictures.

Index

Lightning Source UK Ltd.
Milton Keynes UK
UKHW021038140821
388790UK00004B/142

9 781474 258128